THE CASE FOR COVENANTAL INFANT BAPTISM

THE CASE FOR COVENANTAL INFANT BAPTISM

EDITED BY

GREGG STRAWBRIDGE

P&R

PUBLISHING

P.O. BOX 817 • PHILLIPSBURG • NEW JERSEY 08865-0817

Italics within Scripture quotations indicate emphasis added.

Page design and typesetting by Lakeside Design Plus
Printed in the United States of America

Library of Congress Cataloging-in-Publication Data

The case for covenantal infant baptism / edited by Gregg Strawbridge.
p. cm.
Includes bibliographical references and index.
ISBN-10: 0-87552-554-7 (pbk.)
ISBN-13: 978-0-87552-554-9 (pbk.)
1. Infant baptism. 2. Infant baptism—Biblical teaching. I. Strawbridge, Gregg, 1964–

BV813.3.C37 2003
234′.1612—dc21

2003054942

CONTENTS

Introduction

GREGG STRAWBRIDGE

In my theological mansion are many rooms. I walk down the hallowed halls to rooms named Justin Martyr, Irenaeus, Tertullian, Augustine, Anselm, Aquinas, Luther, Calvin, Ursinus, Rutherford, Witsius, Owen, Bunyan, Newton, Gill, Edwards, Spurgeon, Hodge, Ryle, Alexander, Vos, Machen, Pink, Murray, Van Til—and other rooms yet to be named. As I reflect on the magnificent portraits lining the walls, I see those who have loved our Lord unto death. I see teachers of the church who, though dead, continue to speak. These were all mere men, to be sure, yet saints and teachers of the church. They were not all of one mind regarding the subject of this book.

Our challenge, as we serve our risen and reigning Lord, is to become of one mind and so gain a clearer view from standing on their shoulders. I am among the growing number of those who, like many of our Reformed forefathers, hold that the future of the kingdom, even on this side of eternity, is bright. Jesus shall reign until he has put all his enemies under his feet. That reign has commenced. Now, however, among evangelical and Reformed believers, the discussion of who should be baptized is an intramural debate. Or, to use the language of St. Paul, baptism is not listed as a doctrine of "first importance" (1 Cor. 15:3; cf. 1:13). C. S. Lewis calls to mind an insightful and instructive metaphor in his preface to *Mere Christianity:*

> [Mere or essential Christianity] is more like a hall out of which doors open into several rooms. If I can bring anyone into that hall I shall have done what I attempted. But it is in the rooms, not in the hall, that there are fires and chairs and meals. . . . Even in the hall, you must begin trying to obey the rules which are common to the whole house. And above all you must be asking which door is the true one; not which pleases you best by its paint and paneling. In plain language, the question should never be: "Do I like that kind of service?" but "Are these doctrines true: Is holiness here? Does my conscience move me towards this? Is my reluctance to knock at this door due to my pride, or my mere taste, or my personal dislike of this particular door-keeper?" When you have reached your own room, be kind to those who have chosen different doors and to those who are still in the hall. If they are wrong they need your prayers all the more; and if they are your enemies, then you are under orders to pray for them. That is one of the rules common to the whole house.[1]

I have observed that there are also doors between certain of the rooms. It would seem to be this way between the various Reformed churches. I have moved through the door from the Calvinistic Baptist room to the Reformed Covenantal Paedobaptist room.[2]

After being baptized in a Southern Baptist church at the age of ten, my name was on the roster of several Baptist churches through my college and seminary years. (Let's hope my name is not still on their rolls.) From my undergraduate days, I was confronted with the issue of infant baptism. Initially, I studied the question in preparation for an interview to be a Reformed University Ministries (PCA) intern. I still recall that interchange vividly. I was not yet persuaded of infant baptism, though I was by no means strongly set against it. The examining committee gave me the "thumbs down," but said to call them back if my view changed. Actually, seminary study and many discussions with paedobaptists persuaded me against this view for a time.

1. Preface to *Mere Christianity* (New York: Macmillan, 1952).

2. *Paedobaptist* is the common term for those who believe that the infant children of Christians should be baptized.

The first church in which I served as a pastor actually had a membership of both believer's baptists and paedobaptists. So in the early 1990s I wrote a study guide to help people understand both positions and to articulate how our congregation worked out the practical details.[3] We practiced believer's baptism by immersion, yet we did not require our members to be rebaptized (anabaptism). In this we followed the heart of John Bunyan's argument in his book *Differences in Judgment About Water-Baptism, No Bar to Communion.*[4]

During those few years, I continued to study the baptism question. I fortified my arguments against infant baptism on two substantial points. First, we have an explicit biblical basis for believer's baptism and none for infant baptism. Second, the members of the new covenant are exclusively regenerate people. The second of these reasons became for me the most foundational. In my discussions with paedobaptists, I found that they would appeal to the inclusion of children in the covenant, preeminently in the Abrahamic covenant. They would follow the familiar road from circumcision in the Abrahamic covenant in Genesis 17 to the relationship between circumcision and baptism in Colossians 2:11–12, and then to infant baptism in the Reformed tradition. Covenant members should receive the sign of the covenant. The children of Christians are in the covenant, and so they are to receive the sign of the covenant. This was a compelling argument, except for one thing.

The response that kept me from being persuaded by the argument from circumcision was what I will call the new covenant argument. Who is in the new covenant? Aside from the fact that there is no explicit case of an infant baptism in the Bible, I thought that the older covenant administrations were different from the new covenant precisely at the point that separates the two positions on baptism. The old covenant was broken because not all those taking part in it by physical birth were truly the people of God by spiritual birth. The new

3. This was entitled "A Handbook on Baptism: Essays and Resources."

4. See *The Works of John Bunyan,* ed. George Offor (reprint, Edinburgh: Banner of Truth, 1991), 2:641.

covenant promises are not like the old covenant precisely at the point of covenant membership. The important change is that the new covenant is a relationship between God and his *regenerate* people. So we should not automatically include the children of regenerate people (without indications of conversion) in the covenant. In other words, while all members of the new covenant are to receive the sign of the new covenant, all those members are regenerate. We should not presume that all the infant children of Christians are regenerate. Unless there is clear evidence that they are regenerate, and thus members of the new covenant, we should not baptize them. Our practice of baptism should follow our theology of the covenant.

This argument was unfamiliar to many paedobaptists. In my experience, most paedobaptists had not been challenged on the nature of new covenant membership.[5] But in recent years, this new covenant argument has become an increasingly important part of the Baptist case, especially as it has been stated by Calvinistic Baptists.

My study of the issue took a decisive turn when I began to see that the new covenant includes warnings of apostasy (Heb. 10:28–30).[6] If these warnings are to be taken seriously, then it must be admitted that the new covenant has stipulations for judgment. If these are not merely hypothetical stipulations for judgment, then some members of the new covenant will be "judged" (in the language of Heb. 10:30). This became a central challenge to my Baptist view, supported by the new covenant argument. Such clear statements about the new covenant could not be reconciled with my view that every member of the new covenant was regenerate. Being fully committed to the doctrine of the perseverance of the saints, I believed on biblical grounds that regenerate believers cannot lose their salvation (John 10:27–29; Rom. 8:30). I concluded that unregenerate members of the visible church can be

5. In reading Calvin, I saw an even deeper view of the sacraments than held by paedobaptists that I knew. See Lewis Bevins Schenck, *The Presbyterian Doctrine of Children in the Covenant* (New Haven: Yale University Press, 1940; reprint, with an introduction by Frank A. James III, Phillipsburg, N.J.: P&R Publishing, 2003).

6. This was shown to me in a discussion with Douglas Wilson. In that context, the baptism/covenant epiphany occurred.

covenant breakers in the new covenant. This meant that there was continuity in the way that membership in the covenant was administered. The signs of the covenant are for members of the visible church. Since this is so, even the youngest members, infants, can be included in the visible church and receive the sign of inclusion. This was the critical theological point for me.

After working through this question, I began to see that the basic structure of the Baptist polemic against paedobaptism is this: (1) We have an explicit biblical basis for believer's baptism. (2) There is no explicit warrant (an example or a command) for infant baptism. (3) The new covenant is made exclusively with regenerate individuals. (4) Believers' little children cannot be assumed to be regenerate. Therefore, the baptistic conclusion is that the children of believers are not to receive the sign of the new covenant until they confess their faith (and thus give evidence of their membership in the new covenant).

After due consideration of this argument, I came to see its weak points. (1) The Baptist assumes that the cases of adult converts being baptized are sufficient to deal with the question of the children of believers. But is this true? Are not the children of the faithful throughout Scripture regarded differently than pagan adults? (2) The Baptist lacks explicit warrant to exclude the infants of believers from the covenant, for there is no biblical command or example that demands their exclusion. (3) Their exclusion is *inferred* from what Baptists take to be the nature of the new covenant. Baptists often deny to paedobaptists the right to draw inferences that lead to infant baptism, yet their central theological objection to infant baptism—that the children of believers are not members of the new covenant—is an inference from their view of the new covenant.

The succinct answer to this central line of argument is: (1) Even a million cases of adult converts professing their faith prior to baptism would prove nothing about the baptism of infants. Paedobaptists heartily concur with the practice of adult profession prior to baptism, as is evident in the Reformed confessions![7] Most Baptist polemics just hammer away at the examples of adults, as though this settles the case. Ironically, the childless eunuch (Acts 8:36–39), who clearly believed before he was baptized, becomes the paradigm for settling the question of children's baptism. But, in fact, we do not have anything like a million cases. We have the cases listed in figure 1.

FIGURE 1

Adult Baptisms	Household Baptisms
3,000 (men) at Pentecost (no households present)	Cornelius and household
Samaritans ("both men and women"):	Lydia and household
Simon the sorcerer	
Ethiopian eunuch (no household)	Philippian jailer and household
Paul (no household)	*Corinthians:*
Disciples of John (12 men) (no household present)	Crispus (and household [inferred])
	Stephanas and household
Gaius	

The promise of the new covenant came in its fulfillment "for you and your children" (Acts 2:39) at Pentecost. Only men are said to have been baptized, some three thousand of them. In Samaria, "men and women alike" (8:12) were baptized, including Simon (the apostate sorcerer). The godly Ethiopian eunuch, who (being a eunuch) had no familial household, was baptized (8:38). Paul (who had no household) was baptized (Acts 9:18; cf. 1 Cor. 7:7–8). Cornelius's household was baptized (Acts 10:48; 11:14). Lydia's household was baptized (16:15). The Philippian jailer's household was baptized (16:33). Many Corinthians were baptized, including Crispus, Stephanas's household, and Gaius (Acts 18:8; 1 Cor. 1:14, 16). The disciples of John (adult men) were baptized (Acts 19:5). The explicit cases of baptism, when fully considered, are not evidence for the Baptist view. These examples form a pattern when we consider that the households baptized are Gentiles (Cornelius, Lydia, the Philippian jailer, and Stephanas),

7. For example, the Westminster Larger Catechism, Q. 166.

or at least are in Gentile contexts. In this we see how the gospel goes to the Gentile world—by household (Acts 1:8). This is the covenantal pattern, inclusive of children.

(2) Explicit warrant regarding the baptism of believers' children is lacking in both directions. There is no case of an infant baptism, and neither is there a case of the baptism of a Christian's child as a believer. The question of when to baptize the children of believers must be settled by the proper application of biblical teaching. It cannot be settled by appealing to an explicit text.

(3) There is explicit warrant for the inclusion of children in the new covenant (Deut. 30:6; Jer. 31:36–37), in the church (Eph. 1:1 with 6:1–4; Col. 1:2 with 3:20; 1 Cor. 7:14), and in the kingdom (Matt. 19:14; Mark 10:14; Luke 18:16). Moreover, the covenantal infant baptism view can be argued from truly necessary inferences[8]—drawing upon the continuity of the covenant promise (to be God to your children after you) and the covenant people, as well as the examples of baptism (the households of Cornelius, Lydia, the Philippian jailer, Crispus, and Stephanas). This is a synopsis of the biblical evidence that is convincing to me.

For Christians to progress in this discussion, we need honest hearts, first of all. We need minds that are willing to submit to all the Lord's will as revealed in his Word. As a means to our study, we need substantial discussions on the key passages, theological reflection, and historical data that address central questions. This volume aims to provide such a discussion by well-qualified pastors and scholars.

It will be clear to the discerning reader that the contributors are not in complete agreement on such matters as how to best nurture Christian children, evangelism and baptized children, the efficacy of baptism, and the Lord's Supper and baptized children. They represent several Reformed and paedobaptist denominations. These differences

8. A necessary inference is a logically valid conclusion from given premises, such as: First premise: The children of believers are covenant members. Second premise: Covenant members are to receive the sign of entrance into the covenant. Inference: Therefore (this follows *necessarily* from the premises), the children of believers are to receive the sign of entrance into the covenant.

are a matter of ongoing study. In the house of faith, paedobaptism serves as a kind of hallway that leads to several rooms. And in those rooms many of these matters are being discussed.

Finally, my hope can be stated no better than in the words of George Offor, the editor of John Bunyan's works: "May the time soon arrive when water shall not quench love, but when all the churches militant shall form one army, with one object,—that of extending the Redeemer's kingdom."[9]

9. *The Works of John Bunyan,* 2:593.

1

A Pastoral Overview of Infant Baptism

BRYAN CHAPELL

Why do Presbyterians baptize infants? We must confess that some bring their children for this sacrament because of the sweetness of the ceremony, or because of the expectations of family and church, or even with the misguided expectation that the "holy water" will magically protect their child from hell. However, neither sentiment nor tradition nor superstition is sufficient reason for believers to bring their children to be baptized. And, thankfully, such reasons are not the basis of our church's practice. We baptize infants because we believe that the Bible teaches us to do so.

Mine is the happy task of explaining the scriptural foundation for infant baptism from a pastoral perspective. In fulfillment of that task, I will first present the biblical support for infant baptism as I have presented it in new members' and church officer training classes over the past twenty-five years. Then I will conclude by offering words of explanation that I have often used as a pastor during the administration of the ordinance. My goals are to help explain why we should baptize the infants of believing parents and also to help pastors know how to administer the sacrament in ways that are meaningful and helpful to their churches. Thus, I plan to present this material in terms that are accessible to laypersons and to leave the technical discussions to the able scholars elsewhere in this book.

One further word of preparation relates to my own journey regarding infant baptism. I did not always accept the practice of infant baptism. I was raised among dedicated, faithful, and well-instructed Baptists who believe that the Bible only regards those who decide to follow Christ as proper candidates for baptism. I well understand and respect those who have questions about the legitimacy of a practice that they feel has no biblical warrant. I also do not want to do anything that the Bible does not support. Thus, the paragraphs that follow are more than the recitation of a party line; they are the reflection of the thought process that led me to believe that Scripture teaches that God wants believing parents to present their children to him in baptism.

The biblical explanation will flow as follows:

I. The Biblical Background of Infant Baptism
   Salvation is through the *covenant of faith* in the Old and New Testaments.
   The faithful receive a *covenant sign* in the Old Testament.
   The *covenant continues* in the New Testament.
   The *covenant sign changes* to reflect New Testament blessings.

II. The Biblical Basis for Infant Baptism
   The absence of a contrary command
   The examples of household baptism

III. The Biblical Benefits of Infant Baptism
   The devotion of the parents
   The blessing of the child

THE BIBLICAL BACKGROUND OF INFANT BAPTISM

The Covenant of Faith

Many of the children in our churches enjoy singing the song "Father Abraham Had Many Sons." This song contains a vital New Testament truth: "Father Abraham had many sons—I am one of them and so are you." When they sing these words, our children are not merely echoing a statement of faith that a Jewish child in the Old Testament could make. The truth of these words still applies.

A key concept in the New Testament is that all of God's people (Jew or Gentile—past or present) are blessed in accordance with the covenant that God made with Abraham. The Lord promised in this "everlasting covenant" that Abraham and his descendants would know God's blessings on the basis of faith in his provision (Gen. 15:1–6 and 17:1–8). No one was to receive God's blessings on the basis of personal merit or on the basis of some ceremony. Out of his mercy alone—and before they could qualify for it in any way—the Lord covenanted to be the God of Abraham and his descendants (Gen. 17:7). The people would know and claim the blessings of this covenant by expressing faith in God's provision as Abraham had done (Gen. 15:6). Thus, God promised to bless Abraham and his descendants by grace through faith (cf. Eph. 2:8–9).

But what does a covenant with a Jewish patriarch have to do with people in God's church today? The apostle Paul reminds us that God said to Abraham, "All nations will be blessed through you" (Gal. 3:8; cf. Gen. 12:3). The "everlasting covenant" that God made with Abraham (Gen. 17:7) continues to be in effect and continues to cover us. Paul says, "So those who have faith are blessed along with Abraham, the man of faith" (Gal. 3:9).

This means that we who have faith in Christ as God's provision for our salvation are blessed in accordance with Abraham's covenant. We are Abraham's spiritual descendants and are still covered by the covenant that God first made with him. Paul writes, "Consider Abraham: 'He believed God, and it was credited to him as righteousness.'

Understand, then, that those who believe are children of Abraham" (Gal. 3:6–7). Whether or not they are biological descendants of Abraham, believers today are his spiritual children through the everlasting covenant that God has provided.

There is no other way to be a child of God than to be included in Abraham's covenant. There is no other covenant of salvation, and unless we are part of Abraham's covenant, we are not part of God's people. As the apostle says, "He [Christ] redeemed us in order that the blessing given to Abraham might come to the Gentiles through Christ Jesus" (Gal. 3:14). Those who have faith in Jesus Christ as their Savior receive the covenant promises of Abraham and are his spiritual children, regardless of their time or place of birth (cf. Gal. 3:29).

The Covenant Sign

After making the covenant with Abraham to bless him and his descendants by grace through faith, God provided a covenant sign both to mark those who were recipients of his promise and to signify his pledge to provide for those who had faith in him. It is important to remember that the sign was given *after* the covenant was made; it was neither a precondition of the covenant nor a means of conferring it. Faith was and is the sole condition of knowing the blessings of God's covenant.

The sign of circumcision. The covenant sign that God gave the Old Testament people was circumcision. The removal of the foreskin from the male reproductive organ signified the removal of spiritual uncleanness from God's people and communicated that God's provision for blessing was being passed on to all the children of Abraham from generation to generation (cf. Gen. 17:10–14; Deut. 10:16; Jer. 4:4; Col. 2:13). Circumcision marked God's people as being separated and consecrated unto him and, consequently, as being in union with him and with each other in covenant family and community relationships (Ex. 12:48; Deut. 30:6; Jer. 4:4; 9:26). The rite of circumcision necessarily involved the shedding of blood, and was one of numerous Old

Testament signs that prefigured what would be required of Christ in order for our sins to be removed (cf. Heb. 9:22).

The extent of the sign. Because God's promises extended to Abraham's house, *he was to devote all that he had to the Lord by use of the covenant sign.* This meant that all who were part of Abraham's household in that ancient society were to be devoted to God by circumcision—sons, dependent relatives, and servants (Gen. 17:23; cf. Ex. 12:43–48). In contemporary culture, we are not accustomed to thinking of the head of a household as spiritually representing all its dependent members. Still, the representative role of heads of households has great scriptural precedent and rich implications in both the Old and the New Testaments (cf. Eph. 5:25–27; Heb. 11:7).

The representative principle helps to explain why Abraham devoted all in his house to God through the use of the Old Testament covenant sign, even though some of its members would not yet have expressed their faith. Abraham recognized his need as the head of a household to honor the Lord's promise to be the God of him and his family. The representative principle also explains why, in the New Testament, the apostle Paul could still say that children of a believing parent—even one who is married to a nonbeliever—are "holy" before God (1 Cor. 7:14). Few verses in Scripture more forcefully indicate that God communicates his grace to children while they are in the household of a covenant parent. Scripture does not contend that an adult who has turned from his parent's faith can presume to receive the eternal salvation promised through Abraham's covenant, but, while children remain under the authority of a believing parent, they are represented covenantally by that parent's faith.

The principle of representation by the head of the household also explains why the practice of circumcision was not an indication that women were excluded from the covenant. Both through the act of procreation and through the representative principle implied by circumcision, the rite showed that the covenant promises were extended to all in the house regardless of descent or gender. An adopted child of either gender or even a dependent servant had equal spiritual standing with a biological son through the representative principle that circumcision signified. The ancient people were slow to realize these spiritual implications, but the New Testament drives home the meaning:

> You are all sons of God through faith in Christ Jesus. . . . There is neither Jew nor Greek, slave nor free, male nor female, for you are all one in Christ Jesus. If you belong to Christ, then you are Abraham's seed, and heirs according to the promise. (Gal. 3:26–29)

We must still answer the question why the covenant sign was administered to those who had not yet expressed faith in God's provision. Since the covenant was made to express God's blessings to those who placed their faith in him, and since the covenant could only be experienced through faith, why did God tell Abraham to circumcise all the males in his household even before they knew of God's covenant of faith? Even if all of Abraham's house could have heard of God's provision and placed their faith in him, no one would expect all of Abraham's descendants to put their faith in God by the time they were eight days old and required to be circumcised (Gen. 17:12). Why then was the covenant sign commanded for all?

The relationship between sign and seal. The answer to why those throughout Scripture who were saved through faith alone were still allowed to be circumcised as children (i.e., before they were able to express their faith) has important implications for administering the covenant sign to infants today. Does the requirement of faith for salvation preclude the possibility of administering a covenant sign to the children of believers? It did not in the Old Testament practice of circumcision, and the New Testament tells us why. The apostle Paul says in the book of Romans that circumcision was a "seal" as well as a "sign" of the righteousness that Abraham had by faith (Rom. 4:11). Both terms have important significance for our understanding of the application of covenant sacraments.

We can easily understand how circumcision was a sign of the righteousness provided through God's covenant. The putting off of uncleanness by the shedding of blood and the marking of the faithful as God's special people resonate with many familiar New Testament concepts. However, the concept of a seal is less familiar to us today.

The image that the apostle calls to mind is that of the wax affixed to a letter or document and marked with a signet ring (or other instrument) to authenticate the source and validity of the contents of the document. The seal acted as a visible pledge by the author of the letter to honor what he had covenanted to do in the document when the conditions it described were met. Circumcision was God's way of marking his people with a visible pledge to honor his covenant for those who expressed faith in him. Just as a seal is the pledge of its author that he will uphold his promises when described conditions are met, so circumcision was God's pledge to provide all the blessings of his covenant when the condition of faith was met in his people. Our faith does not actuate God's covenant or cause it to be extended to us—he chose us in Christ before the foundation of the world (Eph. 1:4)—but our faith does claim (and live out) the covenant blessings that God provides by his grace and pledges with his seal.

The validity of a seal is not dependent upon the time that the conditions of the covenant accompanying it are met. Like the seal of a document, the seal of circumcision could be applied long before recipients of promised and signified blessings met the conditions of the covenant. The seal was simply *the visible pledge of God that when the conditions of his covenant were met, the blessings he promised would apply* (cf. Rom. 4:11). For this reason, God did not require that covenant parents wait until a child could express faith before commanding them to administer the covenant sign and seal of circumcision.

The Covenant Continuation

The New Testament apostles and writers take much care to let us know that the principles of the covenant of faith remain in effect for us. When Peter preaches on the Day of Pentecost, he says to his thousands of Jewish listeners, "Repent and be baptized, every one of you, in the name of Jesus Christ for the forgiveness of your sins. . . . The promise is for you and your children and for all who are far off—for all whom the Lord our God will call" (Acts 2:38–39). Peter frames his call to salvation in Christ in covenantal terms by speaking of a promise that applies to his listeners and to their children as well as to others who are yet far off. The apostle assumes that God continues to relate to us as individuals and as families—that the covenant principles are still in effect. Individuals (even in covenant families) are still responsible to express their personal faith, but God continues to work out his gracious promises in families as well as extending the covenant to others.

The apostle Paul is more explicit about the continuation of the Abrahamic covenant and proclaims, "Those who believe are children of Abraham" (Gal. 3:7). He goes on to say that the Law of Moses "does not set aside the covenant previously established by God and thus do away with the promise. . . . If you belong to Christ, then you are Abraham's seed, and heirs according to the promise" (Gal. 3:17, 29).

God's promise to Abraham to save those who have faith in heaven's provision remains in effect. Never do any come to God on the basis of their merit or because they have participated in some ritual. *Both the Old and the New Testaments affirm God's continuing covenant promise to Abraham to bless people by divine grace through faith.*

The Change in the Covenant Sign

While the covenant continues, its sign changes to reflect what God has done to maintain his promises. The bloody sign of circumcision that prefigured the shedding of Christ's blood no longer remains appropriate after the Lamb of God has shed his blood once for all in order to remove our sin (cf. Heb. 10:10; 1 Peter 1:18). Therefore, New Testament believers receive a new sign for the covenant that indicates what Christ has accomplished for them. Baptism with water is the sign of the washing away of our sin (cf. Acts 22:16; 1 Cor. 6:11; Heb. 9:14).

Those who continue to require circumcision as a requirement of God's covenant are condemned by the apostle who says, "For in Christ Jesus neither circumcision nor uncircumcision has any value. The only thing that counts is faith expressing itself through love" (Gal. 5:6). Circumcision no longer remains a requirement for those who desire to obey God (1 Cor. 7:18–19). However, baptism is now required of all those who desire to obey Christ and express their faith in him—men and women, Jews and Gentiles (cf. Acts 2:38; 8:12; 10:47–48).

While the sign of the covenant changes, the features of the covenant of faith do not. God continues to express his love to those who have faith in him, and as a result all believers share in the covenant that God prepared for Israel through Abraham (Eph. 3:6). The promises continue to be extended through parents to their children (Acts 2:38–39)—with the ordinary condition remaining that these children must ultimately express their own faith in Christ in order to reap the full blessings of the covenant.

Emphasizing the continuity of the covenant as well as the changed nature of the sign that accompanies it, the apostle Paul writes to the Colossian believers, "In him [Christ] you were also circumcised, in the putting off of the sinful nature, not with a circumcision done by the hands of men but with the circumcision done by Christ, having been buried with him in baptism and raised with him through your faith in the power of God, who raised him from the dead" (Col. 2:11–12). These words remind us that salvation comes through faith, and also that *the rite of circumcision that once signified the benefits of Abraham's covenant has been replaced by baptism.*

Since the covenant remains, but the sign changes, New Testament believers would naturally expect to apply the new sign of the covenant to themselves and their children as the old sign had been applied. Since the old sign was applied to children prior to their ability to express personal faith, there would be no barrier to applying the new sign prior to a child's personal profession of faith in Christ. Baptism would function both as a sign and a seal of the household's faith in Christ. As a seal, baptism would indicate the visible pledge of God that when the conditions of his covenant were met, the promised blessings would apply.

THE BIBLICAL BASIS FOR INFANT BAPTISM

What evidence is there in the Bible that New Testament parents applied the sacrament of baptism to their children with the understanding that the covenant with Abraham remained in effect with a changed sign? Biblically minded Christians rightly want to see scriptural confirmation of their churches' practices. Thus, we who believe in infant baptism must confess that the lack of any specific example of infant baptism in the New Testament is a strong counterweight to our position. Conscientious Christians who object to infant baptism are not necessarily being superficial, ignorant, or mean spirited. The church would not have argued the issues surrounding infant baptism for centuries if the right answers were obvious. What Presbyterians hope that believers will see in the absence of a named infant being baptized is how strong the other biblical evidences must be to have kept this covenant practice dominant in the worldwide Christian church since the earliest centuries.

The Absence of a Contrary Command

Just as advocates of infant baptism must deal with the absence of an identified infant being baptized in the New Testament, so also must opponents of infant baptism face the absence of a specific command to deny children the covenant sign and seal. As has already been noted, the apostles took great care to emphasize the continuation of the Abrahamic covenant for New Testament believers. Throughout the two-thousand-year history of this covenant prior to the beginning of the apostolic church, the people of God had administered the covenant sign to their children. It seems highly probable that if the apostles had changed that practice, that change would have been recorded in the New Testament, either by example or by precept.

The removal of any sign of the covenant from believers' children would have been an immense change in practice and concept for Jewish families. After two thousand years of covenant family practice (established since Genesis), a believing Jewish parent would not have known how to interpret a continuing Abrahamic covenant that did not administer the sign of the covenant to children. As will soon be discussed, the apostles frequently record households being baptized after the head of the home believes in Christ. Consider how the head of a Jewish household would have reacted when others in the household (including servants and resident relatives) were baptized on the basis of his faith while his own children were denied the covenant sign.

The absence of a scriptural command to prohibit administering the sign of the covenant to children after two thousand years of such practice weighs significantly against the view that the apostles wanted only those who were able to profess their faith to be baptized.

The Examples of Household Baptism

Further undermining the contention that only those who professed their faith were to be baptized are the examples of apostles expecting that entire households would be baptized once the head of the home accepted the gospel. Those who oppose infant baptism fairly ask for an example of an infant being baptized in the New Testament. Already we have acknowledged that there is no specific mention of an infant's baptism. But fairness requires that another question also be asked: Are there any examples of households being baptized because of the faith of the head of the household? Over and over again, the answer to this question is yes.

In fact, when we read the New Testament accounts of baptism, *every person identified as having a household present at his or her conversion also had the household baptized.* These accounts include every baptism of persons described in detail after the appointment of Christ's apostles (including Paul) was complete.

Household membership. Before listing these household baptisms, we should ask who were considered to be members of one's household in the ancient world. Returning to the Old Testament passages in which the covenant sign was first administered in households, we find that a household included all of one's resident dependents: spouse (if living), children (if present), resident relatives, and dependent servants not earning regular wages (e.g., Gen. 14:14–16; 17:23; Ex. 12:3–4). This understanding of households governed Jewish thought and practice for two thousand years, and there is little reason to believe that the Scripture writers would have had any other perspective. There is no evidence that the New Testament writers used the concept of a household in a manner inconsistent with the common understanding of preceding centuries. No effort was made by the New Testament writers to indicate that children were no longer included in households—an exclusion that even today would be alien to our thought.

What is foreign to our thought today is the biblical principle of representative headship. Our lack of familiarity with this principle is one of the reasons why our individualistic culture struggles to accept the covenant family principles and practices of Scripture. But, as has been discussed earlier, the presumption that the faith of the head of the home created obligations for the rest of the family was an historic understanding for God's people. Thus, when the Philippian jailer asked Paul, "What must I do to be saved?" it was natural and scriptural for the apostle to reply, "Believe in the Lord Jesus, and you will be saved—you and your household" (Acts 16:30–31). Paul's words do not mean that the rest of the household would automatically come to faith in Christ, but his presumption was that the faith of the head of the household would ultimately govern the commitments of the rest of the man's family. As a result, the jailer's entire household was baptized that night (v. 33).

Household accounts. The account of the baptism of the Philippian jailer's household is particularly instructive because of the precise description supplied by Luke, the writer of Acts. Luke says that *all* of the jailer's household was baptized (v. 33), but then he uses a *singular* verb to describe who rejoiced and believed in God that night (v. 34). The jailer himself believed (singular verb), and his whole house was baptized. Sadly, this important distinction in the account is not reflected in some of our modern translations (see the English Standard Version for an excellent translation). As a result, some assume that entire households were baptized in the New Testament because everyone in them believed the gospel. While this is not impossible, it is unlikely that all those households consisted only of those who were old enough to make an intelligent faith commitment. Further, the assumption that everyone in those households must have made a faith commitment does not take notice of the careful distinction that Luke makes between those who actually believed and those who were baptized.

The other household baptisms recorded in the New Testament are well known: Cornelius and his household (Acts 10:38), Lydia and her household (Acts 16:15), and the household of Stephanas (1 Cor. 1:16). Crispus and his household should probably also be included in the list when one considers Acts 18:8 and 1 Corinthians 1:14 together.

The purpose for listing these accounts of household baptism is not to contend that individual adult believers were never baptized in the New Testament. Clearly there were baptisms of individuals who apparently did not have households, such as Paul, the Ethiopian eunuch, and Simon the sorcerer (cf. Acts 8 and 9). Others were baptized during their pilgrimages or when household members apparently were not present (Acts 2:41; 19:5). There may also have been times when household members objected to being baptized. We do not know all of the circumstances of the men and women whom Scripture says were baptized (cf. Acts 8:12). What we do know is that when men and women believed in Christ, they were baptized. Further, whenever an individual baptism is described in detail in the New Testament, the members of the household, if they were present, also received the covenant sign of baptism.

Household resistance. The frequency of the household baptism accounts demonstrates that it was normal and consistent with the ancient practice of the continuing Abrahamic covenant for heads of households to see that the covenant sign and seal was applied to all in their home. No evidence indicates that children were excluded from these households. Rather, two thousand years of covenant practice, combined with the absence of any command to exclude children, indicate that household baptisms included infants.

Infant baptism is typically resisted by people in North American culture today because they (1) do not understand the continuation of the covenant of faith made with Abraham and its application to all believers today, (2) are not informed of the representative nature of covenant headship, (3) do not understand how a covenant sign is a seal (i.e., that baptism is a visible pledge that covenant promises will apply when the conditions of faith are met, so that the sign does not have to be tied to the moment that one believes in Christ), (4) do not realize that children would have been included as members of households that were baptized, and (5) cannot conceive of "dunking" a baby, if one's only experience with baptism involves immersion.

Only the issue of immersing babies has not been covered thus far in this chapter. Sadly, there is not space here to deal with the whole question of the proper mode of baptism. Thus, I will simply note that there are churches in the world that do immerse babies (quickly, I might add) in their practice of infant baptism. However, most of the churches that practice infant baptism teach that baptism is a ceremonial sign of Christ's cleansing and union with him, and that the amount of water used is not the key issue.

Various amounts of water are used in the ceremonial cleansings that Scripture describes as baptisms. In addition to examining the gospel narratives of Christ's baptism, we can look at such texts as Mark 7:2–4, Luke 11:38, and Hebrews 9:10–22 to discern a variety of ways in which baptism can be administered. English readers will be aided by knowing that the word often translated "washings" in these verses is a form of the Greek word for baptism. These various ceremonial cleansings involved different rites of pouring, dipping, and sprinkling. The Hebrews passage even refers to an event where thousands of people (as well as their place of worship) were sprinkled at once (cf. Ex. 24:6–8). I am not contending here that sprinkling is the only valid mode of baptism. Other passages relate baptism to the pouring out of God's Spirit (cf. Luke 3:16; Acts 1:5; 2:17–18; Titus 3:5–6). My point is only that *in a ceremonial cleansing the amount of fluid may vary in a manner that is appropriate for the occasion.* A child can still be truly baptized by sprinkling or pouring. Parents do not have to worry about drowning their newborns in order to honor God's covenant.

The Biblical Benefits of Infant Baptism

Should we baptize infants because the sacrament will make children Christians or guarantee that they will become believers? The answer is no, because no sacrament communicates the grace of salvation. The apostle Paul reminded the Corinthian Christians that although the ancient Israelites were all "baptized" by passing through the Red Sea under the cloud of God, they were idolaters who displeased God and experienced his wrath (1 Cor. 10:1–11). No mere ritual will save anyone.

But if baptism will not make our children Christians, then why should we administer the covenant sign and seal to them? The most important answer is that we baptize because God makes promises to believers and to their children. In baptism we honor God by marking out and acting on the promises that reflect his grace both in blessing parents who act in devotion to God and in blessing the child being devoted to him in covenantal faith.

The Devotion of Parents

Parents who love the Lord Jesus desire to devote all that they have to him. As Abraham devoted all that he had to God in the covenant of faith, so parents who trust in Christ want to demonstrate that their most precious gifts, their children, are his. In the sacrament of baptism, *we as parents demonstrate our commitment to be faithful stewards of the precious gift of a child's soul that God grants us to nurture for a season of life.*

Through the devotion that is demonstrated in baptism, parents begin to reap the blessings of obedience that come from building the foundations of a home on the promises of God. The baptism of an infant is the first public testimony of parents that they will trust and follow God in the raising of their child. As an act of devotion, the baptism sets the family on the path of blessing that God promises to those who walk in his ways.

The church witnessing the baptism is also blessed by the parents' testimony of devotion and trust. The church has the encouraging example of the parent's obedience, and fellow worshipers are reminded by the water of baptism that God's grace alone will wash away the sin of this child and fit him for heaven. In the truths signified by the water of baptism, the parents humbly acknowledge that they are dependent upon God's grace, not only to raise the child according to Scripture, but also to do what they cannot do to make the child holy before God.

As a public act of devotion, baptism also makes the parents accountable to the church before which they take vows to raise their child in the nurture and admonition of the Lord. Accountability is not simply a willingness to accept advice and correction from others when things go wrong, but a humble and joyful desire to receive the spiritual resources of the church that will help a child grow in Christian character. In baptism, parents link the spiritual livelihood of their child to the spiritual life of the church. They promise to intertwine their life of faith with the life of the church so that they and the child will hear wise counsel from others (including more experienced parents), encounter the reality of God's presence in worship, and learn from the example of mature saints how God's grace forms the beauty of the soul in both good and difficult circumstances.

It is important to remember, however, that baptism is not merely a sign of God's grace—it is also a seal. Baptism does not simply signify what Christ has done, nor does it only demonstrate the parents' devotion. Baptism is also God's own continuing, visible pledge to his church that he will fulfill his covenant promises to those who place their faith in him. God is present in the sacrament as though the doors of heaven have opened to have him declare anew to his church, "By the marks of this sacrament, I promise that anyone who trusts in my mercy through the blood of Christ will have his sins washed away and will be as pure before me as the water that flows from this font, so that we will be in holy union forever." With this promise indicated by the seal of baptism, God reaches from heaven to embrace the parents and the child with the assurance of his grace, based upon his mercy, not upon their merit. In our moments of great pride in our children, and in our moments of great shame for our failings, *God's pledge of merciful grace that is evident in baptism is always ours by faith to claim* for ourselves and for our children.

The Blessing of the Child

The devotion of the parents who present their children for baptism places each child in a privileged position both to hear and to understand the truths of the gospel. The child first has the example of his parents' devotion demonstrated in their willingness to devote their most precious possession to God. Beyond this initial example, the child lives in a home that through the child's baptism has promised to provide Christian nurture and to use the resources of the church to make that nurture truly biblical in character. The parents publicly promise in the sacrament of baptism to pray with and for their child, so that early in life he might know the realities of God's saving grace in Christ.

The child also has the promise of the church to support the parents in his spiritual nurture and admonition. In the public sacrament of baptism, the people of the church vow to pray for the parents and the child, and to provide godly examples for them.

Some no doubt repeat these vows out of courtesy and convention, but as the church repeats its own testimony year after year, the whole body of Christ learns of its obligation and power to influence the eternity of her children. When the church is truly one in this effort, a child is surrounded and embraced by the testimony of Christ at every turn in life. Thus, the church becomes God's instrument of presenting the reality of himself to the mind and heart of the child. A child with such an experience, fostered at his baptism and nourished throughout his life by a mature body of believers, breathes the truths of grace as naturally and unconsciously as he breathes air.

In this atmosphere, faith naturally germinates and matures so that *it is possible, even common, for the children of Christian parents never to know a day that they do not believe that Jesus is their Savior and Lord.* Such covenantal growth of a child is, in fact, the normal Christian life that God intends for his people, and it is one of the most striking, but infrequently mentioned, reasons that baptism is rightly administered to infants.

Just as children are raised to know the color blue through all about them repeatedly and readily attesting the character of the hue, so children raised in an environment of faith ordinarily mature with an understanding of their Savior. Of course, there are exceptions. True faith remains a supernatural gift, but natural human instruments fulfilling their covenant obligations most frequently communicate it. Thus, as a covenant child grows in natural understanding of his world, it is most common for him to mature with a parallel level of spiritual understanding. This means that it is no more likely that children nurtured in a consistently Christian home can specifically mark when they understood that Jesus was their Savior than they can mark when they knew that blue was blue.

So when would be the proper time to baptize such children? Since Genesis, the proper time that God declared for marking children with the covenant sign has been in their infancy in the covenant community. The early application of the sign indicated that there was not necessarily a definitive moment when a child made a life-altering decision to follow the Lord. Instead, children in believing homes were expected to grow in spiritual maturity and understanding as the covenant community embraced and instructed them. In a similar manner, the sacrament of baptism is rightly administered today to infants to indicate that their whole life is to be one of continually growing in Christ through the family that devotes them to God in faithfulness to the covenant they entered at birth.

A Pastoral Explanation of Infant Baptism

How should pastors explain the concept of infant baptism when administering the sacrament? The truths that underlie the practice are clear, but require an understanding of the scope of Scripture that many in our congregations lack today. As a result, many of the words of institution that are repeated during infant baptisms refer generally to God's love for his children or to Christ's willingness to allow children to approach him (e.g., Matt. 19:14; Luke 18:16). While such references accurately communicate the compassion of God, I have found them unconvincing as the reason we should baptize infants.

Those who disagree with infant baptism agree that Jesus said, "Suffer little children to come unto me, and forbid them not," and we are all aware that Jesus did not baptize the children who then approached him. Making the gospel accounts of Christ's blessing of children the chief emphasis of an explanation of infant baptism seems rather to prove that such ceremonies come more from sentiment and tradition than from any demonstrable biblical principle.

A number of fine books contain forms that will help pastors to frame credible words of explanation prior to an infant baptism. In addition, I have found the following words, though imperfect, to be useful in my ministry:

> Will baptism save this child? No, salvation comes through trusting in Jesus Christ as one's Savior and Lord. Then why do we baptize this child? Not for sentiment, though he/she is sweet. Not for tradition, though it is dear. We baptize this child because we believe the Bible commands us to do so.

Throughout biblical history, God promised to bless through a covenant relationship with his people. He said to Abraham, "I will be a God to you and to your children after you." Abraham believed God's covenant promise and devoted all that he had to the Lord, including the members of his household. In obedience to God, Abraham showed his devotion through practicing the rite of circumcision in his household. This rite demonstrated that God's covenant would pass to future generations, but would necessitate the shedding of blood for sin.

The shed blood did not create the covenant, but rather acted as a seal, a pledge given by God, that he would honor his promise to all who, like Abraham, put their faith in him.

In the New Testament, the apostle Peter, preaching on the Day of Pentecost, assured all that covenant promises of God would continue for the children of believers. He said, "Repent and be baptized, every one of you, in the name of Jesus Christ, so that your sins may be forgiven. . . . The promise is for you and for your children and for all who are far off—for all whom the Lord our God will call."

The promise to bless through faith in God's grace continued, but the apostle Paul told the Colossian believers that the sign of this covenant has changed. No longer foreshadowing the shedding of Christ's blood, the New Testament sacrament of baptism is a sign of what Christ's blood accomplishes, the washing away of sin, and thus our union with him.

This water does not itself wash away sin, but rather, according to the apostle Paul, this sacrament acts as a seal—a visible pledge of God given to the church—whereby heaven assures us that when such children as this one express faith in Christ, all the promises of his covenant of grace will apply to them.

The Bible gives us good reason to express our covenant privileges through such a baptism. In the New Testament accounts of baptism, every person identified as having a household present at his or her conversion also had the household baptized.

Yes, it is sweet to savor God's goodness to this family, but sentiment is not what leads this church or these parents to this holy ordinance.

We baptize this child in obedience to biblical teaching, in keeping with the precedent of centuries of faithful families, and in expectation of God's presence and blessing. God now uses this sacrament to pledge to us his faithfulness as we, in faith, devote this child of the covenant to him.

2

MATTHEW 28:18–20 AND THE INSTITUTION OF BAPTISM

DANIEL M. DORIANI

In Matthew 28:18–20, Jesus institutes Christian baptism. No biblical text is more foundational to the Christian doctrine and practice of baptism than Matthew 28. Mark 16:16 seems to be a second account of Jesus' institution of baptism. Yet, as we will see, no biblical text is less foundational to Christian baptism than Mark 16:16.

By closing with fifty words from the lips of Jesus, Matthew brings his gospel to a magnificent climax in 28:18–20. In those last words, Matthew wraps up several major themes, including Christian mission, faith, discipleship, and the teaching of Jesus. He also locates the institution of baptism within the context of mission and discipleship in the Christian community. Mark 16:16 has been used to promote perhaps the greatest mistake concerning baptism—that it is necessary for salvation. The second portion of this chapter will attempt to correct that misconception in two ways. First, we will see why most evangelical scholars doubt that Mark 16:16 was part of the original text of Mark. Second, we will show that even if Mark 16:16 were genuine, it still would not warrant the teaching that baptism is necessary for salvation.

MATTHEW 28:18–20: THE GREAT COMMISSION

As important as Matthew 28:18–20 is for baptism, the church knows the passage first as the Great Commission. In Matthew 28, Jesus commissions his disciples to disciple all the nations. It is indeed a great commission, and the institution of baptism is best understood as an element of it.

The Context of the Great Commission

The Great Commission completes four major themes of Matthew: coming to faith, mission, making disciples, and hearing the words of Jesus. Let us consider them briefly, to better understand the institution of baptism.

Coming to faith. Matthew 28:17 reports that even in the moment before the Great Commission is given, some at the scene doubt or hesitate. Matthew often stresses that it is difficult to come to mature faith. The disciples are "men of little faith" (*oligopistoi*).[1] Men of little faith worry about food and clothing, instead of trusting God (6:30). When a storm arises on the sea, they have enough faith to cry "Lord, save us," but they are weak enough that they half expect to drown (8:24–26). During another storm, Peter trusts Jesus enough to walk to him on the water, but then hesitates, looks at the waves, and begins to sink (14:25–31). After the Resurrection, some disciples still hesitate. They have received orders to meet Jesus at a mountain in Galilee. They believe enough to obey the command, and some worship, but others still doubt (28:17). Perhaps the women's report seemed too good to be true. Perhaps, seeing Jesus at a distance, altered by his resurrection, they were not quite sure it was he. Whatever the reason, some hesitate in 28:17.[2] As in the storms at sea, the disciples show

1. The Greek *oligopistoi* means "men of little faith." It appears five times in the New Testament, four times in Matthew (6:30; 8:26; 14:31; 16:8) and once in Luke (12:28).

2. Perhaps some of the five hundred who saw Jesus (1 Cor. 15:6) were there. It is hard to see how the eleven disciples could hesitate after Jesus so strikingly removed Thomas's doubts in John 20. See Leon Morris, *Matthew* (Grand Rapids: Eerdmans, 1992), 745.

some faith, but not enough to banish all fear. The journey toward faith is not quick and easy, even for disciples who have witnessed everything. Still, Jesus judges them ready to disciple others. If they are not yet perfectly mature, they are close enough. Then and now, disciples learn and grow fitfully, until they are ready for a commission. Baptism is part of that commission.

Mission. Matthew is often called the gospel for the Jews, and Matthew does say that the good news must go first to the lost sheep of Israel (10:5–6; 15:24). Yet Matthew has an interest in Gentiles from the beginning. His genealogy traces Jesus' lineage through Gentiles such as Rahab and Ruth (1:1–17). In the birth narrative, only Gentiles worship Jesus (2:1–15). Jesus' ministry begins in the far north of Israel, in "Galilee of the Gentiles" (4:15). Jesus performs miracles for Gentiles: a centurion praised for great faith (8:5–13) and a demoniac of Gadara, a pagan region (8:28–34). Because of Jewish unbelief, Jesus says, "The kingdom of God will be taken away from you and given to a people [the Gentiles] who will produce its fruit" (21:43). When the disciples are mature, Jesus predicts, they will testify to Gentiles (10:17–20). After the Resurrection, therefore, it is no surprise that Jesus commands them to disciple the nations. Baptism is part of the mission to the nations.

Teaching and making disciples. Baptism is part of the larger project of making disciples. In Matthew, teaching and baptizing stand together. The example of Jesus is instructive, but Matthew's emphasis falls on words.[3] After teaching his disciples about the kingdom, he compares them to owners of houses who can bring treasures out of their storerooms (13:51–52). Our text charges the apostles to make disciples by "teaching them to obey everything I have commanded you" (28:20). The rest of Matthew's gospel presents those very commands in teach-

3. When he sends the disciples on a mission, Jesus commands them to proclaim the kingdom, heal the sick, expel demons, give freely, and take no money, just as he has done (10:7–10). He says of his example, "A student is not above his teacher. . . . It is enough for the student to be like his teacher" (10:24–25).

ing found in every chapter. Matthew heard it all, while he was still a "man of little faith." He slowly appropriated Jesus' instruction, until he was ready to write the gospel we now use to disciple the nations. Jesus' teachings accomplished in Matthew's life what Matthew wants them to accomplish in us and in the nations. Again, baptism is an element of the teaching and discipling that Matthew sought.

Baptism in the Great Commission

We call Matthew 28:18–20 the Great Commission—and rightly so, for it is great and it is a commission.[4] The institution of baptism is part of that commission:

> Then the eleven disciples went to Galilee, to the mountain where Jesus had told them to go. When they saw him, they worshiped him; but some doubted. Then Jesus came to them and said, "All authority in heaven and on earth has been given to me. Therefore go and make disciples of all nations, baptizing them in the name of the Father and of the Son and of the Holy Spirit, and teaching them to obey everything I have commanded you. And surely I am with you always, to the very end of the age." (28:16–20)

28:16. Mountains are often the scene for a great revelation from God (e.g., Ex. 19; 24; 1 Kings 18–19; Matt. 17:1–8), so it is fitting that Jesus commissioned his disciples from a mountain. Other disciples probably came to the mountain, but Jesus spoke chiefly to the eleven.[5]

28:17. This is the first time in Matthew's gospel that the disciples see Jesus after his resurrection. It is proper for them to worship Jesus

4. Its structure resembles the commissions that God gave to Abraham, Moses, Joshua, and Isaiah. After an introduction, there is a confrontation with God and a reaction by the one commissioned. God then commissions his agent, whom he also reassures. In Matthew 28, we have an introduction (v. 16), confrontation (vv. 17–18a), reaction (v. 18b), commission (vv. 19–20a), and reassurance (v. 20b).

5. Both the angel (28:7) and Jesus (28:10) instruct the women to tell the disciples that Jesus is alive, but neither restricts the message to the eleven, even if they were the prime object of his commission.

when they see him, now that they see that he has defeated death and lives again. Yet some hesitated. Was Jesus far away? Was his appearance altered by his risen glory? Was the news too good to bear? Yet when Jesus approached them, doubts surely evaporated.

28:18. Jesus structures his charge carefully. "Make disciples of all nations" is the central command. Jesus wraps that commission in spiritual reasoning. First, the disciples should obey Jesus because "all authority in heaven and on earth has been given to me." Because of his authority, Jesus has the right to issue commands as broad as life itself, commands that take lifetimes to fulfill.

Jesus also assures the disciples that he sends them out in his strength (28:20). They are not alone; Jesus is "with" them. As simple as it sounds, we dare not minimize the promise, "I am with you always." The idea that Jesus is "with us" appears just three times in Matthew, at three critical junctures. First, at Jesus' birth, we learn that he is Immanuel, "God with us," to save his people (1:21, 23). Second, in the agony of church discipline, Jesus says that he is with us to preserve the integrity of the church (18:15–20). Third, Jesus promises his disciples that he goes with them to disciple the nations.

Jesus modifies the central command, "Make disciples," with three participles that explain how believers execute their task. We make disciples by going, by baptizing, and by teaching proselytes to obey every last thing that Jesus has commanded.

28:19. "Therefore go." Technically speaking, "make disciples" is the only command in this verse: In the Greek, "go" is a participle—"going" (*poreuthentes*). But it would be a mistake to think that this participle lacks imperatival force. Jesus is not saying to make disciples "as you go" or "if you go" or "when you go." Rather, as the major translations render it, he means, "Go and make disciples."[6] The book of Acts shows

6. In Matthew, participles preceding an imperative have imperatival force in 2:8, 13; 9:13; 11:4, 17:27. See Cleon Rogers, "The Great Commission," *Bibliotheca Sacra* 130 (1973): 258–61, who also cites parallel Septuagint (LXX) usage in Gen. 27:13; 37:14; Ex. 5:18. It is a participle of attendant circumstance, so it coordinates with the mood of the main verb. Since the main

that the disciples realized the need to travel the world with their message. Jesus wants his followers to make disciples by going to the nations, not by waiting for the nations to come to them.

"Make disciples."[7] To make disciples is more than preaching the gospel or making converts. To be a disciple is to become Jesus' pupil. Disciples are learners. They take Jesus' yoke. They submit to his instruction. We are disciples if we hear and obey everything Jesus says, because he says it (Matt. 11:29; 12:59; cf. Acts 10:33).

"Make disciples of all nations" means that the assignment has worldwide scope. The term "the nations" typically means "Gentiles," even "pagans," in Matthew (6:32; 10:5; 10:18). But the slightly longer phrase, "all the nations," can refer to all the peoples of the earth, Gentiles and Jews alike (24:9, 14; 25:32). Therefore, the charge is to disciple everyone, so that, as God promised, all tribes, all nations, will be blessed through Abraham (Gen. 12:3; 18:18; 22:18).[8]

"Baptizing them." Here Jesus institutes Christian baptism. It belongs in the context of the Great Commission. It is an aspect of the discipleship of the nations.

The Fourth Gospel reveals that early in Jesus' ministry, his disciples performed baptisms roughly like those of John the Baptist (John 3:22; 4:1–2). Jesus never personally baptized anyone, and it seems that the disciples only briefly imitated John's baptism.[9] Thus, the baptism that Jesus inaugurates is distinct from John's. John's baptism belonged

verb is imperative, the participle is imperatival. The main indicators of a participle of attendant circumstance are present: (1) the participle is aorist; (2) the main verb is aorist; (3) the mood is imperative; (4) the participle precedes the main verb (Daniel Wallace, *Greek Grammar Beyond the Basics* [Grand Rapids: Zondervan, 1996], 640–45).

7. The Greek *mathēteusate* can mean either "be a disciple" (Matt. 13:52; 27:57) or "make disciples." The context demands the sense of "make disciples."

8. The phrase used in Matt. 28:19, *panta ta ethnē,* appears in Gen. 18:18 LXX and 22:18 LXX; Gen. 12:3 LXX differs slightly. See D. A. Carson, *Matthew,* Expositor's Bible Commentary (Grand Rapids: Zondervan, 1995), 596.

9. It is no surprise if the disciples performed baptisms like John's, for Jesus approved of John's ministry and methods, and submitted to John's baptism. But since the Synoptic Gospels, which pass over Jesus' earliest ministry, never mention these baptisms, Jesus' followers probably stopped the practice before long. See G. R. Beasley-Murray, *Baptism in the New Testament* (New York: St. Martin's Press, 1963), 67–72.

to the old covenant. It signified repentance and cleansing from sin. By receiving it, Jewish believers affirmed their loyalty to the old covenant. The baptism that Jesus institutes differs also from his disciples' baptism. Both baptisms show allegiance to Jesus, but Jesus' baptism follows his crucifixion and resurrection.[10] In the Great Commission, Jesus inaugurates something new—baptism into Christ.

Locating baptism within the context of the Great Commission, it is more accurate to say that Jesus instituted or inaugurated Christian baptism, than to say that he commanded it. Strictly speaking, Jesus commanded the disciples to make disciples, not to baptize. In the original, the command to "make disciples" is modified by three participles: "going," "baptizing," and "teaching." As we saw above, the first participle—"going"—functions as an imperative (cf. note 6). But the second and third participles are not as closely connected to the main verb; indeed, the link is debatable.

Since they are participles, "baptizing" and "teaching" both modify or explain the main verb, the command to make disciples. But there are three interpretations of how "baptizing" and "teaching" modify "make disciples." The first option is that the participles are modal. That is, they describe the way, the manner, or the circumstances that accompany the task of making disciples.[11] The second option is that "baptizing" and "teaching" are participles of means. That is, Jesus expects his followers to make disciples *by means of* baptizing them and teaching them to obey all his teachings. Baptism is then an instrument, a method, that Jesus' followers will use to make disciples.[12] The third view is that "baptizing" and "teaching" function as supplementary imperatives. That is, baptizing and teaching are implicitly commanded. We must make disciples by going, baptizing, and teaching.[13]

There is some truth in each of these views. First, teaching is surely a way to make disciples: I will propose that baptism can be, too (below).

10. Ibid., 71–72.

11. Mentioned in Carson, *Matthew,* 597, and Beasley-Murray, *Baptism in the New Testament,* 89.

12. Wallace, *Greek Grammar Beyond the Basics,* 645; Rogers, "Great Commission," 262.

13. Donald Hagner, *Matthew 14–28,* Word Biblical Commentary (Dallas: Word, 1995), 887–89.

Second, since we must make disciples, we ought to use all available means to achieve the goal. So the participles have an imperatival tone, too. Third, this is how Christians make disciples; we baptize and teach as we go.

This explanation suits the grammar of the text.[14] It also fits the wisest explication of the passage, which depends upon the widely accepted idea that many accounts of Jesus' speeches epitomize longer remarks.[15] Thus, the fifty or so words of the Great Commission, which can be uttered in less than thirty seconds, probably summarize a much longer statement. Emphasizing baptism somewhat, we can amplify Jesus' speech in this way:

> You already know that I, the Son of Man, have authority on earth to forgive sins [Matt. 9:6]. You know that the Father has given me authority over all things [Matt. 11:27]. But know now that since my death and resurrection, my authority, my status as ruler over all, my sovereign power over all nations and peoples, will be manifest as never before, so that men of every nation will worship me [Dan. 7:13–14; Matt. 26:64; Rom. 1:4]. Yet I do not simply want them to bow to me; I want them to believe and to bow in faith. For this reason, I charge you to go and proclaim who I am and what I have done for the people of every tongue and nation in my world. Proclaim my death and resurrection. Proclaim that I have given my life as a ransom for sinners. Proclaim my redemption. When people respond in repentance and faith, lead them into full discipleship by baptizing and instructing them.

14. In cases such as Matt. 28:19, where participles follow one another without *kai* ("and") or any other conjunction binding them to the main verb, "they must be viewed as dependent on one another or depending in differing ways on the chief verb" (Beasley-Murray, *Baptism in the New Testament,* 89). F. Blass, A. Debrunner, and Robert Funk, *A Greek Grammar of the New Testament* (Chicago: University of Chicago Press, 1961), 217–18 (par. 421): "The participles are asyndetic if they do not have equal value in the sentence."

15. This is the view of conservative scholars from Darrell Bock to N. T. Wright. In the Synoptics, Jesus' longest speeches, such as the Sermon on the Mount, can be read aloud in twelve minutes—hardly enough time for a crowd to settle. Since summarizing was an acceptable historiographical technique in antiquity, it is reasonable to assume that the Sermon on the Mount lasted for hours. Similarly, a single sentence in Matthew may capture the essence of a few minutes of speech.

Repentance alone is not sufficient. I want them to grow in discipleship, even as you, my first disciples, have done. Therefore, when someone repents and believes, lead them in the way that leads to maturity. First, baptize them, so they will identify with my movement, even as I identified myself with John's movement three years ago, when I asked him to baptize me. Baptize them into my name, so they will understand that they have entered into a personal relationship with me. Baptize them into my name, so they will know that when they repented and believed, they came under my authority. Baptize them into the name of the Father and of the Son and of the Spirit, so they will know that I am equal with the Father God who revealed himself in his covenants with Israel, and so they will also know that I am one with the Spirit by whom they experience new life. Baptize them, so they will know that they belong to me and have become part of the household of faith. Baptize them as a sign of their covenantal relationship with me.

After they repent and believe, instruct them. Present every last lesson you have learned from me.[16] Teach them to keep all my commands. Teach them that I deepen the law by addressing the heart, not just the letter of the law. Teach them that all authority is mine; they have no right to heed one decree and reject another.

The road I am marking out for you is hard. Therefore, be comforted; you do not go alone. I have been with you day and night for three years. The time when you and I walk together daily will soon end. But remember, my name is Immanuel, and so I shall be: God with you. I will be with you all the days of your life. And I will be with the disciples whom you raise up all the days of their lives. So it shall be, to the end of this age.[17]

This paraphrase of the Great Commission suggests how the participles "baptizing" and "teaching" can both be imperatival and describe the means and modes of the task of discipling the nations. The

16. The phrase "every last lesson" reflects a doubling in the Greek, which literally reads, "teaching them to observe everything whatever I commanded to you."

17. This paraphrase multiplies Jesus' words almost tenfold, primarily by unpacking allusions to other Scriptures. Jesus possibly said still more; one can read these words in four minutes or less.

paraphrase also sketches the meaning of the last phases of the commission, so that commentary on it would probably be redundant. But we should comment on the word "all," which appears four times in verses 18–20 in the Greek. We read that Jesus has *all* authority, that his disciples must disciple *all* the nations, that they are to do so by teaching *all* that Jesus has commanded, and that Jesus will be with them *all* the days of this age. The commission is broad indeed, and the institution of baptism participates in that breadth.

The Institution of Baptism

The institution of baptism merits comment in several areas: its newness, its observance, its terms, its authenticity, its recipients, and its effects.

The newness of Jesus' baptism. In Jesus' day, many Jews practiced ceremonial washings or "baptisms." Most were ritual, repeated acts. They were part of the quest for purity at Qumran and among similar groups. Beyond these, John the Baptist announced a baptism of repentance and the confession of sin. But his baptism was preparatory and transitional.[18] He announced, "Prepare the way for the Lord." He baptized with water and awaited one greater than he, who would "baptize you with the Holy Spirit and with fire" (Matt. 3:3, 6, 11–12). Jesus' baptism did not *prepare for* the new age; it *inaugurated* it—when linked with the preaching of Jesus' death and resurrection. Jesus' baptism, sealed by the Holy Spirit in Acts 2, is what John awaited.

The permanent observance of baptism. Biblical history and church history both attest that the church has consistently practiced baptism. The charge to make disciples endures to the end of the age (Matt. 28:20; cf. 2 Tim. 2:2). Therefore, all Christian leaders must use baptism as a means to make disciples.[19] From the beginning of Acts, the

18. John Murray, *Christian Baptism* (Philadelphia: Presbyterian and Reformed, 1962), 4–5.

19. A few Christians hold that Jesus only delivered the commission to make disciples and baptize to his original disciples. But the two who saw Jesus on the road to Emmaus were with the eleven when they received the charge to witness to Christ (Luke 24:33, 45–49). Apparently,

church baptized its converts, whether Jew or Gentile (Acts 2:38–41; 8:12–16; 8:36–38; 10:47–48). History attests that since the end of the apostolic age, with virtually no exceptions, the church has practiced baptism.

The terms of baptism. Jesus charged his disciples to baptize (literally) "into the name of the Father and of the Son and of the Holy Spirit." To baptize "into" a name means a bit more than to baptize "in" that name. In Matthew, the words "in" (Greek: *en*) and "into" (Greek: *eis*) have overlapping, but distinct, meanings. Both imply that the name of the Father, the Son, and the Holy Spirit should be used at a baptism. But "into" further implies that the baptized people come into a relationship with the triune God.[20] They belong to him and submit to him. This is clear from parallel passages in Paul's letters. To be "baptized into Moses" (1 Cor. 10:2) or to be "baptized into the name of Paul" (1 Cor. 1:13) is to enter into a relationship with them. People who are baptized into the name of Jesus enter his covenant family. Baptism is the sign and seal of their union with Christ in his death and resurrection. It is a pledge of submission to the risen Lord.[21] When an adult is baptized, he declares that he belongs to God. When a child is baptized, his parents declare that their child belongs to God.

The authenticity of baptism. Many critics doubt the authenticity of Matthew's account of the institution of baptism.[22] They note that the baptisms recorded in Acts are in the name of Jesus alone, not in the

several others were also present in Acts 1, when Jesus told his disciples that they would be his witnesses to the ends of the earth (Acts 1:8–14; see also notes 2 and 5 above).

20. Nigel Turner, *Grammar of New Testament Greek: Syntax* (Edinburgh: T & T Clark, 1963), 255. Citing 10:41, 12:41, and 28:19, Turner argues that Matthew's use of *eis* has the sense of "because of" or "for the sake of." Thus, the goal of baptism into Jesus' name is to establish a relationship with him.

21. Murray, *Christian Baptism,* 6–7; Beasley-Murray, *Baptism in the New Testament,* 90–92.

22. W. D. Davies and Dale Allison, *Matthew,* International Critical Commentary (Edinburgh: T & T Clark, 1997), 3:685. Radical skeptics propose that the church independently adopted the custom of baptizing proselytes and put the words of 28:19 into Jesus' mouth in order to justify its practice. Full dialogue with radicals belongs in other books.

name of the Father, the Son, and the Spirit (Acts 2:38; 8:16; 10:48; 19:5). The same is true of references to baptism in Paul's letters (Rom. 6:3; Gal. 3:27). The problem, critics say, is that baptism into the name of the Father, the Son, and the Spirit reflects a belief in the Trinity that belongs to the faith of the church, rather than the teaching of Jesus.

It is true that the triune formula may not represent the exact words that Jesus used on the mountain. But, as we saw, it is likely that he said more, not less. Matthew's gospel demonstrates that Jesus thought of himself as equal with the Father. He accepted titles like "Lord" and "Son of God." He assumed privileges and exercised prerogatives that belong to God alone. He received worship, forgave sins, declared himself to be the judge of mankind, and said that a person's destiny depends on his allegiance to him. He taught the truth and performed miracles on his own authority.[23] Discipleship begins with faith in the triune God. Therefore, we baptize into the name of the triune God.

The recipients of baptism. Because discipleship is for all people, baptism is for all people, too. Jesus went first to the Jews and told his disciples to do the same, but Matthew wants his Jewish-Christian readers to take the gospel to the Gentiles, too (Matt. 10:5, 18; 15:21–27). Gentile believers become a borderless nation who will bear the fruit that God seeks (21:43; cf. 13:38; 24:14). To disciple "the nations," one must still evangelize, baptize, and teach the Jews.[24] Like Paul, Matthew never lost interest in his own people.

Some think that the commission to disciple and baptize excludes Jews, and others think that the command to baptize excludes children. Doubtless, the conversion of adults is on Jesus' mind in 28:18–20. The charge to teach them "to obey everything" seems apt for converts who can understand and obey. But what else could we expect at the birth

23. See R. T. France, *Matthew: Evangelist and Teacher* (Grand Rapids: Zondervan, 1989), 279–317; Daniel Doriani, "The Deity of Christ in the Synoptic Gospels," *Journal of the Evangelical Theological Society* 37 (1994): 333–50.

24. There is an exegetical issue here. The term "the nations" (Greek: *ta ethnē*) usually refers to those who are outside of Israel (i.e., Gentiles; see 4:15; 6:32; 10:5–6, 18; 20:19, 25). But it can include Jews. See 21:43; 24:9.

of Christianity? Discipleship necessarily involved new converts. But nothing in Matthew excludes children from discipleship and baptism. Indeed, baptism is a valuable means for discipling children. First, God in his grace can regenerate a child from the earliest age, even in conjunction with baptism itself. Second, wise parents tell their children about their baptism, perhaps on the occasion of an infant baptism in the church:

> We baptized you when you were little, too. We promised to raise you to trust Jesus. The pastor put water on your head. We use water for washing, and when we baptized you, we asked God to wash away your sins. The pastor said "In the name of the Father and of the Son and of the Holy Spirit" for you, too. That means that he asked God to be your God. Now you belong to him. We all want you to believe in God for yourself, but baptism means that you are never all by yourself. See how the family always comes to baptisms and how the whole church is there? Our family came, too, and we pray for you. The people of the church care for you, too. We teach you and pray for you, so you will belong to God all of your life.

The effects of baptism. Other chapters explore the effects of baptism more fully, but Jesus teaches that the institution of baptism is a key element in the process of discipling the nations. The task is large, and we are not worthy of it. Matthew and the eleven were not worthy either, but the same God who fortified Matthew also empowered later generations. The Lord also supplies means for the task, including both baptism and teaching. Of course, the ritual of baptism does not guarantee an effect, any more than the presence of a teacher—even a gifted teacher—guarantees an effect. The recipients must receive the words of teaching and the water of baptism with faith. Then baptism and teaching are means of grace and discipleship. Combined with the faith of an adult convert, or with the faith of parents in the case of an infant, baptism both signifies and mediates a relationship with Jesus. Then baptism brings men and women, boys and girls, into union with Christ and knowledge of him. They follow him, and he is with them forever.

MARK 16:16

Earlier, I asserted that no biblical text is less foundational to our understanding of baptism than Mark 16:16. This verse certainly seems relevant when it says, "Whoever believes and is baptized will be saved, but whoever does not believe will be condemned." The problem is that there is strong evidence that Mark 16:16 does not belong to the original text of Mark. Mark 16:9–20 was probably added to the text many years later by someone who was neither an apostle nor an eyewitness of Jesus' ministry, and so is not inspired.

This is not the place to explain the discipline of textual criticism, which stands behind these assertions, but a few key principles are worth explaining. First, the assertion that Mark 16:9–20 is a later addition in no way undermines one's commitment to the inerrancy of the original text of Scripture. On the contrary, that very commitment has led many scholars to toil to discover the original, inspired text of Mark. Copies and translations are generally highly reliable, but it is the original text, not the copies and translations, that are inspired. Second, it is indisputable that the surviving manuscripts of the New Testament, written out by hand, differ from one another in many minor details. Indeed, the best copies have marginal notes indicating that copyists had texts that read two or even three different ways. Third, major variations between copies are rare. Conservative scholars consider Mark 16:9–20 and John 7:53–8:11 to be the only two extended gospel passages of doubtful authenticity.[25]

25. The case against John's authorship of John 7:53–8:11 is nearly indisputable. The story of the woman caught in adultery is absent from all the best, earliest Greek manuscripts of John and from most early translations. For a thousand years after Christ, no Greek church father referred to the passage and no Greek commentator expounded it.

The Text of Mark 16:9–20

For more than a century, most New Testament scholars have held that the original text of Mark ends at 16:8.[26] Thus, the so-called longer ending of Mark—Mark 16:9–20—is judged to be no part of Mark's original, inspired gospel. The argument in favor of the authenticity of 16:9–20 has three elements. First, the great majority of all extant Greek manuscripts of Mark contain the passage. Even among the earliest manuscripts of the complete New Testament, only two (Codex Sinaiticus and Codex Vaticanus) omit it. Second, most early translations of Mark include 16:9–20. Third, by the late second century, some church leaders, such as Irenaeus and Tatian, were making use of the text in their writings.[27]

These points notwithstanding, there is strong evidence against the authenticity of Mark 16:9–20. First, the two earliest, complete manuscripts of the Gospels, Codex Sinaiticus and Codex Vaticanus, lack the passage. Because of their early date and reputation for accuracy, these are widely regarded as two of the best witnesses to the original text of the New Testament. Second, while only a few later manuscripts omit the passage, many mark it with asterisks or marginal comments, indicating that older Greek copies lacked the passage. Third, some early manuscripts of Mark in Latin, Syriac, Armenian, and Georgian lack 16:9–20. Fourth, Eusebius, the greatest historian of the early church, and Jerome, the greatest linguist of the early church, both judged the text to be spurious. One of Jerome's epistles says, "Almost all the Greek codices do not have this concluding portion." Eusebius said that accurate copies of Mark ended with verse 8 and that 16:9–20 was missing from almost all manuscripts. Thus, Jerome and Eusebius

26. Especially since the landmark work of B. F. Westcott and F. J. A. Hort, *The New Testament in the Original Greek* (Cambridge: Macmillan, 1881).

27. See the evidence in Bruce M. Metzger, *The Text of the New Testament*, 3d ed. (New York: Oxford University Press, 1992), 226–29; Bruce M. Metzger, *A Textual Commentary on the New Testament* (Stuttgart: United Bible Societies, 1975), 122–26; Ned B. Stonehouse, *The Witness of the Synoptic Gospels to Christ* (Grand Rapids: Baker, 1979), 88–110; William R. Farmer, *The Last Twelve Verses of Mark* (London: Cambridge University Press, 1974); William L. Lane, *The Gospel According to Mark*, New International Commentary on the New Testament (Grand Rapids: Eerdmans, 1974), 601–11.

were aware of many copies, now lost, that lacked Mark 16:9–20. Fifth, such early theologians as Clement of Alexandria, Origen, Cyprian, and Cyril of Jerusalem never refer to the longer ending of Mark. Sixth, various manuscripts of the New Testament have three distinct endings of Mark following 16:8, which shows that early Christians were not sure how Mark ended. Seventh, the vocabulary and style of the traditional ending differ significantly from the rest of Mark. For example, there are seventeen words that either appear only in this section of Mark or are used in a sense not found elsewhere in Mark.[28] Stylistically, Mark's customary transitional words, "immediately" (*euthys*) and "again" (*palin*) are absent, and his habit of connecting sentences with "and" (*kai*), called parataxis, is not followed. Eighth, the longer ending does not carry forward the dramatic sequence in 16:6–8, since it never describes the meeting, foretold by the angel (v. 7), between Jesus and the disciples in Galilee. Rather, it reports Jesus' appearance to Mary Magdalene, to two unnamed disciples on a road, and to the eleven at a meal.

In addition, the arguments for the authenticity of Mark 16:9–20 are not as strong as they seem. First, while most manuscripts do include 16:9–20, the great majority of them come from later centuries and belong to one family of manuscript, called the "majority" or "Byzantine" text. Second, even if most Greek copies and most translations into other languages did have 16:9–20, it is easier to see how some would *add* 16:9–20 than it is to explain why others would *delete* it. Third, even if some church fathers do cite Mark 16:9–20, those with access to the best resources deny its authenticity. There are, therefore, powerful arguments against the authenticity of 16:9–20. It seems that the earliest copies of Mark ended at 16:8.[29]

Since the canonicity of Mark 16:9–20 is so doubtful, no doctrine should be founded on it. Most of 16:9–20 repeats parts of the other

28. Lane, *The Gospel According to Mark,* 604, n. 10.

29. As Stonehouse puts it in *The Witness of the Synoptic Gospels to Christ,* 90, "The earliest forms of the Greek New Testament to reach Alexandria, Caesarea and Antioch ended at 16:8." See the appendix for more discussion of Mark 16.

gospels, but there are two new ideas. First, it is stated that whoever believes and is baptized will be saved (v. 16). Second, it is said that disciples will handle snakes and drink deadly poison without suffering harm as a sign (vv. 17–18). Christians should not (and generally do not) construct a doctrine of snake handling from Mark 16. Similarly, Christians should not construct a doctrine of baptism from Mark 16:16.[30] Nonetheless, some try.

A few interpreters hold that one *must* be baptized in order to be saved, since Mark 16:16 says, "Whoever believes *and* is baptized will be saved." Very few putatively Christian groups hold this view. But even if 16:16 were inspired, this interpretation contradicts biblical Christianity by adding something to the gospel. It re-creates the error of the Judaizers, which Paul condemned in Galatians. They held that one must believe *and* be circumcised in order to belong to the covenant and be saved. Paul replied that no one can add to a covenant that has been duly established (Gal. 3:15). But God established a covenant of salvation by faith through grace and will not add conditions to it. This held for Abraham, the father of Israel, and it holds for Christian believers, too. Paul says of Abraham, "He believed God, and it was credited to him as righteousness" (Gal. 3:6; cf. Gen. 15:6). This is an example for us, "So those who have faith are blessed along with Abraham, the man of faith" (Gal. 3:9).

Mark 16:16 does not teach that baptism is necessary for salvation. The first part ("Whoever believes and is baptized will be saved") firmly links baptism and salvation, but when the second part fails to mention baptism ("but whoever does not believe will be condemned"), the link weakens. Perhaps the text expects baptism without requiring it. For new converts, the inward reality of faith should be sealed by the sacrament of baptism, as a sign of union with Christ and his people. Finally, the future tense of the verbs "will be saved" and "will be condemned" gives the passage an eschatological flavor. If so, 16:16 may describe not the moment of salvation, but the start of a way of life, in-

30. Beasley-Murray's *Baptism in the New Testament* may be the best single volume on baptism from a baptistic perspective; he makes no use of Mark 16:16 in his exposition of baptism.

cluding baptism, that results in salvation, rather than condemnation, on the Last Day. Thus, Mark 16:16 adds nothing to the institution of baptism found in Matthew 28:19.

Appendix on the Authenticity of Mark 16

While most scholars favor the view that Mark ends at 16:8, for the reasons given above, there are enough arguments for the longer ending that we may address it another way. Beyond the external evidence afforded by ancient manuscripts, we also have internal evidence to consider. The issue here is which ending best fits the theology and style of Mark.

Advocates of the longer ending judge that Mark would end too abruptly at 16:8. The angel charges the women at the empty tomb to tell the disciples that Jesus has risen and that he will precede them into Galilee, where they will see him. The angel says, "Don't be alarmed" (v. 6), but the women tremble, bewildered and afraid (v. 8). The angel says, "Go, tell" (v. 7), but the women "said nothing to anyone, because they were afraid" (v. 8). The disciples never even see Jesus if Mark ends at 16:8, and so the gospel seems unfinished. Although the final clause, "for they were afraid," is grammatical, it contains only two words and seems to be incomplete.[31] So the book seems to need a more suitable ending, which, some argue, we have in verses 9–20.

There are three problems with this reasoning. First, while the book does end abruptly, there are cases of similar endings in antiquity—even books ending with the same conjunction (*gar*) that ends Mark.[32] Second, the longer ending actually fails to complete Mark any better than the allegedly inappropriate ending at 16:8. As we have seen, it fails to narrate a meeting between Jesus and the disciples in Galilee, as predicted in verse 7. Instead, 16:9–20 recounts occasions when Jesus appeared to Mary Magdalene and to groups of disciples by a road and at a meal. Third, the abrupt ending of Mark is consistent

31. It is grammatical for the last Greek word in 16:8 to be *gar* ("for"), since this word cannot come first in its clause, but *gar* is ordinarily followed by more words in its clause. This word very rarely ends a sentence, let alone a book.

32. Lane, *The Gospel According to Mark,* 583, n. 6.

with Mark's style. The abrupt conclusion echoes Mark's abrupt opening. Both create a stark encounter with the Savior. He is the Christ, the Son of God (1:1). The One who was crucified has been raised (16:6). The gospel ends with fear and astonishment overtaking the witnesses, but witnesses are often said to be frightened in Mark. It is true that 16:8 is not a *tidy* ending, but why must Mark be tidy? Instead, the book ends like some of Jesus' open-ended parables. Since the story is unfinished, it falls to the reader to complete it. The women were frightened and, at least temporarily, disobeyed the angel. So then it falls to us, to every reader, to understand, believe, and be the faithful disciples whom Jesus seeks.[33] Besides, the story is not quite so open-ended as it appears. We know the women eventually told the disciples, who did see Jesus. If they had not, how could Mark report that the women saw an empty tomb? Indeed, if the women had not reported and the disciples had not witnessed, there would be no church and no gospel of Mark. Someone told the apostles the message; otherwise, there would be no Christians to write or read this book.

33. Some say we wrongly read contemporary literary conventions into Mark when we detect a deliberately open ending. Mark, they say, was written in simpler times. Whether such a strategy was too sophisticated for Mark to devise independently, we cannot know. But we do know that Jesus used the strategy of open endings in parables (Luke 12:13–21; 14:15–24; 15:1–32) and ethical instruction (Matt. 6:19–24; 7:24–27). Mark had a Teacher.

3

UNTO YOU, AND TO YOUR CHILDREN

JOEL R. BEEKE AND RAY B. LANNING

"For the promise is unto you, and to your children, and to all that are afar off, even as many as the Lord our God shall call" (Acts 2:39). These words of the apostle Peter were spoken at a critical time in redemptive history. The old dispensation, the time of the "shadow of good things to come" (Heb. 10:1), things promised when "God . . . spake in time past unto the fathers by the prophets" (Heb. 1:1), was passing away. A new dispensation, "these last days" (Heb. 1:2), the day of the fulfillment of those promises in the death, resurrection, and ascension of Jesus Christ, was dawning. Peter himself heralds the new day, saying, "This Jesus hath God raised up, whereof we are all witnesses. Therefore being by the right hand of God exalted, and having received of the Father the promise of the Holy Ghost, he hath shed forth this, which ye now see and hear" (Acts 2:32–33).

Great changes were in store for the church of God in this new era of redemptive history. Significantly, these words of Peter declare that certain things had not changed and would not change in the new era. The pattern of God's dealings with believers and their children, as old as creation itself, would continue as a constitutional principle of the visible church. As the Westminster Confession of Faith says:

> The visible Church, which is also catholic or universal under the Gospel (not confined to one nation, as before under the law), consists of all those throughout the world that profess the true religion; and of their children: and is the kingdom of the Lord Jesus Christ, the house and family of God, out of which there is no ordinary possibility of salvation. (25.2)

It follows that baptism, as "a sacrament of the new testament, ordained by Jesus Christ . . . for the solemn admission of the party baptized into the visible Church" (Confession, 28.1), should be duly administered to believers and to their children. "For the promise is unto you, and to your children" (Acts 2:39).

The Holy Scripture provides four contexts for the proper interpretation of these words of the apostle. Understood in these contexts, these words stand as the biblical and apostolic foundation for the practice of paedobaptism, defined as the administration of baptism to the children of believing parents.

Context 1: Creation and the Unity of the Human Race

In his systematic treatment of the doctrine of man, Charles Hodge devotes an entire chapter to "The Unity of the Human Race."[1] He writes, "As the unity of the race is not only asserted in the Scriptures but also assumed in all they teach concerning the apostasy and redemption of man, it is a point about which the mind of the theologian should be intelligently convinced."[2] This doctrine is best stated in the words of the apostle Paul to the Athenians gathered to hear him on Mars' Hill: "God that made the world . . . hath made of one blood all

1. Charles Hodge, *Systematic Theology* (New York: Scribner, Armstrong, and Co., 1877), 2:77–91.

2. Ibid., 2:77.

nations of men for to dwell on all the face of the earth, and hath determined the times before appointed, and the bounds of their habitation" (Acts 17:24–26).

Sadly, this unity is eroding today, especially for people in Western Europe and North America. In the past, forces such as racism and nationalism obscured this unity, and in the modern era secularism and individualism have all but destroyed it. Characteristic of modern man is his sense of alienation and estrangement from other human beings. He belongs to no one other than himself. To think biblically, today's Christians must recover a due sense of the unity of families, the unity of the church, and the unity of the human race.

The unity of the human race works itself out in Adam's apostasy, which extends to all who descend from him. "Wherefore, as by one man sin entered into the world, and death by sin; and so death passed upon all men, for that all have sinned" (Rom. 5:12).

The unity of the race also works itself out in the new humanity, "created in Christ Jesus unto good works" (Eph. 2:10). Paul tells the Ephesians that he bows the knee "unto the Father of our Lord Jesus Christ, of whom the whole family in heaven and earth is named" (Eph. 3:14–15). The Greek word for "family" is *patria,* "a collective term for the descendants of the same father, immediate or remote," Hodge says.[3] Here Paul refers to the new humanity—not the descendants of "the first man Adam," but those who have been "quickened" or made alive in Christ as the "last" or second Adam. "The first man Adam was made a living soul; the last Adam was made a quickening spirit" (1 Cor. 15:45). Christ is heralded in prophecy as "The Everlasting Father" (Isa. 9:6), and his followers are identified as the children whom God has given him (Heb. 2:13) as his "house" or household (Greek: *oikos,* Heb. 3:6).

It is thus not surprising to read in the New Testament that turning to Christ was not simply the act of individuals but of households. We read of the conversion of Cornelius (Acts 10:1, 2, 33, 44), Lydia (Acts 16:14–15), the Philippian jailer (Acts 16:31–33), Crispus (Acts 18:8),

3. Charles Hodge, *Commentary on Ephesians* (reprint, Edinburgh: Banner of Truth, 1991), 125.

and Stephanas (1 Cor. 1:16; 16:15). In each case, the households are received into the visible church together with the heads of those households. Significantly, we are told that the households of Cornelius, Lydia, the Philippian jailer, and Stephanas were baptized. Similarly, children of believing parents are addressed as members of churches at Ephesus (Eph. 6:1–4) and Colossae (Col. 3:20). These children were also baptized, as Paul affirms in Colossians 2:11–12, where he calls baptism "the circumcision of Christ."

James W. Dale states that "the origin, character, and true value of the Family are elements of essential value in determining the ground and obligation of Household baptism." He explains:

> The Family is from the beginning, and . . . the whole human race is one vast outgrowth of a single Family head. Within this world family there are a thousand times ten thousand other families of miniature dimension, but with identically the same constitution. These families, more or less conformed to their divine original, fill the earth. It is obvious, that this world is founded on a family constitution. Its constitutional unit is not an independent, dissociate individuality, but a conjunct and associate individuality in and under the Family constitution.

Dale concludes that "the constitution of God's gospel kingdom is in harmony with God's constitution of the human race."[4]

This creational context partly explains how the apostolic church understood Peter's words. They struck a deep chord in his hearers in their appeal to the unity of the human race in Adam and the unity of the church as the new humanity in Christ. The promise embraced by believing parents is extended to their children. Just as the children of believing parents are "partakers of the condemnation in Adam, so they are received unto grace in Christ."[5] Could that be why there is not a single case in the Scriptures of a person being born and reared in a

4. James W. Dale, *Christic Baptism and Patristic Baptism* (reprint, Phillipsburg, N.J.: P&R, 1995), 220, 238.

5. "Form for the Administration of Baptism," in *The Psalter,* rev. ed. (Grand Rapids: Eerdmans, 1965; reprint, Grand Rapids: Reformation Heritage Books, 1999), 126.

Christian home and later being baptized upon reaching an "age of accountability"? As Acts 2:39 says, "The promise is unto you, and to your children."

CONTEXT 2: REDEMPTION AND THE COVENANT OF GRACE

If the unity of the human race is assumed in all that the Scriptures teach concerning the redemption of fallen mankind, all that teaching is expressed and summed up in the covenant of grace. As Hodge writes, "The plan of salvation is presented under the form of a covenant." He explains: "Our Lord commanded his disciples to go into all the world and preach the gospel to every creature. The gospel, however, is the offer of salvation upon the conditions of the covenant of grace."[6]

The covenant of grace stretches back to the first promise of a Savior made to Adam and Eve when God said to the serpent: "I will put enmity between thee and the woman, and between thy seed and her seed; it shall bruise thy head, and thou shalt bruise his heel" (Gen. 3:15). The promise was confirmed and amplified in the words that God spoke to Abraham and to his seed: "I will establish my covenant between me and thee and thy seed after thee in their generations for an everlasting covenant, to be a God unto thee, and to thy seed after thee" (Gen. 17:7). In the context of this covenant, God promised David, "Thy seed will I establish for ever, and build up thy throne to all generations" (Ps. 89:3–4).

Hodge therefore asserts what he terms "the identity of the covenant of grace under all dispensations." This has ever been "the common doctrine of the Church," he says. "By this is meant that the plan of salvation has, under all dispensations, the Patriarchal, the Mosaic, and the Christian, been the same. . . . There is the same promise of deliverance from the evils of the apostasy, the same Redeemer, the same condition required for participation in the blessings of redemption,

6. Hodge, *Systematic Theology,* 2:354, 363.

and the same complete salvation for all who embrace the offers of divine mercy."[7]

Luke, the author of both the gospel which bears his name and the book of Acts, places his account of the conception and birth of Christ in this same context. Gabriel announces to Mary the imminent conception and birth of a Son:

> Thou . . . shalt call his name JESUS. He shall be great, and shall be called the Son of the Highest: and the Lord God shall give unto him the throne of his father David: and he shall reign over the house of Jacob for ever; and of his kingdom there shall be no end. (Luke 1:31–33; cf. Isa. 9:6–7)

In her canticle of praise, the Magnificat, Mary says that God's mercy "is on them that fear him from generation to generation" (Luke 1:50; cf. Pss. 103:17; 105:8). Her song concludes with these words: "He hath holpen [helped] his servant Israel, in remembrance of his mercy; as he spake to our fathers, to Abraham, and to his seed for ever" (Luke 1:54–55; cf. Gen. 17:7).

Luke's next witness to the covenant of grace is the father of John the Baptist, Zacharias, whose canticle, the Benedictus, celebrates the covenant of grace as something promised long ago and now wondrously fulfilled:

> Blessed be the Lord God of Israel; for he hath visited and redeemed his people, and hath raised up an horn of salvation for us in the house of his servant David; as he spake by the mouth of his holy prophets, which have been since the world began: That we should be saved from our enemies, and from the hand of all that hate us; to perform the mercy promised to our fathers, and to remember his holy covenant; the oath which he sware to our father Abraham. (Luke 1:68–73)

7. Ibid., 2:366–68.

Finally, Luke calls on Simeon, "just and devout, waiting for the consolation of Israel," whose canticle, the Nunc Dimittis, extols the infant Jesus as the salvation of God: "Mine eyes have seen thy salvation, which thou hast prepared before the face of all people; a light to lighten the Gentiles, and the glory of thy people Israel" (Luke 2:25, 30–32). Clearly, Luke establishes the redemptive-historical context in which he presents not only his gospel but also his account of the acts of the apostles.

Several elements stand out in the words of Acts 2:39. First, it is clear that Peter speaks of "the promise" as rhetorical shorthand for the covenant of grace, which embodies the promise of salvation that he calls upon his hearers to embrace (see Acts 2:21). This promise is the same as the promises made to Abraham, to David, to Israel, and even to the Gentiles. It includes the promise of the Holy Spirit and forgiveness of sins referred to in the previous verse (Acts 2:38).

Second, as the words of Gabriel, Mary, and Zacharias indicate, the covenant promise is always made, as Peter says, "unto you, and to your children." Peter included children in Acts 2:39 on account of the content and structure of God's covenant fellowship with his people ever since the days of Abraham.[8] Mary's Son has a rightful claim to David's throne because he is the seed of David, and the promise was made to David and to his seed. God's covenanted mercy, Mary declares, continues "from generation to generation" in fulfillment of the promise made "to Abraham and to his seed for ever." Zacharias speaks for the children of the covenant (cf. Ps. 105:6, "O ye seed of Abraham his servant, ye children of Jacob his chosen") when he recalls "the mercy promised to our fathers" as "his holy covenant; the oath which he sware to our father Abraham."

The theme of the covenant made with Abraham and his seed recurs throughout Luke's gospel and into Acts. John the Baptist warns listeners not to claim Abraham as their father if they do not bring forth "fruits worthy of repentance" (Luke 3:8). Christ's lineage is traced

8. Cornelis Trimp, "The Sacrament of Baptism," *Mid-America Journal of Theology* 11 (2000): 126.

back through David and Abraham to Adam (Luke 3:23–38). Christ describes a woman healed of a long-standing infirmity as "a daughter of Abraham" (Luke 13:16). Lazarus dies and is carried to the bosom of "Father Abraham" (Luke 16:22, 24). When Zacchaeus repents, Christ declares, "This day is salvation come to this house forsomuch as he also is a son of Abraham" (Luke 19:9). Peter reminds his listeners that they are "the children . . . of the covenant which God made with our fathers," and that is why God has sent his Son Jesus to them first of all (Acts 3:25–26). Stephen recalls the promise, "which God had sworn to Abraham" (Acts 7:17). In the synagogue at Antioch, Paul informs his hearers that God has raised "unto Israel a Saviour, Jesus," and declares, "Men and brethren, children of the stock of Abraham, and whosoever among you feareth God, to you is the word of this salvation sent" (Acts 13:23, 36).

In Acts 2:36, Peter proclaims that Jesus of Nazareth is "Lord and Christ." That fulfills the promise made to David concerning "the fruit of thy body" (Ps. 132:11) and David's own prophecies of the Messiah's resurrection (Ps. 16:8–11) and ascension into heaven (Ps. 110:1). The presentation is intensely covenantal, since the covenant made with David and his seed is rooted in the covenant made with Abraham and his seed.

Peter's words in Acts 2:39 are therefore a covenantal formula. "Unto you, and to your children" simply restates "between me and thee and thy seed after thee" (Gen. 17:7). These words assert the identity of the covenant of grace under all dispensations and the continuity of the covenant pattern in which promises made to believers are extended to their children. As God has always done, so he will continue to do in these last days. "I am the LORD, I change not" (Mal. 3:6).

We have to remind ourselves that the multitude who heard Peter's sermon on Pentecost was Jewish. It included Jews from Palestine, proselytes, and dispersed Jews from other parts of the Roman Empire and beyond. The Old Testament was all they had of the Holy Scriptures. As they listened to Peter preaching from those Scriptures (twelve of the twenty-two verses of Peter's sermon in Acts 2 contain quotations from the Old Testament), they could have understood his words in only one way—as a reference to the promise in God's covenant and the fact that that promise extended not only to believers but to their children as well. To interpret Acts 2:39 in light of the New Testament Scriptures, which did not yet exist, as do many Baptists,[9] is to engage in hermeneutical error and can only lead to a serious misrepresentation of the mind of the Spirit.

The Jewish multitude had Jewish expectations—not just about the Messiah, but also about the way in which God works with people. Suppose that you were one of those Jews, who had grown up knowing all the privileges and encouragements of a God who says, "As the soul of the father, so also the soul of the son is mine" (Ezek. 18:4). You are told that in Christ the covenant has been restated in a new and better way, but children are now left out of the picture. They are no longer included in the way that God deals with people. Would it not at least trouble you to think that God has made such a fundamental alteration to the way in which he offers his grace to men and women?

The bonds of natural family affection are such that for God to cut across them in such a dramatic way would at least have caused people to ask serious, urgent questions. As Francis Schaeffer says,

> If Peter did not mean what the Jews understood him to mean in an Old Testament context—that God establishes His covenant not just with believers but with our children also—then there would have been a riot on that day. Or if it had been a polite crowd, there would at least have been hands going up saying, "Excuse me Peter, what do you mean by that? Could you clarify yourself?" It was such a serious thing for the Jew to be told that God is changing a fundamental way in which He deals with people.[10]

9. E.g., William Cleaver Wilkinson, *The Baptist Principle in its Application to Baptism and the Lord's Supper* (Philadelphia: American Baptist Publication Society, 1881), 158.

10. Francis Schaeffer, *Baptism* (Wilmington: TriMark, 1976), 18–19; cf. Thomas M'Crie, *Lectures on Christian Baptism* (Edinburgh: Johnstone and Hunter, 1850), 60–62.

There are a plethora of books that argue the case for or against infant baptism. But no matter how baptism is presented, one question that Baptists can never answer is this: How could a converted Jew regard the new covenant as a better covenant, if now his children were to be excluded from God's dealings with his people, no longer receiving a sign of God's covenant promise?

If such were the case, Peter and later Paul would surely have had to face that question repeatedly. And yet it is never debated or even mentioned in the New Testament. Peter and Paul are never called upon to answer the question: Do we baptize the infants of believing parents?

Why not? Because Acts 2:39 and other texts underscore that the covenant is the polity or constitution of God's kingdom. It's the way he operates his church, in both the Old and New Testament eras.[11] As David Bostwick, an eighteenth-century Presbyterian minister from New York, wrote:

> Observe, Peter does not say, the promise *was* to you and your children, but it *is still;* otherwise they might naturally be supposed to object, that their children were like to be in a worse condition under the gospel, than they were under the law; which must greatly strengthen their prejudices against the evangelical dispensation. The Apostle therefore precludes any such objection, by informing them, that they can lose nothing by submitting to this new dispensation of the covenant; for the privileges of the gospel should by no means be more confined and lim-

11. The Baptist response, that Acts 2:39 refers to adult children, contradicts Peter's argument. As David Bostwick says, "Why then is their relation to their parents mentioned at all, and why are they joined with them, as the subjects of the promise, if after all they are to stand on their own footing, as adults, as much as the children of heathens? Nor does the construction consist with the plain grammatical sense of the words, for the Apostle does not say the promise is now to you, and shall be to your children when grown and called by the Word, but the promise is now to you and your children; by which he very plainly intends the present privilege the Jewish children enjoy, above the present unconverted Gentiles, who are said to be afar off, and to whom he says the promise shall belong when called into a Church-State, and to their children also" (*A Fair and Rational Vindication of the Right of Infants to the Ordinance of Baptism: Being the Substance of Several Discourses from Acts ii.39* [New York: Edward and Charles Dilly, 1765], 17).

Cf. Gerald R. Procee, *Holy Baptism: The Scriptural Setting, Significance and Scope of Infant Baptism* (Hamilton, Ont.: Free Reformed Church, 1998), 74–75.

ited than those of the law; but on the contrary more enlarged: for under the law the promise was only to them and their children, as descendants of *Abraham;* but now it shall extend to all among the *Gentiles,* and their children also, *whom the Lord our God shall call.*[12]

Thus, in Acts 2:39, after Peter assures Jewish believers that the covenant promise and covenant pattern are still in effect, and that the covenant promise continues to be in force for their children, he boldly proclaims that the promise shall also be to all that are afar off—i.e., afar off from the covenant community and its divine covenant promises. Peter is affirming that God is no longer limiting his saving purposes to one nation in the New Testament era. The gospel is for all to whom it comes without exception or distinction from this time on. God's saving purposes are for all nations, "even as many as the Lord our God shall call" (Acts 2:39), Peter says. Wherever the gospel is preached, sinners are welcome to enter into the covenant that God has established according to his immutable promise. We have no reason to conclude that when they do so the covenant is now restricted to the first generation of converts. As Geoffrey Bromiley says,

> Surely God has not given with one hand, extending the covenant in space, only to take away with the other, contracting the covenant in time. The promise of God in Jesus Christ is still to a thousand generations when the gospel of Jesus Christ is preached and received, so that the children of believers awaken to consciousness with the word of the promise in their ears and the mark of the promise on their bodies. The call to them as to Old Testament Israelites is to enter personally into a covenant-membership which does not come to them as a new thing from without, but of which they have already both the word and the seal by virtue of their Christian descent.[13]

12. Bostwick, *Right of Infants to the Ordinance of Baptism,* 14.
13. Geoffrey Bromiley, *The Baptism of Infants* (London: Church Book Room Press, 1955), 12.

Baptists often dismiss this covenantal argument by harking back to verse 38, arguing that since Peter says, "Repent, and be baptized," baptism may only follow repentance. Since infants are not yet able to repent, they ought not to be baptized. To such reasoning we would posit three responses. First, the word "and" between "repent" and "be baptized" is a coordinate and not a causal conjunction. That is to say, although both things are true, there is not necessarily a causal connection between them. "Repent" and "be baptized" are two coordinate commands. Acts 2:38 does not say that we are to be baptized because we have repented, nor does it imply that it is wrong to baptize someone who has not repented.

Second, the causal conjunction "for" at the beginning of verse 39 indicates that verse 38 is part of a larger thought that is concluded in verse 39. Attempting to understand repentance and baptism in verse 38 without examining verse 39, therefore, is refusing to listen to the whole text. The word "for" in verse 39 indicates that that verse is giving the reason why we are to repent and be baptized, namely, "for the promise is unto you, and to your children, and to all that are afar off." In other words, those who have received God's promise of the remission of sins and the gift of the Holy Spirit are qualified to be baptized, and, Peter clearly says, that includes them and their children.

Third, an argument against infant baptism from Acts 2:38 is also an argument against infant salvation. If infants cannot be baptized because they are incapable of repentance and faith, then they cannot be saved for the same reason. The use of such verses as Mark 16:16 and Acts 2:38 to argue that repentance and faith are required for baptism also argues that repentance and faith are required for salvation, thereby consigning all infants incapable of repentance and faith to perdition.

John Owen asserted that since God has appointed baptism as the sign and seal of regeneration, "unto whom he denies it, he denies the grace signified by it." Thus, God refuses baptism to impenitent sinners (Matt. 3:7–8) because, not granting them the grace, he will not grant them the sign. If therefore God denies the sign to infants of believers, it must be because he denies them the grace. All children of believers who die in their infancy, then, must be hopelessly lost—not that all must be lost who are not baptized, but that all must be lost whom God does not want baptized.[14] Yet most Baptists will admit that the New Testament, like the Old, indicates that small children—even infants (Luke 18:15–17)—are proper subjects of Christ's kingdom (see Matt. 18:6; 19:13–15; 21:16; Luke 10:21).

In all this, Baptists are not faithful to the Scriptures, nor to the Reformers who clearly and unanimously understood infant baptism in the covenantal terms of Acts 2:39. John Knox wrote, "God has promised that He will be a God to us and the God of our children unto the thousandth generation . . . instructing us thereby that our children belong to Him by covenant and therefore ought not to be defrauded of those holy signs and badges whereby His children are known from infidels and pagans."[15] "In baptism," said Calvin, "we have the covenant of God as it were engraved in our bodies."[16] Herman Bavinck, a leading Dutch theologian of a century ago, summarized:

> This covenant was the solid, biblical, and objective foundation upon which all the Reformers unanimously and without exception rested the legitimacy of infant baptism. They had no other deeper and more solid foundation.[17]

The views of the Reformers were formulated in the Reformed Confessions. Perhaps best known is question 74 of the Heidelberg Catechism, "Are infants also to be baptized?" The catechism answers:

14. John Owen, "Of Infant Baptism," in *The Works of John Owen* (Edinburgh: Banner of Truth, 1968), 16:260.

15. *Church of Scotland Interim Report* (1958), 13, cited by G. R. Beasley-Murray, *Baptism in the New Testament* (Grand Rapids: Eerdmans, 1986), 337.

16. *Sermons of Master John Calvin upon the Fifthe Book of Moses called Deuteronomie,* trans. Arthur Golding (reprint, Edinburgh: Banner of Truth, 1987), 421.

17. Translated from *Gereformeerde Dogmatiek,* 4th ed. (Kampen: Kok, 1930), 4:282. Cf. William Goode, *The Doctrine of the Church of England as to the Effects of Baptism in the Case of Infants* (London: J. Hatchard and Son, 1850); Geoffrey W. Bromiley, *Baptism and the Anglican Reformers* (London: Lutterworth Press, 1954), 15–54.

> Yes, for since they, as well as the adult, are included in the covenant and church of God; and since redemption from sin by the blood of Christ is promised to them no less than to the adult; they must therefore by baptism, as a sign of the covenant, be also admitted into the Christian church.

Similar statements appear in the French (Gallican) Confession of 1559 (chap. 35), the Scots Confession of 1560 (chap. 23), the Belgic Confession of 1561 (chap. 34), the Second Helvetic Confession of 1566 (chap. 20), the Westminster Confession of Faith of 1647 (chap. 28.4) and the Larger Catechism of 1648 (Q. 166).[18] The Scripture proofs attached to the Westminster standards form a long catena of evidence rooting infant baptism in the covenant of grace: Genesis 17:7, 9; Matthew 28:19; Mark 10:13–16; Luke 18:15–16; Acts 2:38–39; Romans 4:11–12; 11:16; 1 Corinthians 7:14; Galatians 3:9, 14; Colossians 2:11–12.

The Reformers were aware that their basis for infant baptism was not that of the medieval church. They knew that pre-Reformation practice was largely dictated by custom or church tradition, as well as by erroneous ("superstitious") views of the sacrament. Thus, in Reformed churches, ministers took pains to present a correct view of the sacrament. They confronted parents presenting children for baptism with a frank admonition, saying, "Beloved in the Lord Jesus Christ, you have heard that baptism is an ordinance of God to seal unto us and to our seed His covenant; therefore it must be used for that end, and not out of custom or superstition."[19]

So then, why do we baptize children? Because God's covenant, the framework within which he operates, has not been changed. There has been no explicit instruction which says that God has altered his *modus operandi*, his way of operating, with regard to infants receiving the covenant sign and seal, as John Murray has pointed out.[20] The prom-

18. Cornelis Venema, "The Doctrine of the Sacraments and Baptism according to the Reformed Confessions," *Mid-America Reformed Journal* 11 (2000): 21–86.

19. "Form for the Administration of Baptism," 127.

20. John Murray, *Christian Baptism* (Philadelphia: Presbyterian and Reformed, 1962), 52–53.

ise which says, "I will be your God and you will be my people," given to Abraham to embrace not just him but his family, still stands; and it is still, in the words of Peter, "unto you, and to your children." Children would therefore naturally be regarded as subjects of baptism, just as they were of circumcision in the Old Testament.[21] As Pierre Marcel concludes,

> The covenant, together with its promises, constitutes the objective and legal basis of infant baptism. Infant baptism is the sign, seal, and pledge of all that these promises imply.[22]

CONTEXT 3: PROPHECY, OR THE VISION OF THE PROPHET

Peter heralds the death, resurrection, and ascension of Christ and the outpouring of the Spirit as the fulfillment of prophecy. The prophecies themselves identify and explain these events as signal moments in redemptive history. As Peter says, "This is that which was spoken by the prophet" (Acts 2:16).

Prophecy also provides a context for understanding Peter's formula in Acts 2:39. The prophet Joel speaks of the Spirit being poured out upon entire households and upon succeeding generations: "I will pour out my spirit upon all flesh; and your sons and your daughters shall prophesy, your old men shall dream dreams, your young men shall see visions: and also upon the servants and upon the handmaids in those days will I pour out my spirit" (Joel 2:28–29). David's prophecies also speak of things promised to his offspring (Pss. 18:50; 72:17; 89:4, 29; 132:11). And Isaiah unfolds a bright prospect for the seed of the covenant (Isa. 43:5–7; 44:3; 45:25; 61:9; 65:17, 22–23; 66:22).[23]

21. C. G. Kirkby, *Signs and Seals of the Covenant* (Worcester: n.p., 1988), 66, 78.

22. Pierre Marcel, *The Biblical Doctrine of Infant Baptism: Sacrament of the Covenant of Grace* (London: James Clarke, 1953), 198.

23. Samuel Miller, *Baptism and Christian Education* (reprint, Dallas: Presbyterian Heritage, 1984), 16–17.

Similarly, prophecy identifies the church under the gospel as the "generation" and "seed" of the Messiah (Isa. 53:8, 10). "A seed shall serve him; it shall be accounted to the Lord for a generation" (Ps. 22:30; cf. Heb. 2:13; 3:6). What Christ purchases for his seed will be a lasting heritage for "the seed also of his servants" (Ps. 69:36). So the prophets see the covenant pattern obtaining and continuing in the church under the gospel.

In his assault upon divorce as practiced in the Old Testament church, Malachi declares, "The LORD, the God of Israel, saith that he hateth putting away [divorcing]" (Mal. 2:16). Like Christ himself (Matt. 19:5–6), Malachi appeals to the words of institution for marriage (Gen. 2:24), saying, "And did not he make [the twain] one?" (Mal. 2:15).

Malachi goes on to ask, "And wherefore one? That he might seek a godly seed" (v. 15). Unbiblical divorce not only destroys the unity that God has ordained for man and wife; it also puts at risk the children that the Lord has given them as his heritage (cf. Ps. 127:3) and "a godly seed" (cf. 1 Cor. 7:14). In other words, Malachi appeals to the promise of the covenant made not only to believers, but also to their children.

These prophecies are anchored in the promises of the covenant and confirm those promises "to a thousand generations" (Ps. 105:8). They also reinforce the covenantal pattern or form which the promise takes. At every point, "the promise is unto you, and to your children" (Acts 2:39).

CONTEXT 4: FORENSICS, OR GOD'S LAWSUIT AGAINST ISRAEL

Peter's sermon in Acts 2 goes further than proclaiming Jesus of Nazareth as Lord and Christ. Peter also indicts his hearers as "this untoward generation" (v. 40), who "by wicked hands" have crucified and slain "a man approved of God among you . . . that same Jesus, whom ye have crucified" (vv. 22–23, 36). He repeats this charge in a subsequent sermon (see Acts 3:13–15).

Matthew records what the people said to Pilate when he washed his hands and declared himself innocent of Jesus' blood. The people answered, "His blood be on us, and on our children" (Matt. 27:24–25). Here, too, is covenantal language. "We accept this guilt, and we also accept it on behalf of our children and succeeding generations."

Luke does not report this incident in his gospel, but he does record the charges laid by the high priest against Peter and John in Acts 5:28: "Behold, ye have filled Jerusalem with your doctrine, and intend to bring this man's blood upon us." Significantly, Peter and the other apostles plead guilty as charged, saying, "We ought to obey God rather than men. . . . And we are his witnesses of these things" (vv. 29, 32). The apostles are witnesses for the prosecution as God avenges the blood of his saints, his prophets, and his Son, and visits the guilt of that blood on those who have shed it. As Christ himself said, "Therefore also said the wisdom of God, I will send them prophets and apostles, and some of them they shall slay and persecute: that the blood of all the prophets, which was shed from the foundation of the world, may be required of this generation; . . . verily I say unto you, It shall be required of this generation" (Luke 11:49–51).

Nonetheless, on the Day of Pentecost, the promise of mercy stands. Forgiveness of sins is promised even to those who have "denied the Holy One and the Just" and "killed the Prince of life" (Acts 3:14–15). The covenant accounts for the criminality of what was done to the Mediator of the covenant. At the same time, the covenant embodies the promise of forgiveness of sins even to those who committed the crime.

This offer of grace, the promise of forgiveness, is "unto you, and to your children." Yet the time to repent may be short. So Peter says, in effect, "For your own sake, and for the sake of your posterity, turn from your sins and be saved! Separate yourselves from this crooked and perverse generation, and save yourselves and your children from the wrath about to fall upon it." Sinners have involved their children in their crime and bloodguiltiness; they now have the opportunity to be absolved of that crime and purged of guilt, for themselves and their offspring.

This forensic context stands with the others—creational, redemptive, and prophetic—and is closely tied to them. Indeed, it is difficult to discuss one of these contexts apart from the others. What is implicit in the "family constitution" (Dale) of creation is made explicit in covenant as promises are made to believing parents and their children. What is promised in the covenant is confirmed by all that the prophets have spoken.

Finally, the forensic context reminds us that God is bound by his covenant both to save those who turn to him in Christ and to punish those who spurn the promise and judge themselves unworthy of everlasting life (Acts 13:46). If covenant children do not respond to God's covenant promises and mercies, the sign of baptism will testify against them on the Day of Judgment. "Unto whomsoever much is given, of him shall be much required" (Luke 12:48). Covenant breakers, who fail to appropriate covenant privileges, will reap God's covenant judgment instead of his covenant blessing.[24]

In one way or another, all four contexts fix the meaning of Peter's words as a formula of the covenant. Implicit in his words is the extension of the covenant to all who are embraced in the scope of the promise of the covenant, which ever was, is, and shall be "unto you, and to your children."

THE RESPONSIBILITIES OF THE COVENANT PROMISE

Peter's Jewish audience would have understood from Acts 2:39 that covenant promises entail covenant responsibilities. Believing parents respond to the covenant promise that comes to them and their children by bringing up those children in the fear and admonition of the Lord, as Paul enjoins in Ephesians 6:4. We must not allow our chil-

24. Robert R. Booth, *Children of the Promise: The Biblical Case for Infant Baptism* (Phillipsburg, N.J.: P&R, 1995), 9.

dren to make up their own minds in isolation from covenant truth; rather, we must positively apply the teaching and the discipline of the Lord to direct their minds and feet in the paths of righteousness. We must evangelize our covenant children, calling them to repentance before God and to faith in Jesus Christ.[25]

The promise of Acts 2:39 ought to encourage us in training our children at home, in church, and at school. Through prayer, family worship, catechizing, daily conversation, and godly mentoring, we are commanded to teach the Word of God to our children every day and everywhere. Deuteronomy 6:7 says, "And thou shalt teach them diligently unto thy children, and shalt talk of them when thou sittest in thine house, and when thou walkest by the way, and when thou liest down, and when thou risest up." What God said of Abraham must be the rule for Christian parents: "For I know him, that he will command his children and his household after him, and they shall keep the way of the LORD, to do justice and judgment; that the LORD may bring upon Abraham that which he hath spoken of him" (Gen. 18:19).

Our response to Acts 2:39 is to set the Christ of the covenant before our children, as he is revealed in the Scriptures, trusting that he will grant them faith and repentance by his Spirit. Nor does anything said above obviate the need for personal regeneration as the experiencing of the truth and power of the covenant promise. Covenant promise is no substitute for personal regeneration. Parents who presume that their children are regenerate by virtue of the covenant may see no need to tell them that they must be born again. William Young calls this view "hyper-covenantism," because the relation of children to the covenant is exaggerated to the point where the covenant relation replaces the need for personal conversion. As Young points out, "Doctrinal knowledge and ethical conduct according to the Word of God are [then] sufficient for the Christian life without any specific religious experience of conviction of sin and conversion, or any need for

25. For a practical booklet on how to do this, see Joel R. Beeke, *Bringing the Gospel to Covenant Children* (Grand Rapids: Reformation Heritage Books, 2001).

self-examination as to the possession of distinguishing marks of saving grace."[26]

Consequently, what our Reformed forefathers called experimental religion is deemed largely superfluous. Religious life becomes grounded in external church institutions and activities rather than in the soul's communion with God. "A system for breeding Pharisees, whose cry is 'We are Abraham's children,' could hardly be better calculated," Young concludes.[27]

Rather, as Doug Wilson writes, we "parents who know what the covenant obligations are should tremble at the baptismal font."[28] If we have laid hold of God's promise concerning our children, we are under oath to do everything in our power, in dependence on the Spirit, to lead our children into the realization of the promise.[29] We must stress repeatedly that justification is by faith alone, apart from works of the law (Rom. 3:28); that salvation is by grace alone through faith (Eph. 2:8); that only the blood of Christ can wash away our sins (1 John 1:7; see also Heidelberg Catechism, Q. 72). It is our duty to be the first teachers of our own children. After his conversion, Augustine thanked God for his mother, saying, "Lord, she from whom I received my birth, led me to thy bond; and taught me to know thy own handwriting."

Richard Cecil said:

> We bring our children to Christ, when we teach them to read the Scriptures; when we bring them to the house of God; when we are praying with them, and for them. . . . Do you really wish your children saved? Treat them as you do plants which you would have thrive. You place them in the sun, and give them water: you shelter them from blighting winds. Bring your children under the rays of the Sun of righteousness;

26. William Young, "Historic Calvinism and Neo-Calvinism," *Westminster Theological Journal* 36 (1974): 166.

27. Ibid., 167.

28. *Tabletalk* 22, no. 6 (June 1998): 59.

29. Robert Rayburn, *What About Baptism?* (St. Louis: Covenant Theological Seminary, 1957), 87.

> water them by continual instruction. Keep them from the contagion of the world, from the blasts of temptation, and from poisonous books.[30]

Let us press on, holding fast the promise made to us and to our children, while striving to fulfill our obligations to our little ones. God will be true to his own promise. What an encouragement! Salvation depends upon God's promise, his power, and his faithfulness. "I will and you shall." That is always the language of his covenant. "Faithful is he that calleth you, who also will do it" (1 Thess. 5:24).

30. Richard Cecil, *Remains of the Rev. Richard Cecil* (London: L. B. Seeley, 1813), 198–99.

4

THE *OIKOS* FORMULA

JONATHAN M. WATT

Nobody lives in a vacuum. All of us are born into a context, we grow up in a context, and none of us dies outside of our context—or really, contexts. We are surrounded by the circumstances of our world in everything we do. Some circumstances are easy to observe: we live in this or that town, on such and such a street, with a certain type of family that is responsible for our well-being. By the time we are hastening through adulthood—and often, long before that—we have acquired a host of characteristics and habits that accompany us through life. Many of these characteristics are not easily observed because, instead of relating to concrete things that we can touch, they relate to attitudes and priorities and things we believe to be true. Culture involves the things of life that we can see and touch, as well as the attitudes we carry toward it and our convictions about its value.

The family that raised us molded many of our attitudes. But what made that family the way it was? Part of the answer is the families that raised our parents a generation earlier. However, there is more to the answer, for families do not develop in a vacuum either. Families develop within a *culture,* which is a community's shared assumptions and beliefs about life. A culture may be known to just a small clan, with a few dozen related people living a very homogeneous existence, sharing the same language, religious beliefs, purposes, and even property. Or a culture may be an entire civilization; we often talk of "Western culture," even though it is really a diverse collective. In either case, we are children of our culture to some degree and tend to view other cultures from the perspective of our own. No one lives in a vacuum, so no one looks at the world from outside his own culture.

Consequently, many people mistakenly think they could never really understand another person's culture. After all, if your values are different from mine, your kind of talk has different definitions than mine, and your values are sending you along a trajectory that is different from mine, then we cannot share much because we have different worldviews. At least, that is what many people think. But the Judeo-Christian faith has historically bridged cultural boundaries of all sorts because its starting point is not the differences that exist between people, but the things they have in common. All people derive from the same Creator. We are his creation, and "in him we live and move and have our being." The apostle Paul said this (Acts 17:28), as had the Greek poet Epimenides centuries earlier. Some truths are evident even apart from special revelation.

Cultural differences can erect real barriers between people, but Christ transcends culture, and the truths of Christ can be conveyed in different ways. For example, Jesus said, "I am . . . the truth" (John 14:6), a fact that may be expressed today in more than six thousand different languages. Truth may be garbed in different appearances without necessarily changing its substance, and thus the gospel might be preached in a chiseled stone building or under an open-sided bamboo and banana-leaf shelter. Truth may be modeled by an urban businessman in a three-piece suit or by a tattooed Maori of the Pacific Rim. In either case, the ground-level features of a culture are always subject to the Word of God, which stands in the superior position. However, the Word of God was still "breathed out" by the one God (2 Tim. 3:16) to specific people in particular situations, nestled into living cultures, and so we need to stay on track by identifying their similarities and differences. That means that we always need to try to understand what the people of Bible times meant when they used words. Otherwise, we risk projecting our culture and its assumptions back onto theirs.

The Bible uses various household-related words and kinship terms, and some of these point to concepts that many modern Westerners have not encountered. For example, the history of ancient Israel is replete with references to "tribes" and "clans," yet most of us cannot relate directly to them. The Bible speaks of many family members besides fathers and mothers, such as uncles and nephews, aunts and grandmothers, and of course brothers and sisters. We sense that family experiences described in parts of the Bible were broader than most of us have known. For example, we read that parents sometimes made the arrangements for their children's marriages (e.g., Gen. 24), or that slaves could become permanently placed in a family complex (e.g., Deut. 15:16–18), or that first options in an inheritance settlement could be exercised by a "kinsman-redeemer" (e.g., Ruth 4:1–12). These concepts are foreign to us, so we need to investigate what people in that day brought to mind when they heard certain words.

The New Testament often uses family terminology in connection with baptism. This makes sense when we remember that a number of the metaphors describing conversion to Christ also involve family terms: one is "born again" or "born from above" (John 3:3), and is thereby "adopted" into a new family (Gal. 4:5; Eph. 1:5) with a whole new line of brothers and sisters in Christ (Matt. 12:50), not to mention new mothers and fathers in the faith (Matt. 12:50; 1 Thess. 2:11). Children of God, like adopted and biological children, are not nurtured in a vacuum, but in a *family* context.

So what did Paul and Luke and Peter have in mind when they referred to the family of God? When the New Testament tells us that this or that "household" (as many English translations put it) was baptized in connection with Christian faith, what would the first hearers have thought? Since we live in a culture that emphasizes self, personal choice, and the rights of individuals, we need to consider first the culture that originally put Christian things into the context of family. This is not to claim that everything in an ancient culture was necessarily favored by the church. For example, Paul resisted the abuse of slaves that was widespread in his day. But certain parts of ancient cultures (we have already mentioned the extended family network and marriage) were used positively to convey the gospel—we suspect, because they were part of God's primary plan in the first place.

WORD MEANINGS IN CONTEXT

So what is the relationship between infant baptism and the family household? Christians agree that when an adult professes faith in Christ, baptism is in order, for the direct connection between individual believer and sacrament is obvious (e.g., Matt. 28:18–20). The first generation of the church in Palestine and other parts of the Mediterranean world saw many people come to faith, so it is not surprising that baptisms of people who "owned" the faith and could articulate it went on to receive the sacrament. The more difficult matter has to do with the implications of one adult's profession for the baptism of someone else. Narrowing our subject a little further, we ask whether the concept of "household" that prevailed in ancient societies influenced the way first-century Christians perceived baptism. To answer this question, we should remember how words are used.

Words are built around a root, which is a kind of core that allows other pieces of information to be added on. In English, the word *rebuilding* has the root *build,* with the prefix *re-* attached at the beginning and the suffix *-ing* attached at the end. The root conveys a central idea, perhaps pointing to a thing (a noun) or to an action or state of being (a verb). Word elements can be combined in a variety of ways, so we can create related words, such as *builder, rebuilt,* and *building.* Of course, we can also combine different word roots. The result of the combination may be a related meaning (e.g., *cross* and *piece* together make *crosspiece*) or a whole new meaning (e.g., *butterfly* is not obviously related to its two roots). In Greek, however, we are often able to see a close relationship between the roots and the meaning. And we need to understand that meaning in the word's context, not our own.

If we want to understand what the New Testament writers meant by this or that word, we need to start by asking how it was being used in their setting, by them and by their contemporaries. We need to consider their culture before we start to paste our meanings onto theirs. A couple of cultural settings come to our attention when we investigate the New Testament. The broad cultural setting was the first-century Greco-Roman world, which happened to be enjoying a remarkable degree of linguistic unity because Hellenistic Greek (a dialect spoken from about 300 B.C. to A.D. 300) had become the language of wider communication, or the *lingua franca.* Greek was the native language for many, and it was becoming a second language for even more, all across the Mediterranean world. No matter where you came from, it was almost expected that you would know some Greek, and if you wanted to establish your relevance to the world, competence in Greek was a necessity. Greek was to the first-century Mediterranean world what English is today—the language that opens doors across cultures. Thus, the Greek-speaking Greco-Roman world provided a vital context, and understanding it helps us comprehend the Bible.

Another important context for the New Testament, the primary religious context, was provided by the Jewish Scriptures, which we call the Old Testament. Central doctrines and questions about life had been identified and addressed in this Jewish heritage many centuries before the New Testament was written. The Old Testament had identified and defined such prominent things as creation, sin, redemption, and—what will be helpful to us now—the "household of God." Something that is especially helpful as we keep these contexts in mind is that, a few centuries before the apostles were spreading the gospel of Christ, they came together in a wonderful way: the Hebrew Old Testament was translated into Greek in Alexandria, an Egyptian city that had developed into the second largest urban center of the Mediterranean world. The translation was made because so many Jews were using Greek as their first or second language, while Hebrew was barely being used anymore (except by Jewish scholars). That Greek translation came to be known as the Septuagint, which means "seventy," because of a popular story that claimed it had been translated by seventy Jewish scholars.

The two main contexts of the New Testament writings thus converged: the theology of the Jewish Scriptures came to be expressed in the primary language of the Greco-Roman world. We will be greatly aided as we try to understand what the Bible is telling us today if we can see what it was saying to those who first received it. Theologian Oscar Cullmann once stated, based on the way certain words were used in the ancient world and in the Greek Scriptures, that "the New Testament knows of Baptisms—whether adult or infant makes no difference—which do not presuppose faith before and during the act itself."[1] This study is a selective investigation of that claim.

THE *OIKOS* WORD GROUP

We begin our investigation by looking for a direct connection in the text between baptism and Christian households. About two dozen words appear in the New Testament that somehow are built around the word root *oik,* which often relates to the household. These words include: *oikeios* ("family member"), *oikeō* ("to live, dwell"), *oiketeia* ("slave household"), *oiketēs* ("servant"), *oikēma* ("prison cell"), *oikētērion* ("dwelling"), *oikiakos* ("household member"), *oikodespoteō* ("to run the household"), *oikodespotēs* ("master"), *oikodomos* ("building"), *oikodomeō* ("to build, strengthen"), *oikodomē* ("building, strengthening"), *oikonomeō* ("to be manager"), *oikonomos* ("steward"), *oikonomia* ("responsibility"), *oikoumenē* ("inhabited earth"), *oikourgios* ("devoted to home duties"), *epoikodomeō* ("to build up"), *katoikeō* ("to inhabit"), *katoikia* ("place in which to live"), *katoikizō* ("to place, put"), and *katoikētērion* ("home" or "haunt"). Most of these words re-

1. Oscar Cullmann, *Baptism in the New Testament,* trans. J. K. S. Reid (London: SCM Press, 1950), 52.

tain the general meaning of the root, having something to do with the home or its related functions and responsibilities. There are various other kinship and family terms in the Bible that have a different root, of course, but we will not examine them in this chapter.

We then narrow our attention to *oikos* and *oikia,* which are usually translated "home," "house," or "household." The first is a masculine noun; the second is feminine. Greek, like many languages, coded all nouns for gender. What do these words denote in the Septuagint (that early Greek version of the Old Testament)? Sometimes they refer to the place in which someone lives, whether a tent (Gen. 9:21, 27) or a permanent house (Gen. 12:1). They also refer to a place of worship (Gen. 28:17), especially a permanent sanctuary, and usually appear in combination with other words, such as "house of the LORD" (2 Sam. 12:20) or "house of prayer" (Isa. 56:7). The house may be literal or metaphoric (as in the house that wisdom is said to have built for herself, Prov. 9:1). The words can also refer to God's people, as in the common phrase "house of Israel" (e.g., Amos 5:25, which is used in Acts 7:42).

What do these words denote in the New Testament? The pattern is quite similar. They may refer to the temple as "the house of God" (Mark 2:26; 11:17) or to God's heavenly dwelling, as when Jesus talked about "my Father's house" (John 14:2). They also refer to the Christian community, as in "the household of God" (1 Tim. 3:15; 1 Peter 4:17; Heb. 3:6), which is "a spiritual house" (1 Peter 2:5). In John 8:35, the "house" of God seems almost to be God's entire kingdom. Other passages in the New Testament make reference to the people of God by means of these words. We read about "the house of Israel" (Matt. 10:6; Acts 2:36) or of Jacob (Luke 1:33), or elsewhere of a royal dynasty (Acts 7:10).

Centuries earlier, the two words had been used a little differently.[2] The feminine form usually denoted the place of residence, while the masculine form could also refer to the possessions that a deceased

2. See Otto Michel, "*oikos,*" in *Theological Dictionary of the New Testament,* vol. 5, ed. Gerhard Friedrich, trans. Geoffrey W. Bromiley (Grand Rapids: Eerdmans, 1967), 119–59.

person had left behind. However, by the time the Septuagint was being translated, or a little later when the New Testament was written, either word could refer to a place of residence or to the group of people who occupied it. And that brings us to the New Testament usage.

Oikos and Baptism

On four occasions described in the New Testament, baptism was explicitly administered to people from the same household, including those of Lydia (Acts 16:15), a jailer in Philippi (Acts 16:32–33), a synagogue leader named Crispus (Acts 18:8), and a man in Corinth named Stephanas (1 Cor. 1:16). As shown already, there seems to be no particular difference between the way the feminine (*oikia*) and the masculine (*oikos*) words are used in the New Testament. *Oikos* is used more frequently, though, and designates either the residence (Acts 16:15b, 34) or the people who presumably lived in it (Acts 16:15a; 18:8; 1 Cor. 1:16). *Oikia,* on the other hand, appears in Acts 16:32, in reference to the people in a household.

Some details from each of the contexts are important for our consideration. The Crispus account (Acts 18:8) says that he believed, and adds that his household believed also, along with others living in Corinth. Similarly, in 1 Corinthians 1:16 Paul says that he baptized the household of Stephanas, but gives none of the details. Stephanas's household could have included infants, of course, though we cannot be sure (we shall return to this issue a little later). The same could be said for all of the people who were part of Cornelius's family group mentioned in Acts 10, though with *oikos/oikia* not being used there, it lies outside this assignment.

For now, we shall direct our attention to the other two passages, both in Acts 16. During his second missionary journey, Paul (assisted by Timothy) itinerated through parts of (modern) Turkey. The Spirit of God compelled them (v. 6) to bypass much of the territory that they might otherwise have visited in western Turkey, which at that time was in the Roman province of Asia Minor. So they proceeded westward to the port city of Troas, skirted the northeast corner of the Aegean Sea (v. 11), and arrived (via some other towns) at a "leading city" (though not the capital) of Macedonia, Philippi (v. 12). Philippi was located near a Roman highway called the Via Egnatia, which started a little to the southeast at the port city of Neapolis and stretched westward more than five hundred miles toward the empire's capital. It was one of the transportation arteries that prompted the popular saying, "All roads lead to Rome."

Two household baptisms in Philippi are described in Acts 16. Lydia's situation is described in verses 14–15 (which I translate literally): "The Lord opened the [her] heart to respond . . . and she was baptized and the household (*oikos*) of her." Her own faith came with mature understanding and the apparent ability to profess it, yet baptism was extended to her whole household. The account of profession and baptism in the jailer's situation is similar. Verses 32–33 (which I again translate literally) read: "And they spoke to him the word of the Lord with all those in his house (*oikia*) . . . and he was baptized, and all those of him immediately." Again, the connection between mature hearer-believers of the *oikia* and the whole baptismal situation is tantalizing.

To explore the possibilities of what was being designated in these "household" references, we need to consider what the word designated in the culture(s) of that day. In the Reformed tradition, we are constrained somewhat when it comes to this avenue of exploration. The Judeo-Christian biblical context is most important, for we want to follow this principle of interpretation: Let the clear passage(s) of Scripture interpret the unclear. The cultural context may clarify something or open up some possible interpretations, but those possibilities remain subject to the guidelines and constraints supplied by the *scriptural* context. There is a place for "exegeting a culture," especially one's own, so that we can be discerning and insightful. But our central task is exegeting the words of God conveyed through men: we seek cultural clarification only if it explains how those writers were using a word to express the ultimate truths that God was revealing to them.

In the Greco-Roman world, a person was most broadly part of a people group, or *ethnos*. This word is often translated "nation" in our Bibles, but that English word fits modern times better than it did the ancient world. Then, it pertained more "to cultural than biological or kinship" features.[3] Below the level of *ethnos* would come one's tribe (*genos*), and then framed within that tribal level were various clans identified by extended blood-relative connections.[4] Within the clan, one could identify close blood relatives, and those most immediately related to you could be designated your *oikos*, or household, an "important kinship unit in the ancient world."[5]

What might this household look like? Horrell says that *oikos* and *oikia* denoted "some kind of structured and stratified group,"[6] but advises that the exact nature of the group would have to be clarified by literary context. When a person comes to Christ, he becomes a part of a new household, one based on spiritual union rather than physical connection. Can we press further? DeSilva states that the "hub" of the household was the master, father, or husband.[7] Of course, one person could fill all three of those roles. Now this is where we note a divergence from the kind of household that many North Americans have known. The Greco-Roman household could include not only the master/husband/father and, of course, the mother and children, but also the older generation (grandparents) and extended family, such as uncles, aunts, cousins, and various in-laws. Aristotle stated that a complete household included not only husband, wife, and children, but also slaves.[8] Although he lived four centuries prior to the New Testament, he was closer to the world of the New Testament than we are.

3. Per Bilde, ed. *Ethnicity in Hellenistic Egypt* (Aarhus: Aarhus University Press, 1992), 32.

4. David DeSilva, *Honor, Patronage, Kinship and Purity* (Downers Grove, Ill.: InterVarsity Press, 2000), 165.

5. Ibid.

6. David G. Horrell, "From *Adelphoi* to *Oikos Theou*: Social Transformation in Pauline Christianity," *Journal of Biblical Literature* 120 (2001): 298. For more detail, see Dennis C. Duling, "Matt. 18:15–17: Conflict, Confrontation, and Conflict Resolution in a 'Fictive Kin' Association," *Biblical Theology Bulletin* 29 (1999): 4–22.

7. DeSilva, *Honor, Patronage, Kinship and Purity,* 173.

8. Aristotle, *Politica* 1.3 (1253b2–7).

DeSilva notes that in the classical world, households might also include married offspring with their families, various in-laws, and even slaves.[9] Guests and even clients (beneficiaries supported by special arrangement) could also be construed as part of the household.[10] Although not all of these were present in every ancient household, such diversity was possible when the Greco-Roman "household" is mentioned. The household of the biblical world must have been a colorful pastiche of personalities and activities! We ought to have in view this diversity, rather than a simple nuclear family, when we read of a "household" in the Bible.

The diversely stocked family known to much of the ancient Mediterranean world—the head of the household (normally the husband/father, though, in the case of his absence, a woman might fill that role) and its many related people—became a wonderful avenue for explaining what happens when a person comes to Christ. It became what missionary Don Richardson calls a "cultural compass"—a respected societal institution that can be used to illustrate redemption. Of course, this household was more than an incidental feature of ancient societies; it was an outworking and application of the basic marriage institution based in God's creation. Not everyone today has experienced the ethos of the so-called "household code" familiar to the world behind the New Testament and implicit in such passages as 1 Timothy 3:15, which is just one of the sections describing "how one ought to behave in the household of God."

Jeremias, like Stauffer before him, points to the so-called "*oikos* formula" in combination with the adjective "all" in the accounts of the Philippian jailer (Acts 16:33) and Crispus (Acts 18:8) in order to claim that "no single member of the household was excluded from baptism."[11] He thinks that the wording most certainly includes children, though probably not slaves. Bringing in Old Testament usage to affirm the claim, he reasons that since "every male" of Abraham's house-

9. DeSilva, *Honor, Patronage, Kinship and Purity,* 174.

10. James F. White, *A Brief History of Christian Worship* (Nashville: Abingdon Press, 1993), 19.

11. Joachim Jeremias, *Infant Baptism in the First Four Centuries,* trans. David Cairns (London: SCM Press, 1960), 19–20.

hold includes infants (Gen. 17:23), then the "New Testament *oikos* formula" must predate Paul, being an adoption of "Old Testament cultic language."[12] But he is careful not to push this argument too far, adding: "This does not mean . . . that in every particular case in which the baptism of 'a whole household' is mentioned, small children were actually present. But it does mean that Paul and Luke could under no circumstances have applied the *oikos* formula, if they had wished to say that only adults had been baptized." Jeremias keeps family solidarity at the forefront of the matter: individual decisions were not as decisive as those of the master of the household who was responsible to speak for his family.[13]

We conclude that many people in ancient societies experienced the powerful role of an extended family that included "stem" members (father, mother, children, grandparents) along with more distant relatives (single aunts, uncles, cousins, etc.) and sometimes even domestic servants or slaves. By analogy, we can say that this household picture helped elucidate the nature of redemption into Christ and our new relationship with God and his people—our new family under the Master—and that a primary person's profession of faith in Christ held implications not only for his own baptism, but for his family's as well. The household metaphor in ancient Greco-Roman or Jewish societies was far more suggestive and illustrative than it would be today.

A THEOLOGY OF HOUSEHOLD BAPTISM

The church has historically practiced infant baptism.[14] The use of household language in the biblical world opens up the possibility of the baptism of infants, but by itself may not decide the matter once

12. Ibid., 21.

13. Ibid., 22–23.

14. See discussion in W. F. Flemington, *The New Testament Doctrine of Baptism* (London: SPCK, 1953); James W. Dale, *An Inquiry into the Usage of* Baptizo*: and the Nature of Christic and Patristic Baptism* (Philadephia: Presbyterian Board of Publication, 1874); G. W. H. Lampe, *The Seal of the Spirit* (London: SPCK, 1967); Rowland S. Ward, *Baptism in Scripture and History* (Brunswick, Australia: Globe Press Pty, 1991); Carl A. Volz, *Faith and Practice in the Early Church* (Minneapolis: Augsburg, 1983).

and for all. We always need to keep a word study in the context of the whole picture of interpretation. The same holds true for *oikos/oikia* when it comes to infant baptism: the words played a strong supporting role that was illustrated and strengthened by the connection they shared with the cultures of the biblical world.

However, we still need to keep the whole biblical picture before us in order to confirm our case. The complex of biblical doctrine, not one single word, gives us a full picture. This can be seen by interaction with an articulate opponent of infant baptism, G. R. Beasley-Murray, who objects to Jeremias's attempt to make a tight case for infant baptism based on the *oikos* passages.[15] Beasley-Murray states that if the word "all" in Acts 16:33 is taken to mean every last person in the jailer's household (as Jeremias argues), including the infants, then "infants were brought out of their beds at this early hour of the morning and listened to the instruction before being baptized." Perhaps neither writer is exactly correct. The word "all" in Greek and Hebrew—and in English today—is used flexibly. It could mean "including everything and excluding nothing," as in the statement "The surgeon believed he had removed all traces of the cancer." Or, we can use it to mean "all kinds of," as in the sentence "All nationalities are represented in this city." This is why we often translate the Greek word *pas* ("all") in Matthew 5:11 in this way: You are blessed when people utter "all kinds of evil against you falsely." Here the word connotes a wide variety of possibilities. So when we turn to the phrase "all the household" in certain baptism narratives, we can see that makes quite a strong statement because it is almost redundant. The word "household" is already quite inclusive, while the addition of the word "all" makes it even stronger still. The hitch is this: we do not know exactly who comprised that household. Even if "all the household" does mean "every last person," which is quite possible, we still do not know for sure that infants were in that particular family group. In this connection, Beasley-Murray pokes fun at Jeremias for his insistence on that point, but he errs in the opposite direction. He says sarcastically that

15. G. R. Beasley-Murray, *Baptism in the New Testament* (Grand Rapids: Eerdmans, 1962), 315.

if that were so, "infants were brought out of their beds at this early hour of the morning and listened to the instruction before being baptized."[16] But with short narrative summaries being what they are, we ought to show restraint before we confidently nail down unspecified details. His claim that the *oikos* formula is a "myth"[17] is simply unhelpful, and, besides, parents know all too well that there is nothing implausible about infants being up in the middle of the night.

Households—of God, of Israel, of the Spirit, of faith, or of Greco-Roman society—were so familiar to the ancients, that they could hardly have avoided drawing parallels between the family structure they saw everywhere around them and its counterpart in the Christian life. It seems inconceivable that the writers of the Bible would have opened so wide a door into human imagination if they intended to exclude an important piece of the picture. Yet, we still must allow Scripture to interpret itself. We still need to follow other lines in Scripture—such as the line connecting Old Testament circumcision and the new covenant sign of baptism—to determine the propriety of infant baptism. The *oikos* idioms strongly favor the likelihood of infant baptism, even as they fall short of proving it beyond any shadow of a doubt. The household nuances carried by these phrases are consistent with, and encouraging of, the application of baptism to infants in covenant households. How strange it would be if a patriarch such as Abraham, or a lawgiver like Moses, or some other believing Israelite father, could present his infant son for circumcision, but not for baptism. Men who possessed the "rights of dispensation" spoke on behalf of their household. Robert Booth has put it this way: "Since God has not changed the terms of church membership, new covenant believers and their children are likewise included in his church. . . . The people of God in the Old Testament and the people of God in the New Testament are one and the same people."[18] And he adds: "God . . . required Abra-

16. Ibid.

17. Ibid., 316.

18. Robert R. Booth, *Children of the Promise* (Phillipsburg, N.J.: P&R, 1995), 73. For a similar line of thinking, see Geoffrey W. Bromiley, *Children of Promise* (Grand Rapids: Eerdmans, 1979), and Frederick S. Leahy, *Biblical Baptism* (N. Ireland: Outlook Press, 1992), chaps. 1 and 5.

ham to give that same sign and seal to all who came under his household authority, including his children."[19]

Although the household words of the New Testament, by themselves, do not seal the case for infant baptism, they make such a powerful presumption in favor of including children that they lay the burden of proof on those who would claim that children were *not* participants in *oikos* baptisms. For the culture of that day assumed that children were usually part of the family. Family solidarity, not individualism, had been the norm for the cultures of the patriarchs, the Israelite monarchy, Herodian Jews, and even pagan societies nestled around the ancient Mediterranean. The preference is for, not against, the inclusion of all family members. It had been that way since the time of Noah (Gen. 7:1), Abraham (Gen. 17:12–13), Joshua (Josh. 24:15), and David (2 Sam. 12:10), all the way to those overseers of the early churches (1 Tim. 3:4) whose leadership and example—or bad behavior and errors (cf. 1 Sam. 3:12–14)—left an impressive legacy for subsequent generations and relatives. From patriarchs to patresfamilias, the master of the family spoke for those who were his. When he was baptized, so were they.

19. Booth, *Children of the Promise,* 80.

5

Baptism and Circumcision as Signs and Seals

MARK E. ROSS

It is commonplace in Reformed theology to refer to the sacraments as signs and seals of the covenant of grace.[1] For example, the Westminster Shorter Catechism defines a sacrament as "an holy ordinance instituted by Christ; wherein, by sensible signs, Christ, and the benefits of the new covenant, are represented, sealed, and applied to believers" (Q. 92). Curiously, neither baptism nor the Lord's Supper is ever directly called a sign or a seal in the New Testament. Both terms, however, are used in Romans 4:11 with reference to circumcision: "[Abraham] received the sign of circumcision, a seal of the righteousness of the faith which he had while uncircumcised." Our discussions of infant baptism will be significantly advanced by our getting a clearer notion of just how sacraments in general, and baptism in particular, serve as signs and seals of the covenant. To that end, I want to examine carefully how circumcision served as a sign and seal of the covenant that God made with Abraham.

1. The best discussion is still book 4 of Calvin's *Institutes,* chaps. 14–18.

CIRCUMCISION AS A SIGN AND SEAL

When Paul calls circumcision a sign, he is no doubt echoing the language of Genesis 17:11, which calls circumcision "the sign of the covenant" between God and Abraham. Similar language is used of the rainbow in Genesis 9:13. The rainbow is to serve as a reminder of the covenant that God made with Noah and with all flesh. It stands as a visible reminder of the promise that God made. There is, consequently, a vital and close connection between the sign and a promise from God.[2] The function of the sign is to confirm the promise to us, making it, as it were, more firm in our minds (i.e., giving us greater confidence in its truth). The sign of circumcision was thus intended to remind Abraham of the covenant that God had made with him, and of the promises (and obligations) contained in that covenant. The sign itself adds nothing to the promise, and we should not think that God is under greater obligation to perform his promise when a visible sign is attached to it. The sign is for our benefit, giving us greater assurance.

Signs in general function this way in the biblical revelation. When Moses went down to Egypt as God's ambassador, he was given signs to perform so that Israel and Egypt might know that he had come as the messenger of the Lord (Ex. 4:1–9). The signs would authenticate him as God's messenger. We have the same idea in the New Testament. The Greek word for "sign" (*sēmeion*) is used frequently in the New Testament (seventy-seven times), often with reference to the miracles of Jesus and the apostles. Numerous times it occurs in conjunction with other words, such as "wonders" and "miracles." In these cases, a sign is a supernatural confirmatory or attesting mark, an indicator of the genuineness, authenticity, or veracity of something or someone as having originated from God. The Jews sought from Jesus a sign from heaven, so that they might know the truth of his message

2. Notice Calvin's first definition of a sacrament: "an outward sign by which the Lord seals on our consciences the promises of his good will toward us in order to sustain the weakness of our faith" (*Institutes,* 4.14.1). Also, "a sacrament is never without a preceding promise but is joined to it as a sort of appendix, with the purpose of confirming and sealing the promise itself, and of making it more evident to us and in a sense ratifying it" (4.14.3).

(John 6:30). Jesus' signs (miracles) prove that he is a messenger sent from God (e.g., John 2:11; 3:2; 20:30). The signs performed by Paul were "the signs of a true apostle," authenticating him as an apostle (2 Cor. 12:12). We should pay close attention to the word of the gospel communicated to us because it has been confirmed to us by signs (Heb. 2:1–4).

A sign need not be miraculous, however, in order to serve as an attesting mark. Judas used a kiss as a sign to point Jesus out to his captors (Matt. 26:48). Paul, while apparently dictating his letters to an amanuensis, often closed the letter in his own handwriting as a sign of its authenticity (cf. 2 Thess. 3:17).[3] So whether a sign is miraculous or not, its primary meaning is that of authentication, something which validates or guarantees the genuineness or veracity of something else. As an authenticating mark, it can then serve to confirm the truth of something. A sign of a covenant thus confirms the terms of the covenant, whether as promises of blessing, threats of cursing, or both.[4]

A representative or symbolic function can also be attached to a sign. Jesus multiplied the loaves and fishes, giving bread in the wilderness, to show that he was the bread of life (John 6). He performed the sign of opening the eyes of the man born blind in order to prove that he was the light of the world (John 8 and 9). Jesus claimed to be the resurrection and the life, and in attestation of this he raised Lazarus from the dead (John 11). In these cases, the miracles not only proved his claim, but gave an exhibition of it.

As the sign of the covenant that God made with Abraham (Gen. 17:11), circumcision perhaps represents in miniature both what is promised to those who keep the covenant and what is threatened against transgressors. For those who keep the covenant, God removes the uncleanness of their flesh, circumcising their hearts to love the Lord their God (Deut. 30:6). Those who break the covenant will be

3. Leon Morris, *The First and Second Epistles to the Thessalonians,* New International Commentary on the New Testament, rev. ed. (Grand Rapids: Eerdmans, 1991), 263–64.

4. On this whole question of covenant signs and their connection to both blessing and curse, Meredith Kline's *By Oath Consigned* (Grand Rapids: Eerdmans, 1968) is must reading.

cut off from their people, even as circumcision "cuts off" the foreskin of the flesh (Gen. 17:14). Also, because God's covenant with Abraham promised a seed (descendants) to Abraham, the circumcision of his foreskin drew attention to the promise of a seed, while at the same time highlighting the threatened curse to cut off the seed of covenant breakers.

For all this, whatever representative or symbolic function a sign might perform, the principal idea remains that of authentication or validation. The sign of circumcision certifies some truth or truths. Just what that truth is will be key to our understanding of how sacraments function as signs.

The same idea of authentication or validation is connected with the term *seal* (Greek: *sphragis*). Jesus urged the people to trust in him because the Father had set his seal upon him (John 6:27). Believers are sealed or validated as the true children of God by the presence of the Spirit given to them (2 Cor. 1:22; Eph. 1:13; 4:30). Paul regarded the Corinthians themselves as the seal of his apostleship (1 Cor. 9:2), meaning that the work of the Spirit among them through him was proof that he was a genuine apostle. In Revelation 7, the bondservants of God are sealed on their foreheads with the seal of the living God (Rev. 7:1–3), marking them out as the true servants of God, so that the agents of destruction will not harm them.

In many of these cases, the idea of ownership is probably also present, along with the idea of authentication and validation. God's seal upon us not only validates us as his children, but also marks us as belonging to him. The seal placed upon Jesus' tomb was the emblem of Rome, marking the tomb as being under the authority of the empire. As a seal, circumcision no doubt also emphasizes the idea of ownership. It is the sign of God's covenant with Abraham, in which Abraham is called to perfect, perpetual obedience (Gen. 17:1–2). Abraham has an obligation to keep God's covenant. He belongs to God by covenant. He is God's vassal.

Now the specific claim made by Paul in Romans 4:11 is that Abraham "received the sign of circumcision, a seal of the righteous of the faith which he had while uncircumcised." In this passage, it would seem that Paul is not making two claims about circumcision—namely, that it was both a sign and a seal—but rather making one claim, and explaining that claim in greater detail. Paul says that circumcision was a sign to Abraham, an authenticating mark, validating or confirming the terms of his covenant with God. He then elaborates on circumcision's role as a sign by saying that this sign was "a seal of the righteousness of the faith which he had while uncircumcised."

Although it is commonplace in Reformed theology to distinguish (but not separate) the ways in which sacraments function as signs and seals, this does not seem to be Paul's intent in Romans 4. If we focus upon signs that somehow represent the blessings and/or curses of the covenants to which they are attached, we can make such a distinction between sign and seal. There is indeed a difference to be noted between representing a claim and confirming a claim, but Paul is not making that distinction in Romans 4:11. Rather, he is stressing the idea of confirmation by explaining that circumcision was a sign in the sense that it sealed or confirmed the promise of God.

Understanding what Paul is saying here is absolutely critical to a correct understanding of sacraments as signs and seals. Agreement here could go a long way toward improving, if not resolving, the debate over infant baptism. Far too many expositors have been led astray on just this point. Quite a number, on both sides of the debate over infant baptism, assume that circumcision is said in Romans 4:11 to be a sign and a seal of Abraham's *faith*, or of his *righteousness*, or *both*. Whichever, the idea is that the sign authenticates or validates something about Abraham, confirming that he has faith, or that he has righteousness, or that he has both. For example, the paedobaptist John Murray says:

> Although circumcision contributed in no way to the exercise of faith nor to the justification through faith, for the simple reason that it did not yet exist, yet circumcision did sustain a relationship to faith. Circumcision, he insists, was not a purely secular rite nor merely a mark of racial iden-

> tity. The meaning it possessed was one related to faith. . . . Its significance, he shows, was derived from its relation to faith and the righteousness of faith. . . . In a word, it signified and sealed his faith.[5]

Murray goes on to say, "For if circumcision signified faith, the faith must be conceived of as existing prior to the signification given and, in a way still more apparent, a seal or authentication presupposes the existence of the thing sealed and the seal does not add to the content of the thing sealed."[6] Murray's claim is that Paul intends us to think that Abraham's circumcision signified and sealed Abraham's faith, and thus authenticated and validated it, guaranteeing its existence and genuineness, and thus also confirming that Abraham had righteousness by virtue of his faith.

James Montgomery Boice, another paedobaptist, follows the same path. In explaining what is meant by the phrase "a seal of the righteousness that he had by faith while he was still uncircumcised" (NIV), Boice says:

> That is, after Abraham had believed God and God had imparted righteousness to him, God gave the seal of circumcision to validate what had happened. In the same way, baptism is a seal that the person being baptized has been identified with Jesus Christ as his disciple, and the elements of the Lord's Supper, when received, indicate that the person has taken Jesus to himself as intimately and as inseparably as eating bread and drinking wine.[7]

Boice adds, "The sacraments are important as signs and seals of what has happened spiritually and invisibly."[8] For Boice, then, Abraham's

5. John Murray, *The Epistle to the Romans,* New International Commentary on the New Testament (Grand Rapids: Eerdmans, 1968), 1:137.

6. Ibid.

7. James Montgomery Boice, *Romans,* vol. 1, *Justification by Faith, Romans 1–4* (Grand Rapids: Baker, 1991), 458.

8. Ibid.

circumcision validated "what had happened," namely, that Abraham *had believed,* and that God *had imparted righteousness to him.*

For an example from the Baptist side, John Piper says in a sermon on Romans 4:9–12, "Circumcision is a sign and seal of a faith that Abraham had before he was circumcised." Piper also refers to circumcision as "a sign of faith," "a sign and seal of Abraham's righteousness of faith," and "a sign of faith and righteousness."[9] Like Murray and Boice, Piper understands Paul to be saying that circumcision signified and sealed, authenticated and validated, something about Abraham, namely, that he had faith and was accounted righteous.

But if we understand circumcision in the manner proposed by Murray, Boice, Piper, and a host of others, it is difficult to explain why the covenant sign of circumcision was applied to Abraham's seed without reference to the faith of the recipients, or to the inward spiritual change supposedly signified and sealed by circumcision. Did Ishmael have faith? Had he experienced a spiritual and inward transformation? Had he also believed, and because of that had God imparted righteousness to him? If so, he would have been heir to the covenant blessings; but he was not an heir to the covenant blessings and he was not "of faith" (Gal. 4:21–31). What about Esau, who likewise would have been circumcised? He was not "of faith" either, though he was born into the covenant and bore its mark (Rom. 9:6–13). Circumcision was not in these cases, or in the case of countless others, a guarantee of faith, righteousness, or justification, as Paul is at pains to stress (cf. Rom. 2:25–29; 1 Cor. 7:19; Gal. 5:6; 6:15, Phil. 3:2–3). If circumcision is taken directly as a sign and seal of faith, or of imputed righteousness, or of an inward spiritual transformation, it fails miserably. Far too many circumcised Jews of the Old Testament, and of the New Testament, proved to be hostile to God. Their circumcision was no guarantee of their faith or their salvation. Their unbelief and disobedience turned their circumcision into uncircumcision (Rom. 2:25–29).

9. John Piper, "How Do Circumcision and Baptism Correspond?" (sermon delivered on August 29, 1999). Available online at Desiring God Ministries, www.desiringGOD.org.

Surely, whatever meaning circumcision had for Abraham, it had also for Ishmael and for every other male in Abraham's household circumcised on the same day as Abraham (Gen. 17:23). This must be the starting point in our understanding of circumcision, baptism, or any other sacrament: there is one meaning for all who rightly receive the sign. If we understand Abraham's circumcision to certify that he had faith, or that God had given him righteousness, then we are at a loss to explain what Ishmael's circumcision meant, or Esau's, or Saul's, or any other candidate Jew who is an unbeliever and cut off from the blessings of God's covenant.

It bears saying that we have the same problem with baptism in the New Testament. If baptism is understood to be a sign of faith, or a sign that one has received the forgiveness of sins, then it too fails miserably. This problem is not averted by waiting until people make professions of faith at an age of maturity, as Simon Magus illustrates (Acts 8:9–24), and as countless others since have demonstrated. Baptist and paedobaptist churches alike must deal with this problem. There are just too many baptized people around who do not have faith, and/or whose lives demonstrate that they are unregenerate, to make credible the claim that baptism is a sign of faith. Taking any sacrament to be a sign of faith, righteousness, justification, salvation, inward spiritual transformation, or other such things leads inevitably into problems. There are just too many people who have been admitted to the sacraments by what seemed at the time to be credible professions of faith who later demonstrated, as Demas did, that they have loved this present world and have deserted the gospel (2 Tim. 4:10).

I suppose that if we thought of the sacraments as only *probable* signs and seals, indicating that to the church's best judgment the people who have received these sacraments are recipients of the blessing of God, then we could live with the problem of unregenerate covenant members as simply an indication of the weakness and fallibility of the church. But the very purpose of the sacraments is to authenticate and validate something, giving us assured grounds to believe some truth.

A conception of the sacraments as probable signs runs directly contrary to their purpose.

If we cannot take circumcision to be a sign of faith, or of righteousness, then how are we to understand Paul's claim? For surely there must be some connection between circumcision and faith and righteousness; otherwise, why would Paul call circumcision "a seal of the righteousness of the faith which he had while uncircumcised"? We must take a closer look at Paul's words. Let us begin by looking at what he means by the phrase "the righteousness of the faith."

One possibility is that he is saying something about the kind of faith possessed by Abraham, namely, that it was a righteous faith. In other words, Paul ascribes a certain quality to Abraham's faith, namely righteousness, and the sign of circumcision sealed or authenticated it to be of such a quality. If so, we could paraphrase the verse to say, "a seal of the righteous faith which Abraham had while uncircumcised." But it is not Paul's concern to discriminate between types of faith in the present context. He speaks simply of faith, and his aim is to show that Abraham was justified by faith, pure and simple, not by a certain kind of faith.

A better possibility would be that Paul is speaking of the righteousness which belonged to or came from faith—that is, the righteousness reckoned or credited to Abraham on the basis of his faith. In Philippians 3, Paul speaks of "not having a righteousness of my own derived from the Law, but that which is through faith in Christ, the righteousness which comes from God on the basis of faith" (v. 9). Taken in this sense, which surely is the correct one, Paul is saying that circumcision is a sign and seal of the righteousness which Abraham had by faith.

Given what Paul says, however, there must be some connection between circumcision and righteousness. What would that connection be? Romans 4 is intended by Paul to provide Old Testament proof for the claims made in Romans 3 that justification is on the basis of faith, that people are accounted righteous before God, not on the basis of their works, but through faith in Jesus Christ (Rom. 3:21–31). The key text is Genesis 15:6, as quoted in Romans 4:3 (and v. 22): "Abraham believed God, and it was credited to him as righteousness." How is circumcision connected to this? Circumcision is not a guarantee that Abraham has faith, nor even that Abraham has righteousness. What circumcision guarantees is the word of God's promise: that *righteousness will be given on the basis of faith.* In other words, circumcision is the authenticating mark that certifies the truth of God's promise, that he will give righteousness to the one who has faith. What is certified is not so much a truth about Abraham, or any other circumcised person, but a truth about God. In particular, circumcision certifies the truth of God's word in the gospel, namely, that all who believe will be accounted righteous.

We can perhaps see this point more clearly if we ask ourselves which proposition is certified to be true by the circumcision given to Abraham. Is it "All who are circumcised are accounted righteous" or "God gives righteousness to all who have faith"?

It cannot be the first, given the example of Ishmael and countless others. It can only be the second. Circumcision is, and can only be, a sign and seal of the truth of God's promise, his promise to give righteousness to all who have faith. If Abraham has faith, then he can conclude that he has righteousness. He can conclude this because God has promised to give righteousness to all who have faith, and he has given circumcision to attest to this promise, guaranteeing its truth. However, Abraham cannot conclude that he has righteousness simply because he is circumcised. God's promise is not that all who are circumcised are given righteousness, but that all who have faith will be given righteousness.

On this understanding of circumcision as a sign and seal, there are no problems of meaning in giving circumcision to those not known to have faith, nor to those who later show themselves to have no faith. Since the sign and seal of circumcision is not a guarantee of either the faith or the righteousness of the one circumcised, the discovery that a circumcised person is an unbeliever does not invalidate the circumcision as an authenticating mark. God's promise is not invalidated by the unbelief of his covenant children. His word stands: those who believe will be accounted righteous.

Indeed, unbelieving members of the covenant family testify to the other side of circumcision. As a covenant mark, it testifies not only to a blessing (namely, that righteousness is given to those of faith), but to a curse: namely, that those who break the covenant will be cut off. As sinners, we stand continually under the threat of God's curse in the covenant of works, that disobedience will bring death. Circumcision testifies to this as much as it does to the promise of righteousness being given to those who believe. Abraham's circumcision in Genesis 17 bound him to keep God's covenant. That covenant called him to perfect, perpetual obedience (Gen. 17:1–2). Breaking the covenant would be punished by death; the transgressor would be "cut off" from his people (v. 14).

Circumcision thus testified to the truth of another proposition, namely, that transgressors of the covenant would be cut off. Thus, when Abraham was circumcised, and when he circumcised Ishmael and later Isaac, they were to look at the mark in their flesh as certifying to them the words spoken by God in his covenant with them. He promised them righteousness on the basis of faith, *and* he threatened death to anyone who broke his covenant. Just as a bride can look at her wedding ring and recall the promises made to her by her husband, so they could look at their circumcision and recall the promises of God. In the face of their many sins, circumcised believers could look at their circumcision as a visible guarantee that the God of Abraham, the true and living God, would accept them as righteous if they, like Abraham, would believe God, trusting in his promise.

Now for those who hold to an evangelical understanding of the sacraments,[10] surely we must understand baptism and the Lord's Supper to be signs and seals in the sense that we have found in Romans 4:11. Baptism does not signify and seal that a given individual has cer-

10. I mean by this that the sacraments have no inherent power to convey blessing to the recipients, but do so only where faith is present. Where there is no faith, circumcision becomes uncircumcision, baptism becomes unbaptism, etc.

tainly been forgiven of sins and accounted righteous in the eyes of God. It signifies and seals that those who believe will be washed from their sins and accounted righteous before God. The Lord's Supper does not signify and seal that those who partake are truly united to Christ and partake of his death and resurrection. It signifies and seals that those who believe are united to Christ and truly partake of his death and resurrection. The sacraments are visible reminders and assurances of the truth of God's word to us. They are not stamps of approval placed upon us to validate that we are truly believers, that we are truly righteous in the eyes of God, or that we are truly saved. Thus, we cannot conclude simply from the fact that we are baptized that we are washed from our sins and accounted righteous before God. Before we can conclude that, we must be able to assert that we have faith.

Perhaps this point can be made clearer if we think in terms of a simple syllogism. The major premise is supplied by the sacrament:

MAJOR PREMISE: All who have faith in Christ will be accounted righteous.

The minor premise must be supplied from our own hearts (perhaps supported by the confirmation of the church, through its leaders, admitting us to the church):

MINOR PREMISE: I have faith in Christ.

The conclusion can then be drawn:

CONCLUSION: I am accounted righteous.

The role of the sacraments in this scheme is to support the major premise, assuring us of its truth by the addition of a visible token from God, who gives it to remind us and to certify to us the promises he has made. We cannot reason directly from possession of the token—namely, having been circumcised, having been baptized, having partaken of the Lord's Supper—that we possess the blessings that God has promised. Faith must be added to the token. We have assurance of the blessings only when we have faith.

Abraham's circumcision, then, provided him with an enduring, visible sign in his flesh of the promises made to him by God (and of the obedience he owed to God). Whenever his faith weakened, he had available to him a sign from God, sealing to him the promises that God had made. To Ishmael, Esau, and others who likewise became members of the covenant, circumcision testified the very same truths that Abraham's circumcision testified to him. They too were assured of the truth of God's promises, namely, to give righteousness to those who have faith and to cut off all who disobey. The circumcisions of Ishmael and Esau should have served as grim reminders of the judgment awaiting all who turn aside in unbelief. Had they turned to God in faith, their circumcisions would have assured them of acceptance. But they were children of the flesh, and so the word they heard in the sacrament did not profit them, since it was not united by faith in those who heard (cf. Heb. 4:2).

Baptism and Circumcision

Now that we have a clearer understanding of the way in which sacraments in general function as signs and seals, we take up the question of how circumcision and baptism are to be understood and related. Those who subscribe to covenantal infant baptism maintain that baptism has now replaced circumcision as the mark of covenant membership, and that baptism's meaning and application are essentially the same as circumcision's in the Old Testament period.[11] Included with this is the idea that the children of covenant members today are members of the covenant, as in the Old Testament period.

11. While they are *essentially* the same, there are some obvious differences. Baptism, for example, is administered to both males and females, unlike circumcision. The point is that the sign is administered to those who rightly have a place in the covenant community, and that the meaning of baptism (as a sign and seal) is the same as the meaning of circumcision.

Before endeavoring to justify these claims, we need to be a little more clear on what is being claimed and what is not.[12] Because the fundamental ideas here are frequently misunderstood—a problem that paedobaptists themselves often encourage through their statements—we must point out that, in the position taken here, *to have a place in the covenant does not mean that one is in fact saved and in possession of all the covenant blessings.* No guarantee of salvation is attached to a covenant member simply by virtue of his or her place in the covenant. Furthermore, one does not even possess a presumption of salvation, or of election, by virtue of covenant membership. Salvation comes only through faith. Without it, covenant membership brings curses down upon the unbeliever.

Membership in the covenant does, of course, bring some blessings to the person in it. A covenant member is in a vastly more privileged position than an unbeliever, if only because covenant membership brings exposure to the means of grace. This is a point that Paul emphasizes about the Jews in Romans 3:1–2, immediately after dismissing the idea that circumcision guarantees acceptance with God and making the point that real circumcision is of the heart (Rom. 2:29). "Then what advantage has the Jew? Or what is the benefit of circumcision? Great in every respect. First of all, that they were entrusted with the oracles of God" (Rom. 3:1). We must even keep in balance the two ideas that circumcision is not, just by itself, a guarantee of one's acceptance with God and that having circumcision is a great benefit and blessing to one. Possessing circumcision is no guarantee that one is saved, yet it does provide a level of exposure to the gospel that those without it do not have. And if faith comes from hearing, and hearing by the word of Christ (Rom. 10:17), then being within earshot of the gospel puts one in a much more privileged position than one who is far from the means of grace.

12. There is considerable variation among paedobaptists on this point, as may be seen in Paul K. Jewett's treatment and critique of a number of variations in his *Infant Baptism and the Covenant of Grace* (Grand Rapids: Eerdmans, 1978), 144–60.

Now before we take up the evidence for the claims made by covenantal paedobaptists, let us consider what sort of evidence we are looking for. What would it take to convince us of these claims? The most obvious evidence, and surely the most convincing, would be a direct statement of Scripture to the effect that baptism has replaced circumcision. It would be even better to have this statement made in a context where a new convert's infant children were then baptized. As we all know, we don't have anything like that in the New Testament. Would that we did! It has been argued, for instance by John Piper, that the council of Jerusalem (Acts 15) provided an opportune time to state that baptism had replaced circumcision, if in fact it had.[13] But it is not even mentioned. Does this cast grave doubt on the paedobaptist position?

I do not think that we should rush to such a conclusion. There is a true development of doctrine within the church. It was only gradually that the New Testament church came to appreciate that the Gentiles were fellow heirs with the Jews. The vision received by Peter in Acts 10 had not fully settled the question for him as to whether circumcision in addition to baptism should be administered to the Gentiles. That was the question of Acts 15. Working out the implications of the new thing that God was doing, even though it had been prophesied in the Old Testament, took time.

Likewise, the doctrine of the Trinity took time to develop. All the data are to be found in the Scriptures, but the exact way in which all those data are to be organized and formulated into a concise summary (such as we have in the great creeds of the church) took considerable time. It would be wonderful if we had a text like the expansion of 1 John 5:7 found in the KJV, but if we do not, the doctrine of the Trinity is not lost to us. Similarly, a specific text plainly identifying baptism as the replacement for circumcision is not necessary to establish the doctrine. As has often been pointed out by paedobaptists, no specific text of the New Testament establishes that a woman should receive the Lord's Supper. It may appear probable in Paul's handling of

13. Piper, "How Do Circumcision and Baptism Correspond?"

the subject in 1 Corinthians 14, but it is not explicit. Surely no one is disposed to question the entitlement of women to the Lord's Supper just on the grounds that no New Testament text explicitly states this. This is to set the bar too high, and in a way not justified by the Scriptures themselves. Other proof than an explicit statement can suffice for the establishment of doctrine. While Acts 15 might have been a convenient setting for making the point that baptism had replaced circumcision, the fact that it does not, or that no other passage does either, is not by itself a reason to set aside the claim that baptism does replace circumcision in the paedobaptist sense.

If no direct proof of the sort discussed above can be given for the paedobaptist position, what kind of evidence can be given? I would maintain that the case fundamentally rests on establishing two principal contentions: first, that baptism and circumcision have essentially the same meaning; and second, that the covenant community is similarly constituted in the Old and New Testaments (specifically, that children are members of the covenant community in both). The second point is treated elsewhere in this collection, so my discussion of it here will be comparatively brief.

I would argue that if baptism and circumcision signify and seal the same truths of God, and if the children of believers are members of the covenant people in the New Testament, then those children, as members of the covenant, are entitled to the sign and seal of the covenant.

What then do baptism and circumcision mean? I would argue that their meanings can be summarized in terms of two fundamental concepts: cleansing and consecration. By "cleansing" is meant cleansing from sin, the forgiveness or washing away of the guilt of sin, so that a sinner may be reconciled to God. By "consecration" is meant that the person is now claimed by God as his own, devoted to God for obedience and service, bound in duty to serve God with all his heart, soul, mind, and strength, to live as God's person, acknowledging God's rule over him. The idea is not that one has consecrated or pledged himself to God, but that God has claimed him, imposing upon him the duties of wholehearted devotion and service.

As for cleansing in circumcision, what has already been argued above about circumcision as a sign and seal in Romans 4:11 indicates that cleansing from sin is a part of the meaning of circumcision. As we have seen, it is a part of circumcision not in the sense that those who are circumcised are thus identified as having been cleansed from sin, but in the sense that the circumcision signifies and seals that God does or will cleanse from sin all those who believe. Various texts in the Old Testament certainly connect circumcision with the idea of cleansing. In Deuteronomy 30:6, Moses says that the Lord your God will circumcise your heart to love the Lord your God with all your heart and with all your soul, so that you may live. This language is comparable to the new covenant language of Jeremiah 31:31–34 or Ezekiel 36:25–38. It is Old Testament language for what the New Testament calls regeneration and points toward the renewal of the heart necessary for faith and obedience.

The uncircumcised heart in the Old Testament is not clean, but polluted with sin. Leviticus 26:41 speaks of an uncircumcised heart becoming humble, so that the person makes amends for iniquity. Here too is the idea of a change of heart and purification. Isaiah 52:1 associates the uncircumcised with the unclean: "For the uncircumcised and the unclean will no longer come into you."

The New Testament builds on the idea of cleansing in circumcision. In Colossians 2:11, Paul says that the believing Colossians have themselves been circumcised in a certain sense—not in the physical sense of having their foreskins removed, but in "a circumcision made without hands, in the removal of the body of the flesh by the circumcision of Christ." Here is cleansing from the pollution of sin, "the removal of the body of the flesh." This the Colossians have received in "the circumcision of Christ," that is, the circumcision which comes from Christ, performed by him.[14] It was not the result of the Colossians' own effort, but was received as a gift from Christ.

14. F. F. Bruce, *The Epistles to the Colossians, to Philemon, and to the Ephesians,* New International Commentary on the New Testament (Grand Rapids: Eerdmans, 1984), 103–4.

Baptism likewise speaks of our cleansing. In Acts 22:16, Paul reports that Ananias commanded him, "Get up and be baptized, and wash away your sins, calling on His name." Baptism and cleansing are clearly united in this passage. Acts 2:38 speaks of being baptized for the forgiveness of sins. Of course, we should not think that baptism brings about the forgiveness of sins. Although the language of these two passages could be understood in that way, such an interpretation would contradict other passages of Scripture. The thief on the cross certainly received the forgiveness of sins, yet he had no opportunity to be baptized. Similarly, Acts 2:38 promises the gift of the Holy Spirit to those who repent and are baptized, but baptism cannot be a precondition for receiving the Holy Spirit if the Gentiles in Cornelius's house received the Spirit prior to their baptism (Acts 10:47–48). Peter had preached to these Gentiles that all who believe in Christ receive the forgiveness of sins (Acts 10:43). Their baptism served to signify and seal this fact; the baptism did not produce it.

As we saw above, Paul used the idea of circumcision to speak to the Colossians of the cleansing or purification that they had received in Christ. They had received a circumcision made without hands. This circumcision consisted in the removal of "the body of the flesh." It had been effected by Christ and was therefore called "the circumcision of Christ." All this took place, Paul says in verse 12, when they were buried with Christ in baptism, in which they were raised up with him through faith in the working of God, who raised him from the dead.

It is imperative that we look more closely at this verse in the Greek text. Colossians 2:12 is a continuation of verse 11, which itself is a continuation of the sentence begun in verse 9. Verse 12 is a series of participial phrases, all of which are related to the main verb in verse 11, "you were circumcised." Thus, in verse 12 Paul is explaining more fully just how it is that the Colossians have been circumcised in this circumcision made without hands. They were circumcised, "having been buried with [Christ] in baptism." Thus, verse 12 explains how the Colossians were "circumcised."

It is also important to say at this point that in *both* verse 11 and verse 12 Paul is not speaking of any physical rite or ceremony. The baptism in view in verse 12 is just as spiritual as the circumcision in verse 11. The physical rite of baptism signifies and seals that believers are raised up with Christ by faith in the working of God, who raised him from the dead, but water baptism in and of itself does not accomplish this. People can receive water baptism, and many have, without receiving what is signified and sealed by it. Again, Simon Magus is the classic example. He received water baptism, presumably after making a profession of faith (Acts 8:12–13), but shortly thereafter Peter perceived that he was still in the bondage of iniquity (v. 23). The baptism of Colossians 2:12 can only be the reality of the Spirit's working to regenerate the heart and free the soul from the dominion of sin. In Ephesians, this is called making one alive who has been dead in sin and raising him up with Christ (Eph. 2:4–7). This is precisely how Paul puts it in Colossians 2:13, that they were dead in their transgressions and in the uncircumcision of their flesh, but have now been made alive together with Christ, having been forgiven for all their transgressions. As we have seen, baptism can signify and seal this transaction, but it does not produce it.

So we see that both circumcision in the Old Testament and baptism in the New Testament signify a cleansing from sin, a removal of the uncleanness of sin. In neither case does the sign produce such cleansing; rather, the signs testify to the truth that God cleanses from sin when one believes.

Now let us consider the other fundamental concept connected with circumcision and baptism: consecration to God. Genesis 17 marks the introduction of circumcision as a sign of the covenant. There the idea of consecration to God is prominent. (Indeed, the idea of cleansing is nowhere prominent in the chapter; it remains implicit in the promise to fulfill the covenant blessings in the giving of the land and the multiplication of the seed.)

Genesis 17 opens with a call to Abraham to walk before God and be blameless. Beginning with verse 9, there is repeated emphasis on the necessity of Abraham and his seed keeping God's covenant. Judgment is threatened against those who do not keep the covenant. To use the language of the New Testament, Genesis 17 is a call to discipleship. Abraham's circumcision thus signified his consecration to God.

Again, because there is so much confusion on this issue, I must emphasize that in saying that Abraham's circumcision signified his consecration to God, I am not saying that Abraham consecrated himself to God, that is, committed his life to following God. Abraham had, it is true, done that long before, for when he was called, he obeyed, going out to a land he did not know (Heb. 11:8). Still, the consecration marked by Abraham's circumcision was not the consecration of himself to God, but God's consecration of Abraham to God. In other words, the consecration marked by circumcision is that God has set this person apart to himself, bringing him into a covenant relationship with himself and obligating him to be faithful in that covenant. As we have seen, that covenant also has promises attached. What God promises to Abraham and his seed, and what Abraham and his seed owe to God, are thus side by side in the covenant.

It is worth saying at this point that the covenant made with Abraham is a conditional covenant. In Genesis 17, the same promises are made to Abraham as are found in Genesis 12 and 15. But Genesis 17 makes it clear that faithfulness to the covenant is demanded of Abraham and his seed, for if they fail to comply, they will be cut off. There has of course been much debate over the question of whether the covenant with Abraham is conditional or unconditional. Since I cannot argue the point at length here, I beg the reader's indulgence in providing just a short treatment of this topic.

The fundamental reason for claiming that the covenant with Abraham is conditional has already been given: Genesis 17 promises the same blessings as are promised in Genesis 12 and 15. Yet Genesis 17 makes it clear, as neither Genesis 12 nor Genesis 15 does, that the fulfillment of the covenant promises will depend upon the obedience of Abraham's seed. Those who do not keep the covenant are to be "cut off" from their people (17:14). If this is so clear, why do so many claim that the Abrahamic covenant is unconditional?

The main reason is that neither Genesis 12 nor Genesis 15 emphasizes the conditional nature of the covenant. Genesis 12 does imply it, because Abraham must leave his own country in order to inherit the land that God promises to give him. Genesis 15, however, seems to put the whole weight upon God. God promises Abraham that his seed will inherit the land, and in confirmation of that promise he undergoes a ceremony in which he invokes a curse upon himself, should his word prove to be false. The fact that God alone passes between the animal pieces certainly leaves the impression that this covenant is one-sided. A promise is made, and God confirms it with an oath, swearing by himself (cf. Heb. 6:13; Gen. 22:17). If we look at Genesis 15 by itself, the covenant does appear to be unconditional. But we must always compare Scripture with Scripture, and when we do so, we find that Genesis 17 is just as clearly conditional as Genesis 15 appears to be unconditional. How then are we to reconcile these differences?

I would argue that Genesis 15 should be seen not as an unconditional promise, but as an *absolute* promise—that is, a promise which cannot prove to be false. What is promised to Abraham will certainly come to pass. That is, he will certainly have a great seed who will inherit the land that God has shown to him. Although these results are conditional upon the obedience of Abraham's seed, God can make this absolute promise concerning the results of a conditional covenant because he is capable of insuring that the conditions are met. This is precisely what he does in Christ, sending him into the world as the seed of Abraham in order to fulfill the conditions of the covenant that God has made with Abraham. God's promise cannot be proved false, only because he is capable of insuring that the conditions are met which are necessary for the fulfillment of the promise.

Returning now to Abraham's circumcision, we see in Genesis 17 that it stood as a sign of the covenant made with Abraham. In that covenant, God promised certain blessings to Abraham, but he also demanded obedience from Abraham and his seed. Abraham's circumcision thus functioned as a mark of ownership upon him, marking him as belonging to God and under obligation to do God's will.

Baptism in the New Testament carries an identical meaning. Our Lord institutes baptism for his church in the Great Commission (Matt. 28:18–20). Disciples are to be made of all nations, baptizing them into the name of the Father, the Son, and the Holy Spirit. These disciples are to be taught to obey all that Christ has commanded. These instructions are preceded by the assertion that all authority has been given to Christ in heaven and on earth. This is virtually an echo of Genesis 17:1, "I am God Almighty; walk before Me, and be blameless." Baptism has a clear connection to discipleship.

But again, what is that connection? Does baptism signify that one has made a choice and a commitment to be a disciple? Or does it signify that the one who is baptized is bound in duty to be a disciple? To understand baptism as a sign of our commitment to discipleship is to turn a sign and seal of God's covenant into a human pledge or badge of commitment. Our baptism then signifies that we have made a choice in life, or in infant baptism that this choice has been made for us by our parents. Many paedobaptists have represented the baptism of infants in just this way, and Baptist critics have rightly seen in this nothing more than the dedication of a child to God. But when we understand baptism as a sign of God's covenant with us, we see that it is more the mark of our duty to God than of our commitment to do that duty. What is signified and sealed by baptism is what God demands of us, not what we have pledged to God.

I conclude that baptism and circumcision have the same meaning. Both signify and seal that by faith we are cleansed from our sins, and that we have been consecrated to God to be his own. Therefore, the claim that baptism has replaced circumcision stands upon firm ground. The remaining issue, then, is whether the sign of the covenant is to be administered in the new covenant in the same way as it was in the old covenant. This depends upon how the church or covenant community is constituted in the New Testament. Specifically, do the children of believers have a place in the visible church, just as Abraham's children had a place in the nation of Israel?

Since this issue is treated at length elsewhere in this collection, I will just make two brief observations here in favor of the view that children are members of the new covenant church in the way that they were members of the old covenant church. First, children are directly addressed in the new covenant Scriptures (Eph. 6:1–3). While Paul may be addressing only believing children, that is not stated in the text. His failure to be explicit on this matter does not entitle us to assume that children as such, irrespective of any profession of faith, may be properly considered to be members of the church. We shall have to settle the question otherwise.

Help is provided by 1 Corinthians 7:12–14. In this passage, Paul is at pains to distinguish between a believing spouse and an unbelieving spouse. He says that the children of a believing spouse are "holy," not "unclean." Paul is surely using these terms in their established Old Testament sense, for he is not claiming that the children of a believing parent are automatically believers and thus "holy" in the sense of having been washed from sin and having received the imputed righteousness of Christ. That would be against the teaching of the New Testament. If neither circumcision nor uncircumcision means anything, but faith working through love, then being a covenant member through circumcision does not make one "holy" in the sense of being saved from sin. Similarly, the "holy," but not "unclean," children of one believing parent are not automatically saved. Even so, they are different from children who are not from believing parents. They are covenant members, and as such are more privileged (in view of their life inside the covenant), but they are not automatically saved by their covenant membership.

Our investigation so far has shown that members of the new covenant are heirs of the covenant promises made to Abraham and are rightly regarded as belonging to Abraham's seed. We have also found that the New Testament regards the children of believing parents as "holy" in an important sense, namely, that they have standing within the covenant that God made with Abraham. If baptism is the sign of that covenant in the New Testament, having the same meaning that circumcision did in the Old Testament, then surely the newborn infants of believers in the New Testament are just as entitled to receive the sign of covenant membership as their predecessors were in the Old Testament.

To conclude, let me make an application of the meaning of baptism in the lives of covenant children as this meaning is understood in the light of circumcision. A common question posed to me as a pastor, as I teach and instruct people about the meaning and significance of baptism in their own lives and the lives of their children, is, "What does the baptized child have which the unbaptized child does not?" The answer which I give is rather surprising to most parents, and it leaves them puzzled. I reply, "Why, they have baptism, of course." Stunned silence follows. Then they reply, "Well, yes, no doubt; but what difference does it make?" "Well," I say, "it makes whatever difference baptism makes in the life of any person. What difference does baptism make in your life, compared with someone who is not baptized?" If baptism is a sign and seal of God's covenant, then those who have been baptized possess this sign and seal, while the unbaptized do not. The unbaptized do not have any visible token certifying to them the promises of God. They do not have the name of God placed upon them, by which they are called as members of his covenant people. If indeed baptism marks us as those who have received God's covenant, then those who do not have baptism do not stand in God's covenant.

Here my questioners demand of me something more. "But," they say, "let's assume that the unbaptized children we are talking about have Christian parents, just like the baptized children. And let's further assume that these parents are just as dutiful as the other parents, so that their unbaptized children are exposed to every blessing in the church that the baptized children are exposed to, with the exception of baptism itself. What is the real difference between these children?"

Before answering this question, let me strengthen the implicit objection to infant baptism that it contains. Oftentimes these parents perceive that the duties owed to God that are signified in baptism are just the obligations we owe to God in the covenant of works. Consequently, these obligations are already upon the child irrespective of baptism. Furthermore, they point out, the promises that are signified and sealed in baptism are just the promises of the gospel, which are in fact given to all who would call upon the name of the Lord Jesus Christ. "So," they say, "if the baptized and the unbaptized have the same obligations to God, and have received the same gospel promises, what is the real difference?"

At this point, I say, "Let me give you another illustration. Take two young ladies. Both have special young men in their lives. Both men are talking about marriage, making big promises: lifelong faithfulness, joint ownership of all that the man possesses, etc. (all on the condition, of course, of marriage and faithfulness from her). The ladies are treated equally in every respect but one: one lady has received an engagement ring, while the other has not. Now what does the engaged lady have that the other does not?" The answer is obvious. The engaged lady has a ring. Does that make a difference? Well, just ask any lady without one. The visible token of the ring does not alter the promises made, but it surely makes those promises more firm in the mind of the recipient. Likewise, the ring makes more firm the duties owed. For the engaged lady, receiving the ring has brought home to her both the promises and the duties in a much more tangible way.

It is in just this way that the baptized child has something that the unbaptized child does not. Baptism signifies and seals truths that are most precious. It shows that we do have a place within God's covenant, that we are called by his name, that his promises have indeed been given to us. The baptism does not guarantee that we have possession of what is promised. That can only be guaranteed by faith. But the baptism can assure us that faith is enough. As a visible token of God's promise, it gives tangible expression to the certainty of God's promise to us, and that is something more than just the promise itself. God could have left things simply as a promise. That would have been enough. But he didn't. He gave us more, choosing to give us a tangible reminder to assure us of his promises and to mark us out as his own. The child who grows up with that (and whose parents and church rightly apply it through instruction and training) has something that the unbaptized child does not have, and it is "great in every respect" (Rom. 3:2).

Critics of the covenantal paedobaptist position do not easily yield at this point. They object that we have many explicit cases of baptism being administered in the New Testament, and in no case are children clearly involved. Moreover, in many (if not all) of these cases, baptism follows a profession of faith. Surely, they argue, if baptism is to be applied to covenant children, as circumcision was in the Old Testament, this would have been made explicit in the New Testament. Since it is not, infant baptism must be rejected.

Again, we cannot jump to that conclusion so quickly. If the inclusion of children within the covenant had represented a *departure* from Old Testament practice, then we might have expected some indication in the New Testament that this change was to be made. For example, when the dietary restrictions are lifted, this is noted (Mark 7:19; Acts 10:9–16). Or, when circumcision and complete adherence to the Mosaic law are rejected, this is noted (Acts 15). Luke, it might be said, notes a departure from the Old Testament practice of only males receiving the covenant sign by pointing out that both men and women were being baptized (Acts 8:12).

If the children of covenant members were no longer to be covenant members themselves, a good way to show that would have been to have children brought to the apostles for baptism, only to be refused on the ground that they were not entitled to it until they had professed faith. We don't have this. This is not to say that the absence of such an account is enough to establish that the position of the children of covenant members remains unchanged in the New Testament. We need much better evidence than just this lack of any contrary example in order to maintain that the children of covenant members are still covenant members themselves. Still, it is worth noting that the argument from silence can work both ways here. Just as Baptists might claim that the lack of any example of an infant being baptized casts doubt on the practice, so a paedobaptist can claim that the lack of any example excluding an infant from baptism casts doubt on the claim that the children of covenant members are excluded from the church until they profess faith.

6

THE MODE OF BAPTISM

JOSEPH PIPA

What does Romans 6:3–6 teach about the purpose and mode of baptism? Baptist writers maintain that Romans 6:3–6 teaches that baptism symbolizes conversion by picturing the sinner as buried and risen with Christ. They do not deny that baptism may represent more than it symbolizes, but they insist that it symbolizes the death, burial, and resurrection of Christ. For example, Tom Wells writes:

> Let us note first that baptism may represent more things than it pictures. To make my point clear, let me illustrate what I mean. An American penny represents several things. For example, it represents purchasing power . . . it also represents the government of the USA. But it does not picture these things. It pictures Abraham Lincoln on one side and the Lincoln Memorial building on the other.[1]

The case for immersion is based upon two primary arguments: (1) The Greek term *baptizō* and its cognates always refer to immersion. (2) Baptism is related to the death, burial, and resurrection of

1. Tom Wells, *Does Baptism Mean Immersion? A Friendly Inquiry into the Ongoing Debate* (Laurel, Miss.: Audubon Press, 2000), 24.

Christ in Romans 6:3–6 and Colossians 2:1–12.[2] I contend, on the basis of Romans 6:3–6, that baptism represents union with Christ through the washing of regeneration.

In order to understand Paul's argument in Romans 6:3–6, we need to look briefly at his argument in verses 1–14.[3] In the book of Romans, the apostle Paul lays the foundation for what we call the doctrines of grace. In the first two and one-half chapters, he establishes the depravity of all people in order to lay the foundation for the glorious doctrine of justification received by faith. According to Paul, a sinner is justified, not through law keeping, but on the basis of the atoning, propitiatory work of the Lord Jesus Christ. Paul carefully explains that justification is received by faith alone. In chapter 4, he proves his doctrine from the Old Testament, and in chapter 5 he demonstrates some of the practical outworking of justification and shows how it relates to the covenant headship of the Lord Jesus Christ. In chapter 6, he begins to develop the doctrine of sanctification, not in isolation from justification, but by showing the relationship of the two doctrines. Paul teaches in Romans 6:1–13 that our union with Christ has secured not only our justification, but also our sanctification.

In verses 1 and 2, the apostle Paul anticipates the objection that free grace leads to the practice of sin by declaring that it is impossible for a justified person to continue deliberately in sin, because we have died to sin. He says that if you are in Christ, you are dead to sin and alive unto God. Therefore, the gospel declares that justification is not an end in itself, but part of God's glorious work of perfecting his saints. Justification does not lead to lawlessness, but rather to power over the dominion of sin. "How shall we who died to sin still live in it?" This applies to everyone who is truly in Christ Jesus.

In verses 3–6, Paul proves this assertion by appealing to our baptism and conversion:

2. For arguments in addition to those made by Wells, see J. L. Dagg, *A Treatise on Church Order* (1858; reprint, Harrisonburg, Va.: Gano Books, 1990), 13–73.

3. I have adapted part of this material from a chapter in a book entitled *Sanctification: Growing in Grace,* edited by Andy Wortman and Joseph Pipa (Greenville, S.C.: Southern Presbyterian Press, 2002).

> Or do you not know that all of us who have been baptized into Christ Jesus have been baptized into His death? Therefore we have been buried with Him through baptism into death, so that as Christ was raised from the dead through the glory of the Father, so we too might walk in newness of life. For if we have become united with *Him* in the likeness of His death, certainly we shall also be *in the likeness of* His resurrection, knowing this, that our old self was crucified with *Him*, in order that our body of sin might be done away with, so that we should no longer be slaves to sin.

In verses 3–4, Paul asserts that union with Christ is the basis of our victory over sin, and that our baptism testifies to us that we are united with Christ. Notice how often Paul speaks of union with Christ in Romans 6: "All of us who have been baptized into Christ Jesus" (v. 3); "if we have become united with Him in the likeness of His death, certainly we shall also be in the likeness of His resurrection" (v. 5); "if we have died with Christ, we believe that we shall also live with Him" (v. 8). In fact, the apostle Paul characteristically describes what it means to be a Christian as being united with Christ. Think how often in his epistles he uses such phrases as "in him," "in the beloved," and "in Christ Jesus." For Paul, union with Christ is the bottom line, the essence of truly being a Christian.

Paul points out that because we are united to Christ as our covenant head, not only did he act on our behalf, but we also acted in him. Therefore, when he died, we died; when he was buried, we were buried; when he rose again, we rose again. He summarizes these things in verses 8–10:

> Now if we have died with Christ, we believe that we shall also live with Him, knowing that Christ, having been raised from the dead, is never to die again; death no longer is master over Him. For the death that He died, He died to sin once for all; but the life that He lives, He lives to God.

How can I know that I have died and been raised with Christ? Paul answers, "By your baptism." In Romans 6:3–4, he reminds us that our baptism testifies to us of our covenant connection to Christ: "Or do you not know that all of us who have been baptized into Christ Jesus have been baptized into His death? Therefore we have been buried with Him through baptism into death, so that as Christ was raised from the dead through the glory of the Father, so we too might walk in newness of life."[4] Paul uses the verb *baptizō* twice in verse 3 and the noun *baptisma* once in verse 4.

Before looking at these verses, let us establish two things. First, Paul is not saying that baptism regenerates.[5] He is not describing the nature of baptism, but refers to baptism in one of its fundamental, sacramental senses. He says that in baptism God makes a statement to those who are in Christ. Hodge writes, "It is not of the efficacy of baptism as an external rite, that he assumes his readers are well informed: it is of the import and design of that sacrament, and the nature of the union with Christ, of which baptism is the sign and the seal."[6] In our baptism, God declares that we are in union with the Lord Jesus Christ. Second, although *baptizō* and its cognates often refer to immersing or dipping, these terms are also used to describe washing and cleansing. Thus, no conclusion about the mode of baptism may properly be drawn from the mere fact that these words are used.[7] To follow Paul's argument in Romans 6:3–4, it is imperative not to equate baptism with immersion. Think of baptism here as the sacramental application of water.

First, let us note that Paul is not saying that baptism is a burial. In fact, his words do not relate baptism to burial: "We have been buried with Him through baptism into death" (v. 4). Our baptism into Christ's

4. Some writers maintain that Paul is using *baptizō* to express the work of regeneration. See also Robert Rayburn, *What About Baptism?* (1957; reprint, Greenville, S.C.: A Press, 1990), 41ff.; James W. Dale, *Christic Baptism and Patristic Baptism* (1874; reprint, Phillipsburg, N.J.: P&R, 1995), 242–45.

5. Paul is not discussing infant baptism in Romans 6:3–4, but rather the role of baptism as a believer reflects on his baptism.

6. Charles Hodge, *Commentary on the Epistle to the Romans* (1886; reprint, Grand Rapids: Eerdmans, 1974), 193.

7. John Murray, *Christian Baptism* (Philadelphia: Presbyterian and Reformed, 1962), 29. See also Rayburn, *What About Baptism?* 25; Robert L. Dabney, *Systematic Theology* (1878; reprint, Edinburgh: Banner of Truth, 1985), 758–77; Dale, *Christic Baptism and Patristic Baptism.*

death shows that we were buried with him. In the context, Paul refers to burial to show the absolute character of Christ's death, and thus ours. Some point to the parallel passage in Colossians 2:12 as proof that Paul equates baptism with burial: "having been buried with Him in baptism." In Colossians 2:13, however, Paul also refers to union with Christ. In Colossians, the burial of Christ stands for the totality of his redeeming work. Notice in verse 13 that Paul contrasts death and resurrection: "When you were dead in your transgressions and the uncircumcision of your flesh, He made you alive together with Him, having forgiven us all our transgressions." In Romans 6, Paul refers to burial to show the absolute character of the death. He uses the same imagery here. Moule writes:

> Union with Christ is primarily union with Him as the Dead and Buried, because His Death (consummated as it were and sealed in His Burial) is the procuring cause of all our blessings in Him, as it is our Propitiation and Peace. The Christian, joined to Him, shares as it were the atoning Death and the covering, swallowing, Grave of his blessed Representative; he goes to the depths of that awful process with and in his Lord.[8]

We were baptized into Christ's death, burial, and resurrection.

Moreover, the fact that baptism does not refer to the burial of Christ is seen in the consideration of the parallel terms in the text: "buried with," "implanted with," and "crucified with." Of these terms Murray writes:

> It is very easy to point to the expression "buried with him" in verse 4 and insist that only immersion provides any analogy to burial. But such procedure fails to take account of all that Paul says here. It should be noted that Paul not only says "buried together" (*synetaphēmen*) but also "planted together" (*symphytoi*) and "crucified together" (*synestaurōthē*).

8. H. C. G. Moule, *Studies in Colossians and Philemon* (reprint, Grand Rapids: Kregel, 1977), 104–5.

> These latter expressions indicate the union with Christ which is symbolised and sealed by baptism just as surely as does "buried together." But it is only too apparent that they do not bear any analogy to immersion. . . . When all of Paul's expressions are taken into account we see that burial with Christ can be appealed to as providing an index to the mode of baptism no more than can crucifixion with him. And since the latter does not indicate the *mode* of baptism there is no validity to the argument that burial does.[9]

Fairfield adds:

> All argument for immersion, drawn from the word, "buried," depends upon the conception of a *literal burial* in the waters of baptism. But when we bear in mind that the *death* spoken of in both of these passages is not literal death, but figurative; that the *resurrection* in like manner is not literal, but figurative,—is it not a plain violation of every law of language to understand the burial alone as literal?[10]

In Romans 6:3–4, Paul uses baptism to confirm our union with Christ. Although Baptists insist that *baptizō* always means "immerse" or "dip," some of them concede that at times *baptizō* must be understood metaphorically to refer to union. Because of the relation of the thing baptized to the element with which it is baptized, the term *baptizō* may be used metaphorically to express union. Commenting on Matthew 3:11, Wells resorts to the metaphorical meaning of *baptizō*. He admits that the baptism of the Spirit is described as a pouring out, but he argues that the Spirit surrounded the apostles, as if they were immersed in him.[11] He builds here on Dagg, who wrote:

> Both promises [i.e., the promise of outpouring and the promise of baptism or immersion in the Spirit] were fulfilled on the day of Pentecost;

9. Murray, *Christian Baptism,* 30–31.

10. Edmund B. Fairfield, *Letters on Baptism* (1893; reprint, Nashville: Publishing House of the M. E. Church, South, 1925), 189.

11. Wells, *Does Baptism Mean Immersion?* 26–27.

> but the two promises exhibit the influence of the Spirit then communicated, in different aspects. In one it is viewed as proceeding from God, and is likened to water poured out; in the other, it is viewed as affecting all the powers of the apostles, surrounding and filling them, as water surrounds and imbues substances which are immersed in it.[12]

Although Dagg's interpretation stretches the meaning of the text, he is willing at least to posit a metaphorical meaning of *baptizō* that in reality describes union, not burial. Wells concedes the metaphorical use of *baptizō* in 1 Corinthians 10:1–2:

> The Israelites were, "in the cloud and in the sea," only figuratively. The same figure is used in verse 1 where they are said to have, "passed through the sea." The sea and a cloud were all around them. *It was as if they were immersed in these waters.* That is all that Paul's language requires.[13]

The great Baptist commentator John Gill, commenting on Mark 10:38 ("Are you able to drink the cup that I drink, or to be baptized with the baptism with which I am baptized?") interprets *baptizō* metaphorically for being engulfed in sorrow. He writes:

> Which Christ speaks of in the present time, partly because his sorrows and sufferings were already begun: he had already been drinking of the cup of sorrows, being a man of sorrows and acquainted with griefs, all his days; and he was wading in the waters of affliction, though as yet they were not come into his soul, and he was as it were immersed in them; he was not yet baptized with the bloody baptism he came into this world for . . . and the baptism of his sufferings was to be surely accomplished.[14]

Paul uses *baptizō* to express the radical nature of union. As baptism brings us in contact with water, it expresses union. Rayburn writes,

12. Dagg, *A Treatise on Church Order,* 65.
13. Wells, *Does Baptism Mean Immersion?* 11.
14. John Gill, *Gill's Commentary* (1852–54; reprint, Grand Rapids: Baker, 1980), 5:373.

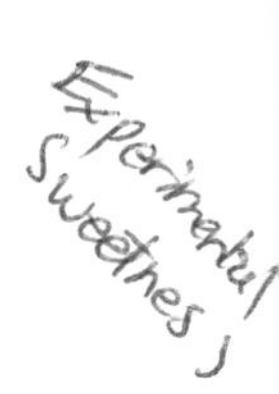

"Actually, the Scriptures prove that the word we render *baptize* actually means to *impart to,* or *apply to an object an element* used, whether it be water or fire or something else, in *any way*—not just by immersion in the element."[15] "Baptism" metaphorically describes being engulfed in suffering (Mark 10:38–39) or being overwhelmed by the Holy Spirit (John 1:33; Matt. 3:11).

Thus, the word itself suggests our radical union with Christ. The concept of union is made even clearer when we examine the particular phrases that Paul uses: *baptizō eis* and *baptisma eis.* One of the meanings of *eis* is "into" or "with respect to," implying relationship.[16]

Moreover, the biblical writers often use the formulas *baptizō eis* and *baptisma eis* to express union.[17] Paul uses this phrase to express union several times. In 1 Corinthians 10, he uses the figure of baptism to show the union of the Old Testament church with Moses, the covenant head. In verses 1 and 2 he says, "I do not want you to be unaware, brethren, that our fathers were all under the cloud and all passed through the sea; and all were baptized into Moses in the cloud and in the sea." The "baptism into" teaches that they were in union with Moses, the mediator of that old covenant. In a sense, he was their covenant head. This union is expressed a little differently in Galatians 3:27, "For all of you who were baptized into Christ have clothed yourselves with Christ." Paul again expresses the concept of union, this time using the covering of clothing to picture union. So to be baptized into Christ brings one into union with him. Consider one other example in 1 Corinthians 12:13, "For by one Spirit we were all baptized into one body, whether Jews or Greeks, whether slaves or free, and we were all made to drink of one Spirit." Here baptism expresses the unity of the body of Christ. Immersion as a mode fits none of these illustrations.[18]

15. Rayburn, *What About Baptism?* 26.

16. See Walter Bauer, *A Greek-English Lexicon of the New Testament and Other Early Christian Literature,* trans. and augmented by William F. Arndt and F. Wilbur Gingrich (Chicago: University of Chicago Press, 1979), 230; Henry George Liddell and Robert Scott, *A Greek-English Lexicon,* rev. and augmented by Henry Stuart Jones (Oxford: Clarendon Press, 1982), 491–92.

17. See Bauer, *Greek-English Lexicon,* 131–32.

18. See also Matt. 28:19; Acts 8:16; 19:3, 5; 1 Cor. 1:13, 15.

Returning to Romans 6, notice the development of Paul's argument. First, he points out that we were baptized into Christ. Thus, our baptism declared our union with him. He adds in verse 3 that to be baptized into Christ means that we have been baptized into his death; union with Christ secures union in every aspect of his work. This is made even more particular in verse 4: our burial with Christ is signified to us by our baptism into his death. (The noun *baptisma* with the preposition *eis* is used only here, and it has the same significance as the verb with the preposition.) If our baptism declares our union with Christ, then it expresses union with Christ in every aspect of his work: obedience, suffering, death, burial, resurrection, ascension, and session.

Thus, in our baptism, God declares to us that we are in union with the Lord Jesus Christ. We have explained above the reality of this union. It is a covenantal union, secured by God's election of us in Christ from before the foundation of the earth. Election is never divorced from union with Christ. God never looked upon any of us in favor, divorced from his looking upon Christ with love and favor. God testifies to us of this union in our baptism. Thus we see that Paul is speaking of what baptism means, rather than what it symbolizes. Pierre Marcel, commenting on Romans 6:3–6 and other passages, nicely summarizes this point:

> One is not here concerned with a question of *imitation,* as though the death of Christ ought merely to serve as an *example to* us following which we ought to die to sin and rise to a new life. The question here is primarily one of *participation.* On the one hand, we are made *partakers* of His death: the death of Christ has power to extinguish the enmity of our flesh and to cause us to die to sin. On the other hand, we are made *partakers* of His resurrection, for His resurrection has power to arouse in us a new condition which makes it possible for us to live a new life. The efficacy of Christ's death and resurrection is *communicated* to us.[19]

19. Pierre Ch. Marcel, *The Biblical Doctrine of Infant Baptism,* trans. Philip Edgcumbe Hughes (London: James Clarke, 1953), 145.

Recognizing that baptism in Romans 6:3–4 expresses union, we understand that the act of baptism is more than merely a symbol or a sign. Paul says that our baptism testifies to us about our union with Christ. If the consideration of one's baptism argues for union with Christ, then baptism is a sealing ordinance as well as a signifying one. Cranfield writes:

> What then did Paul mean by his claim that Christian baptism is essentially baptism into Christ's death? Not that it actually relates the person concerned to Christ's death, since this relationship is already an objective reality before baptism takes place, having been brought into being by God's gracious decision, which is implied by the *hyper hēmōn* in 5.8; but that it points to, and is a pledge of, that death which the person concerned has already died—in God's sight. On God's side, it is the sign and pledge that the benefits of Christ's death for all men really do apply to this individual in particular, while, on man's side, it is the outward ratification (we are thinking of course of adult baptism here) of the human decision of faith, of the response already begun to what God has done in Christ. That Paul thought of it (in its aspect of divine pledge) as an automatic, mechanical, magical guarantee is impossible in view of I Cor 10. But it does not therefore follow that he thought of it as a "mere sign", a *signum nudum*. It seems likely that he thought of Christ Himself as present and active personally in freedom and in power in the visible word of baptism as well as in the spoken word of the preached message.[20]

The sealing element of baptism is expressed in the Westminster Confession of Faith, 28.1:

> Baptism is a sacrament of the new testament, ordained by Jesus Christ, not only for the solemn admission of the party baptized into the visible Church, but also, to be unto him a sign and seal of the covenant of

20. C. E. B. Cranfield, *A Critical and Exegetical Commentary on the Epistle to the Romans* (Edinburgh: T. & T. Clark, 1985), 1:303.

> grace, of his ingrafting into Christ, of regeneration, of remission of sins, and of his giving up unto God, through Jesus Christ, to walk in newness of life.

Having seen that the phrase *baptizō eis* expresses union, let us consider the second line of evidence, that baptism expresses our regeneration and conversion.[21] In Romans 6:5–6, our baptism also speaks to us about the nature of our conversion: "For if we have become united with Him in the likeness of His death, certainly we shall also be in the likeness of His resurrection, knowing this, that our old self was crucified with Him, in order that our body of sin might be done away with, so that we would no longer be slaves to sin."

Although Paul applies baptism to union, he implies its relation to conversion by the close connection of verse 5 ("For . . .") to what precedes. Our baptism testifies to us of union with Christ, because we have truly died with him and been raised with him.

In these verses, Paul applies the language of Christ's death to our conversion. In our conversion, our covenant death and resurrection become living realities. He says that our old man has been crucified with Christ. It is difficult for us to grasp the audacity of this language. Centuries of Christian use have sanitized the term *crucifixion.* But when Paul introduced the term here in the book of Romans, it had a great deal of shock value. Crucifixion was the worse form of capital punishment ever invented. There was no way that one hanging on a cross could escape death. Although death came slowly and painfully, it came with certainty.

With this language, Paul teaches the absolute, transforming nature of regeneration. At regeneration, what Christ did for us covenantally becomes ours in reality, and we die to sin. When God regenerates us, we die; our old nature dies totally and completely. The Bible does not allow for the idea of the Christian having two natures, the old man and the new man. We often hear that the Christian has a new nature

21. As noted above, a number of writers take the reference to baptism in verses 3 and 4 to refer to the work of regeneration.

and a sinful nature, and that these two natures are like two dogs, a black dog and a white dog. The dogs are constantly fighting, and whichever one you feed the most on a particular day gets the upper hand. But such an idea is contrary to the biblical doctrine of human nature. We have one nature. Before conversion, it is an unregenerate nature; from the perspective of conversion, it is the old man. In Christ, the regenerate nature is the new man. Paul is reminding us that if we are converted, the unregenerate nature has been put to death, and therefore we are dead to sin.

I am not saying that we are sinless. God in his providence has left a remnant of sin within us. One helpful analogy to explain the reality of the remnant of sin is that of smoldering embers. When firemen extinguish a great fire, they leave some men to watch the scene of the fire. They must watch, because under the rubble could lie smoldering embers, which the slightest breeze could cause to flame up with raging fierceness. God in his providence has left within us the embers of the remnant of sin. Thus, we must watch ourselves and wrestle with sin. But the sinful nature has been put to death in the Lord Jesus Christ.

Our baptism testifies to our regeneration, as well as to our union. Murray wisely comments:

> There does not appear to be in the New Testament any passage which expressly says that baptism represents purification from the defilement of sin, that is to say, regeneration. But since baptism is washing with water, since it involves a religious use of water, and since regeneration is expressed elsewhere in terms of washing (John 3:5; Titus 3:5; I Cor. 6:11), it is difficult, if not impossible, to escape the conclusion that this washing with water involved in baptism represents that indispensable purification which is presupposed in union with Christ and without which no one can enter into the kingdom of God. There is also the consideration that baptism is the circumcision of the New Testament (Col. 2:11, 12). Circumcision, without doubt, symbolised purification from defilement. We should infer that baptism does also.[22]

22. Murray, *Christian Baptism,* 7–8.

One of the Bible's primary ways of referring to regeneration is to speak of it as cleansing or washing with water. See Ezekiel 36:25, Titus 3:5–6, and John 3:5. This symbol is based on the Old Testament concept of ritual cleansing by water: see Numbers 19:17–19 and Hebrews 9:13, 19; 10:22. Peter joins baptism with the concept of cleansing in 1 Peter 3:21. Picking up on Wells's reference to the symbolism of a penny, I maintain that baptism directly symbolizes cleansing with water. We confirm this by comparing baptism with the Lord's Supper. As bread and wine materially represent the body and blood of the Lord given for us, so water in baptism materially represents washing.

How do we relate the two concepts of union and regeneration? Union with Christ is achieved through regeneration. Through the washing of regeneration, we are brought into union. Therefore, *baptizō eis* verbally signifies union and materially symbolizes the washing of regeneration.

Union through the washing of regeneration provides the basis for inferring the mode of baptism. Hebrews 9:13, 19 teaches that washing was by sprinkling: "For if the blood of goats and bulls and the ashes of a heifer sprinkling those who have been defiled sanctify for the cleansing of the flesh . . . For when every commandment had been spoken by Moses to all the people according to the Law, he took the blood of the calves and the goats, with water and scarlet wool and hyssop, and sprinkled both the book itself and all the people." Earlier in verse 10, the writer refers to these ceremonial cleansings by a term translated "washings." The term he uses is the noun *baptismos.* The relation between the "baptisms" of verse 10 and the ceremonial sprinkling in verses 13 and 19 seems quite clear. Murray writes:

> The significance of this passage as it bears upon our present interest is that the "divers baptisms" referred to in verse 10 must surely include the lustrations expressly referred to in the succeeding verses. . . . In a word, the imperfection of the Levitical lustrations is contrasted with the lustration once for all perfected by Christ. In this sustained contrast every lustratory rite that comes within the writer's purview must

> be included in the "divers baptisms" of verse 10. And that simply means that the lustratory rites mentioned in the succeeding context must come within the scope of the "divers baptisms."[23]

There really is no reason not to relate the cleansings to baptism. The case is strengthened by the consideration that the majority of the Old Testament references to cleansing are by sprinkling or pouring. Wells, by appealing to the noncanonical rabbinical practice of cleansing by immersion,[24] asserts "that there was a good deal of immersion connected with the tabernacle rites."[25] But the Old Testament clearly teaches that the majority of Old Testament ceremonial cleansings, if not all of them, were by sprinkling or pouring.[26]

The link between cleansing and union is the Holy Spirit, as Paul points out in Titus 3:5–6, "He saved us, not on the basis of deeds which we have done in righteousness, but according to His mercy, by the washing of regeneration and renewing by the Holy Spirit, whom He poured out upon us richly through Jesus Christ our Savior." He cleanses and indwells. Thus, we may not ignore the relation of the baptism of the Holy Spirit to our baptism. Rayburn comments:

> To try to separate baptism from the work of the Holy Spirit is to do violence to the whole revelation of the Scriptures upon the subject. Real baptism is the work of the Holy Spirit, and water (ritual) baptism is that which symbolizes His work. Yet the most uneducated reader cannot fail to see that in the New Testament believers were not dipped into the Spirit, nor were they immersed in Him, nor plunged down into Him; but, to the contrary, the Spirit was shed forth, was poured out, fell, came, or rested upon them, and as a result they were baptized with the

23. Ibid., 21.

24. Ibid., 8–9; see also p. 17.

25. Wells, *Does Baptism Mean Immersion?* 7.

26. Rayburn says, "The idea of immersion is foreign to the Jewish economy. The word *immerse* does not even appear in the original Greek or Hebrew of the Bible in any of its forms" (*What About Baptism?* 28). Wells seeks to refute this by appealing to archaeological finds that suggest that immersion was practiced to some degree. Note that Rayburn is referring to the Old Testament when he speaks of "the Jewish economy."

> Holy Ghost. Baptism then is not the person's being put into the element, but rather the elements being put upon the person. It is impossible to prove anything from Scripture if this point is not proved: that a person is properly baptized when the element of the baptism is put upon him.[27]

Thus, our union with Christ is effected by the Spirit (by being poured out, Titus 3:5–6), who washes (by sprinkling, Ezek. 36:25–27). Water baptism signifies and confirms our union with Christ, effected by regeneration, by the power of the Holy Spirit, who was poured out on the church on the Day of Pentecost and continues to be poured out in regeneration. Although Romans 6 does not speak explicitly to the question of the mode of baptism, but rather to the meaning of baptism (not burial with Christ, but union through cleansing), we may nonetheless infer the mode of sprinkling or pouring. The meaning of baptism is a sealing of one's union with Christ, effected by the regenerating work of the Holy Spirit. The mode of baptism is inferred from its meaning, not the meaning of *baptizō* or its relation to burial. Thus, the mode should reflect that of ceremonial cleansing (sprinkling) or the regenerating work of the Holy Spirit (pouring).

27. Rayburn, *What About Baptism?* 24.

7

The Newness of the New Covenant

JEFFREY D. NIELL

"Behold, days are coming, says the Lord,
when I will effect a new covenant
with the house of Israel and with the house of Judah;
not like the covenant which I made with their fathers
on the day when I took them by the hand
to lead them out of the land of Egypt;
for they did not continue in My covenant,
and I did not care for them, says the Lord.
For this is the covenant that I will make with the house of Israel
after those days, says the Lord:
I will put My laws into their minds,
and I will write them on their hearts.
And I will be their God, and they shall be My people.
And they shall not teach everyone his fellow citizen,
and everyone his brother, saying, 'Know the Lord,'
for all will know Me,

> from the least to the greatest of them.
> For I will be merciful to their iniquities,
> and I will remember their sins no more."
>
> When He said, "A new covenant," He has made the first obsolete. But whatever is becoming obsolete and growing old is ready to disappear. (Heb. 8:8–13)

What is *new* about the new covenant?[1] And what does that question have to do with baptism? With ever increasing frequency, Hebrews 8 and particularly the quotation from Jeremiah 31:31–34 is being used to argue against paedobaptism (covenant baptism). This recent contention is one that concerns *membership* in the new covenant: Just who are to be considered part of the new covenant and, therefore, recipients of the covenant sign of baptism? This question is part of the discussion of who should receive baptism. The assertion is that membership in the new covenant is qualitatively different from membership in the old covenant, and Hebrews 8 supposedly sets forth this difference.

Those who argue for this position claim that membership in the new covenant is significantly different from membership in the old covenant, and that, therefore, the children of believers should not be recognized as covenant members and be baptized. It is of course true that something is new in the new covenant. However, in appealing to the latter portion of Hebrews 8:11—"for all will know Me, from the least to the greatest of them"—it is asserted that membership in the new covenant (and thus the signs of membership, baptism and the Lord's Supper) is restricted to those who "know the Lord." Since "knowing the Lord" is something that must be evident and discernible in all the members of the covenant, it follows that infants cannot be

1. I thank my dear friend Randy Booth for all of the years of laboring together on this topic. Also, the congregation of Emmanuel Covenant Church, which has delighted in this material (as they do in the whole counsel of God), is greatly appreciated for their encouragement and assistance, especially Eric Finley, Kevin Johnson, Richard Klaus, and Mike Munoz.

members. Since infants are not able to show evidence of any faith, they should not be baptized.

This position suffers from many weaknesses. Apart from the limited (if any) historical support for such an interpretation, it is based on poor exegesis. This novel interpretation fails to take into account the true nature of the old covenant and fails to adequately take into account the context of the epistle to the Hebrews, and therefore it founders in the immediate context, where the Jeremiah quotation is found.[2]

Hebrews 8 is being touted as the passage that denies covenant membership to the children of adult covenant members. In 1997, when John MacArthur debated R. C. Sproul on the topic of baptism, he noted the "watershed" importance of the Jeremiah passage. MacArthur asserted:

> You don't have a whole group of covenant people in which there is a little believing remnant in the New Testament, and if you ever do question that, then you need to deal with the text of Jeremiah 31:31–34, which is the watershed issue, I believe, on this whole discussion. In Jeremiah 31:31–34, he promises the New Covenant, and here's what Jeremiah says, "There is a covenant coming. It's not like the covenant you know; it is a new covenant," and he says this, "Here's how it's different." And of all the options Jeremiah could have picked, of all the things that Jeremiah could have said, of all the choices that he could have made to distinguish the New Covenant from the Old, this is what he said (verse 34): "They shall all know Me, from the least of them to the greatest of them." The essence of the New Covenant is everybody in it knows God savingly. That is, I think, the significant distinction between belonging to the Abrahamic Covenant ethnically and belonging to the New Covenant savingly. And so a sign that suited an ethnic covenant is not parallel to a sign that suits a saving covenant, and therein bap-

2. Ironically, by appealing to this passage in this way, Baptists admit that baptism can be discussed by using "dry verses," that is, passages that do not mention baptism. No longer is this approach restricted to the proponents of covenant baptism.

tism is to be made distinct from circumcision, and again I remind you that Scripture does make no such connection.[3]

Hebrews 8 has, in many circles, moved to center stage in the discussion of baptism. Supposedly, Hebrews 8 has become the millstone around the neck of paedobaptism. This brief article shall concern itself with the Jeremiah quotation that is found in Hebrews 8 and show that an interpretation derived from the context of Hebrews does nothing to discredit paedobaptism. Initially, we will have to deal with many misconceptions. Due to the influence of dispensationalism, significant misunderstandings surround this Hebrews passage. Simply stated, the eighth chapter of Hebrews is often thought to teach certain things that are new about the new covenant that simply are not new at all. We will begin by clearing the table of many false ideas about the newness of the new covenant. Then we will be able to set the table for proper understanding; our discussion will then present an interpretation of the passage that accords with the immediate context of Hebrews (6:20 through 10:39), the overall context of the epistle, and biblical, covenant theology in general. These points will show that God has implemented no change whatsoever in covenant membership in the new covenant: children of believers are *still* included in the congregation of God's people, just as they have been throughout redemptive history. The exclusion of children from the covenant community is not a characteristic of the new covenant.

WHAT IS *NOT* NEW ABOUT THE NEW COVENANT

In striving to know what is new about the new covenant, part of the answer is found in Hebrews 8. However, many things that are said about the new covenant in this passage are *not* new, though they are often presented as if they were. Many of the things described in this quotation from Jeremiah were already precious realities in the old covenant. Many misunderstandings arise because of the failure to

3. Baptism Audio Debate Series (Orlando, Fla.: Ligonier Cassette, 1998).

properly understand the experience of the regenerate in the older covenant. At the outset, note that the author of the epistle to the Hebrews quotes Jeremiah 31:31–34 to assert the truths of the new covenant. The *entire* quotation is concerned with its newness, not just Hebrews 8:11. Thus, whatever interpretation is derived from this text must come from the entire quotation. One cannot take a single verse and declare, "This is what is new!" without regard for the rest of the passage. The author is making a point about the newness of the new covenant, and the quotation from Jeremiah corroborates that point. Let us now begin to consider some specific matters that are not new in the new covenant.

A Different People

The passage does not teach a radical separation between the peoples of the Old and New Testaments:

> I will effect a new covenant with the house of Israel and with the house of Judah. (Heb. 8:8)

> For this is the covenant that I will make with the house of Israel. (v. 10)

The passage is clear: this new covenant will be made with the house of Israel and with the house of Judah. The church of this new covenant era is referred to as Israel and Judah, the people of God. This fact is consonant with the teaching of the rest of the New Testament. The apostle Paul refers to the saints as "the Israel of God" (Gal. 6:16). He refers to himself and the disciples in Philippi as members of "the true circumcision" (Phil. 3:3). The church in the new covenant era is frequently described in the same terms used to refer to the people of God during the old covenant administration (1 Peter 2:9–10; Rom. 9:24–26). Additionally, note that God did not initiate a new standard of conduct for his people in the new covenant era. The text is clear: "I will put My laws into their minds, and I will write them on their hearts" (Heb. 8:10). God's law, the transcript of his holiness and his expectations for his people, was already on the hearts of his people, and so is not new in the new covenant.

If we are going to assert that the newness of the new covenant is found, in part, in this passage in Hebrews, then we must first take into account that the people of God in the Old and New Testaments are referred to by the same designation. Furthermore, an accurate interpretation of the newness of the new covenant will properly account for the old covenant nomenclature being applied to the saints of the new covenant era. We must also note that the standard of conduct is the same: God will write his law upon their hearts and place it in the minds of his covenant members.

No Differences

The passage does not teach that the new covenant is exactly the same as the previous covenant:

> [It is] not like the covenant which I made with their Fathers. (Heb. 8:9)

Differences do exist between the old and new covenants. The new covenant is distinct from the previous one. This passage demands this recognition. Covenant theology clearly and emphatically acknowledges that the new covenant is distinctive. All too often, covenant theologians have been accused of treating the New Testament as if it were the Old. This misrepresentation of covenant theology is not helpful. But the question remains, How is the new covenant different? Does the newness pertain to its *essential nature*, making it qualitatively different from the previous covenant, or does the newness pertain to *membership*—or both? Those who would utilize the Hebrews passage to argue against paedobaptism would say that the new covenant is new in both respects.

Support for this assertion is said to be found in the quotation from Jeremiah that is under consideration. Both its membership and its essential nature are supposedly different because "all will know Me, from the least to the greatest of them" (v. 11). However, the phrase "from the least to the greatest of them" will not sustain this interpretation, and it founders upon the rocks of the rest of the New Testament as well. For example, new covenant disciples are warned—with the very same warnings given to our fathers—to not prove themselves to be covenant rebels (Heb. 2:1–3; 3:7–4:2; 6:4–8; 10:26–31; 12:25–29; John 15:1–7; Rom. 11:17–24; Acts 14:22). Hebrews 8:11 cannot mean that every single member of the new covenant knows the Lord savingly, for that would be contrary to the rest of the New Testament. We must avoid equating covenant membership with election while we recognize that Scripture exhorts new covenant disciples to continue on in the faith. We will see that the distinction between the new covenant and the previous one does not relate to its essential nature or membership. The distinction is something altogether different.

Internal Religion

The new covenant is concerned with internal religion, in contrast to the external, but that is not what is new in the new covenant:

> I will put My laws into their minds, and I will write them on their hearts. (Heb. 8:10)

Internal religion has been a precious reality throughout redemptive history. It is not true that the new covenant is new because matters of religion and faith are now internal rather than external. Once again, dispensationalism has led biblical interpretation astray. The Shema[4] is clear: "Hear, O Israel! The LORD is our God, the LORD is one! You shall love the LORD your God with all your *heart* and with all your soul and with all your might. These words, which I am commanding you today, shall be on your *heart*" (Deut. 6:4–6). Internal, "heart" religion is not new in the new covenant era, yet MacArthur comments on the text of Hebrews 8 as if the newness of the new covenant pertains to its internal character:

4. *Shema* is a transliteration of the Hebrew word "hear," the first word of Deut. 6:4.

> The New Covenant will have a different sort of law—an internal not an external law. Everything under the old economy was primarily external. Under the Old Covenant obedience was primarily out of fear of punishment. . . . Even when the old law was given, of course, it was intended to be in His people's hearts (Deut. 6:6). But the people could not write it on their hearts like they could write it on their doorposts. And at this time the Holy Spirit, the only changer of hearts, was not yet given to believers. . . . In the New Covenant true worship is internal, not external, real, not ritual.[5]

Leon Morris comments similarly:

> The first point is that the new covenant is inward and dynamic: it is written on the hearts and minds of the people. A defect in the old had been its outwardness. It had divinely given laws, indeed; but it was written on tablets of stone (Exod. 32:15–16). The people had not been able to live up to what they knew was the word of God. It remained external.[6]

And Philip E. Hughes is similarly incorrect:

> This new covenant, *not like the covenant* made with the people through Moses, would be of grace, not of works; radical, not external; everlasting, not temporary; meeting man's deepest need and transforming his whole being, because from beginning to end it would be the work, not of man, but of God himself. In other words, the law which formerly was external and accusing now becomes internal, an element of the redeemed nature, and a delight to fulfill.[7]

These writers surprisingly assert that the internal operations of divine grace were not present for the old covenant saint. MacArthur de-

5. John MacArthur Jr., *Hebrews,* MacArthur New Testament Commentary (Chicago: Moody Press, 1983), 183.

6. Leon Morris, "Hebrews," in *The Expositor's Bible Commentary,* ed. Frank E. Gaebelein, vol. 12 (Grand Rapids: Zondervan, 1981), 78.

7. Philip E. Hughes, *A Commentary on the Epistle to the Hebrews* (Grand Rapids: Eerdmans, 1977), 300.

clares that old covenant obedience was out of fear of punishment, that the Holy Spirit had not yet been given to believers, and that worship at that time was not real. The Bible militates against such ideas. Morris and Hughes assert that the law was not internal until the new covenant, implying that this internalized aspect is much of the newness of the new covenant. But the Bible teaches otherwise.

Regeneration is impossible apart from the work of the Spirit of God—truly, "the only changer of hearts" (MacArthur)—and since regenerate persons walked the earth during the time before Christ, they must have been made alive by the work of the Spirit of God. Abraham is presented to the new covenant church as an example of justification by faith (Rom. 4). The saints mentioned in Hebrews 11 are included because of faith, and they all are saints of the older covenant church and examples for us. Walter C. Kaiser's comments are helpful:

> But a moment of careful reflection will reveal that something has been left out. If the Holy Spirit was not active in the individual lives of believers in the OT, would this mean that they were unregenerate? Since the Holy Spirit is the only One who can bring new life and effect subjectively the salvation that Christ would secure for them objectively, did this mean that OT believers did not possess faith—which is always said to be the gift of God (effected by the Holy Spirit) and not of works, lest any man or woman . . . should boast (Eph. 2:8–9)?[8]

The Holy Spirit was clearly present prior to Christ's ascension; otherwise, blasphemy against the Holy Spirit would have been a nonsensical concept (Matt. 12). Nehemiah, in his corporate prayer of confession, knows of the work of the Spirit in guidance and conviction (Neh. 9:20, 30; cf. Zech. 7:12). Proverbs 1:23 speaks of the Spirit being poured out upon the penitent. Stephen, in his discourse on Jewish history, refers to the rebellion and resistance of the Jews as a resisting of the Holy Spirit (Acts 7:51). Furthermore, Jesus expected Nicodemus, a teacher of the law, to have been familiar with the work

8. Walter C. Kaiser, *Toward Rediscovering the Old Testament* (Grand Rapids: Zondervan, 1987), 136.

of the Spirit in regeneration: "Are you the teacher of Israel and do not understand these things?" (John 3:10).

Even more compelling is the fact that the experience of the old covenant saint was one in which the law of God was written on his heart. The psalmist is clear:

> The righteous will inherit the land
> And dwell in it forever.
> The mouth of the righteous utters wisdom,
> And his tongue speaks justice.
> *The law of his God is in his heart;*
>
> His steps do not slip. (Ps. 37:29–31)
> I delight to do Your will, O my God;
> *Your Law is within my heart.* (Ps. 40:8)

To state the matter as simply as possible, the writing of the law of God on the hearts of his people is *not new* in the new covenant, nor are the internal operations of God's Holy Spirit upon the hearts and minds of his people new in the new covenant. These were precious realities for the old covenant saint as well.[9] Since these aspects of the new covenant are not new, what then is new about it? Before answering this question, we must deal with a few other areas of misunderstanding.

Divine Initiative

God takes the initiative in the new covenant, but that is not new:

> I will effect a new covenant. (Heb. 8:8)

9. See also Deut. 10:12; 30:14; Pss. 78:8; 119:11, 111; Isa. 51:7. The internal operations of the Spirit of God were especially recognized during times of covenant renewal and restoration (Jer. 24:7; 32:39; Ezek. 11:19; 18:31; 36:26; Joel 2:16). Furthermore, the covenant sign of circumcision, rather than pointing chiefly to something external or national, pointed primarily to what was to be an inward, spiritual reality of a circumcised heart (Deut. 10:16; 30:6; Jer. 4:4; 9:25–26; Rom. 2:25–29).

> For this is the covenant that I will make. . . . I will put My laws . . . I will write them. (v. 10)

> For I will be merciful . . . and I will remember their sins no more. (v. 12)

Without divine initiative, no one would be saved. Throughout the Bible, God shows himself to be the One who accomplishes everything according to the counsel of his will, and nothing can thwart his purposes (Eph. 1:11; Pss. 115:3; 135:6; Job 42:2). Our salvation—our justification and sanctification—begins and ends with our merciful, heavenly Father. The regeneration (new life) granted by our Lord is infectious. It infects the entirety of our being, so that the life we now live, we live by faith (faith, too, being a gift from God) in the Son of God, who loved us and gave himself up for us (Gal. 2:20). "We love, because He first loved us" (1 John 4:19). We live for his glory because he first gave us life. Divine initiative is not new. Abraham was justified by faith, the gift of God (Rom. 4; Gal. 3:8–9). God, throughout redemptive history, has chosen his people—"I have loved Jacob; but I have hated Esau" (Mal. 1:2–3)—and hardened others, such as Pharaoh (Ex. 4:21; Rom. 9:11–18).

Covenantal Relationship

God establishes a covenant relationship between himself and his people in the new covenant, but that is not new:

> And I will be their God, and they shall be My people. (Heb. 8:10)

This precise terminology, as with the law being written on the hearts of God's people, is used throughout redemptive history to speak of those in covenant with the Lord. It is the very language of covenant relationship throughout the Bible and is applied to people in both the Old and New Testaments:

> I will also walk among you and be your God, and you shall be My people. (Lev. 26:12)

> Hear the words of this covenant, and speak to the men of Judah and to the inhabitants of Jerusalem; and say to them, "Thus says the LORD, the God of Israel, 'Cursed is the man who does not heed the words of this covenant which I commanded your forefathers in the day that I brought them out of the land of Egypt, from the iron furnace, saying, "Listen to My voice, and do according to all which I command you; so you shall be My people, and I will be your God."' " (Jer. 11:2–4)

> What agreement has the temple of God with idols? For we are the temple of the living God; just as God said, "I will dwell in them and walk among them; and I will be their God, and they shall be My people." (2 Cor. 6:16)

> And I heard a loud voice from the throne, saying, "Behold, the tabernacle of God is among men, and He will dwell among them, and they shall be His people, and God Himself will be among them." (Rev. 21:3)

From the Old to the New Testament, those in covenant with the Lord have been described as "My people," the people of God, and those among whom God walks. This truth is not new in the new covenant era. If Hebrews 8 is truly referring to something new, it must be referring to something else.

Knowledge of the Lord

Knowledge of the Lord characterizes the new covenant, but it is not new:

> And they shall not teach everyone his fellow citizen, and everyone his brother, saying, "Know the Lord," for all will know Me, from the least to the greatest of them. (Heb. 8:11)

Throughout redemptive history, the people of God have been taught and marked as a people who know the Lord. God has sent his prophets and provided scribes and experts in the law for the instruction of his people. This fact ought to be unquestioned. Nonetheless, the phraseology is stated negatively: "They shall *not*." Something is going to cease; it will disappear in the new covenant era, and it will pertain to teaching and the knowledge of the Lord. It has to do with a form of teaching that occurred among the covenant people of the Lord.

Let's consider a couple of points of clarification before we proceed any further. First, the passage speaks of a form of teaching, but it does not mean that the Israelites went about saying to one another, "Hey, fellow citizen, know the Lord." Such a practice is not found in the Old Testament. Moreover, there *was* a problem with the assumption of divine acceptance on the basis of physical descent from Abraham (Matt. 3:9–10; Rom. 9:8). Second, whatever the "teaching" that is to cease is, it cannot be the teaching gifts that have been given to the church (Eph. 4). Neither can it refer to the teaching responsibilities given to parents with regard to their children (Eph. 6:1–4). Such teaching is still present among the new covenant saints.

For now, we are simply determining what is *not* new about the new covenant. What this teaching and knowledge actually refer to will be dealt with below. Some fail to give an accurate interpretation of this passage because they fail to consider the first portion of Hebrews 8:11. Frequently, readers will make an uninformed jump to the latter portion of the verse ("for all will know Me, from the least to the greatest of them"), interpreting it without regard for that to which it is connected.[10] We do not question that this knowledge will have a universal effect within the new covenant. The text is clear: "for all will know Me, from the least to the greatest of them." We also admit, however, that this statement pertains to some type of teaching and knowledge that was present during the old covenant administration. Before examining the meaning of this quotation from Jeremiah, one more misunderstanding needs to be cleared away.

10. The word translated "for" is the Greek word *hoti*, which can legitimately be translated "because," thus showing the relationship between the first and later portions of this verse: "And they shall not teach . . . because. . . ."

Divine Mercy

God's grace, mercy, and forgiveness are prominent in the new covenant, but not new to it:

> For I will be merciful to their iniquities, and I will remember their sins no more. (Heb. 8:12)

God's full pardon for sinners was just as present and real for saints in the Old Testament as it is for saints in the New. We have already pointed out that the apostle Paul puts Abraham forth in Romans 4 as an example of one who is justified by faith. We have also referred to Hebrews 11, the "hall of faith," for numerous examples of Old Testament redeemed saints. Salvation has always been by grace and through faith. This was true for Ruth the Moabitess, Uriah the Hittite, and Onesimus. Full pardon, full remission of sins, and God's abundant grace and mercy poured out on the sinners he receives has been a precious reality throughout redemptive history. The psalmist declares this truth frequently:

> HOW blessed is he whose transgression is forgiven,
> Whose sin is covered!
> How blessed is the man to whom the LORD does not impute
> iniquity,
> And in whose spirit there is no deceit! (Ps. 32:1–2)
>
> The LORD is compassionate and gracious,
> Slow to anger and abounding in lovingkindness.
> He will not always strive with us,
> Nor will He keep His anger forever.
> He has not dealt with us according to our sins,
> Nor rewarded us according to our iniquities.
> For as high as the heavens are above the earth,
> So great is His lovingkindness toward those who fear Him.
> As far as the east is from the west,

So far has He removed our transgressions from us.
Just as a father has compassion on his children,
So the LORD has compassion on those who fear Him.
For He Himself knows our frame;
He is mindful that we are but dust. (Ps. 103:8–14)[11]

The Old Testament saint delighted in this truth: "The LORD, the LORD God, compassionate and gracious, slow to anger, and abounding in lovingkindness and truth" (Ex. 34:6). So, the question must be asked, What *is* new about the new covenant? No one can assert that Old Testament saints were only partially redeemed, whereas those in the New are fully redeemed. Forgiveness from the sovereign wellspring of God's abundant mercy has been placed upon saints throughout the ages,[12] so what then is new about the new covenant?

WHAT IS NEW ABOUT THE NEW COVENANT?

We have seen that Hebrews 8 is pivotal in our understanding of the newness of the new covenant and that we must consider it in any attempt to answer the question before us. First of all, we have had to clear away many misunderstandings and misconceptions in order to pursue a proper interpretation of this passage. We have seen that the people of God, in the new covenant era, are still spoken of as the house of Israel and the house of Judah. Furthermore, we have seen that many things are *not* new in the new covenant. For example, God's standard for covenant obedience remains his law; it is written upon the hearts and minds of his disciples in both testaments.[13] The internal operations of divine grace are not new in the new covenant era, nor is divine initiative or the language of covenant relationship: "I will be their

11. Once again, the blessedness of singing the Psalms comes before us. The new covenant saint who obediently sings the Psalms (Col. 3:16) would not question the fact that full pardon has been received *throughout* redemptive history.

12. See also Deut. 7:7–9; Mic. 7:18–19; Neh. 9:17, 27, 31.

13. It is simply being pointed out that many interpret the law mentioned in Hebrews 8:10 as the moral law, which is certainly not new in the new covenant.

God, and they shall be My people." These truths are precious realities for the disciples in both testaments, as is the role of teaching and the privilege of being taught. Finally, we noted that full pardon, the remission of sins by a gracious God, is not new in the new covenant. All of these things—since these matters are not new in the new covenant—demand an explanation. The writer of the epistle to the Hebrews is making a point about the newness of the new covenant, yet everything mentioned in the Jeremiah quotation can, in one sense, be understood as not new at all. The writer must mean something else, and whatever this "something else" is, it must accord with the context of the epistle. To this explanation we now turn.

Jesus Has Fulfilled the Ceremonial Law

In accordance with the immediate context of the epistle to the Hebrews, particularly 6:20 through 10:39, the newness of the new covenant pertains to the outward administration of the covenant of grace in worship and obligation. More particularly, the ceremonies of religious observance have been abrogated—they have been "put out of gear," for they have been fulfilled. While the meaning and the intention of the ceremonies have been eternally validated, their practice is no longer required. These ordinances pointed forward to the person and work of the Messiah, Jesus Christ, who has now come. Jesus Christ is our High Priest, our final sacrifice, and the One who dwelt (tabernacled) among us. All of the shadows of the old covenant administration of the covenant of grace, since they were by nature temporary, have ceased with the coming of the substance, the reality they prefigured. This interpretation accords best with the immediate context (6:20–10:39) and with the overall argument of this epistle, which firmly establishes the supremacy of Jesus Christ. This assertion can be stated both negatively and positively. To state it negatively: the newness of the new covenant is seen in *the cessation of the ceremonial aspects of the law.*[14] To state it positively: Jesus Christ has fulfilled the law. He

14. The law spoken of in the passage (Heb. 8) must be the ceremonial law, for the moral law was in force before the ceremonial law was given on Sinai, and it had to be kept alongside the

has become our perfect High Priest and has accomplished our redemption (atonement) through the perfect sacrifice of himself. It now remains for us to establish this interpretation as that which best accords with the context.

This interpretation, which understands Hebrews 8 as referring to the ceremonial aspects, that is, the outward elements, of the covenant of grace, is not a novel interpretation. The Reformed Baptist A. W. Pink, explained that the passage does indeed refer to the outward, ceremonial administration of the covenant. He wrote:

> But at this point a difficulty, already noticed, may recur to our minds: Were not the things mentioned in Heb. 8:10–13, the grace and mercy therein expressed, actually communicated to God's elect both before Sinai and afterwards? Did not all who truly believed and feared God enjoy these same identical blessings? Unquestionably. What then is the solution? This: the apostle is not here contrasting the internal operations of Divine grace in the Old and N.T. saints, but as Calvin rightly taught, the "reference is to the economical condition of the Church." The contrast is between that which *characterized* the Judaic and the Christian dispensations in the *outward* confirmation of the covenant.[15]

Previously, Pink had explained:

> The apostle's object is obvious. It was to the old covenant that the whole administration of the Levitical priesthood was confined. . . . But the introduction of the new Priesthood necessarily abolished that covenant, and put an end to all the sacred ministrations which belong to it. This is which the apostle here undertakes to prove.[16]

---

ceremonial observances. Admittedly, Jesus Christ also fulfilled the moral law for his people; however, the point here, relevant to the context of Heb. 8, pertains to the ceremonial aspects of the law. Suffice it to say that Christ's perfect fulfillment of the moral law does not change our responsibility to obey it.

15. A.W. Pink, *An Exposition of Hebrews* (Grand Rapids: Baker, 1954), 454.

16. Ibid., 436.

> What we shall here endeavor to treat of is the *administration* of that covenant, as it was made known by God, and the various *forms* in which it was established among His saints.[17]

> Instead, in Heb. 8 the apostle is treating of such *an establishment of* the new covenant as demanded the revocation of the Sinaitic constitution. What this "establishment" was, is made clear in Heb. 9 and 10: it was the *ordinances of worship* connected with it.[18]

Pink's comments are precisely in line with those of John Calvin as he commented on Jeremiah 31. Calvin wrote:

> He afterwards says, *I will put my Law in their inward parts.* By these words he confirms what we have said, that the newness, which he before mentioned, was not so as to the substance, but as to the form only: for God does not say here, "I will give you another Law," but *I will write my Law,* that is, the same Law, which had formerly been delivered to the Fathers. He then does not promise anything different as to the essence of the doctrine, but he makes the difference to be in the form only.[19]

> Since it is so, it cannot be inconsistent with the truth and faithfulness of God, that the ceremonies should cease as to their use, while the Law itself remained unchanged. We now then see that the Apostle [the writer of Hebrews] faithfully interpreted the design of the Prophet [Jeremiah] by accommodating his testimony to the abrogation of the ceremonies.[20]

Remarkably, one of the most learned and gifted communicators among the Anabaptists, Balthasar Hubmaier, understood the context of Hebrews to be referring to the removal of the ceremonial aspects of the

17. Ibid., 448.

18. Ibid., 450.

19. John Calvin, *Calvin's Commentaries,* vol. 10, *Commentaries on the Book of the Prophet Jeremiah and the Lamentations,* trans. John Owen (reprint, Grand Rapids: Baker, 1979), 4:131–32.

20. Ibid., 4:140. It is also helpful to see Calvin's explanation in the *Institutes,* 2.9.1–4.

law.[21] In this, we affirm that the Bible does not teach two ways of salvation.[22] The one covenant of grace is simply administered differently in the new covenant than in the old. This understanding is the one required of these words in Hebrews 8.[23] The immediate context of the epistle and Jeremiah's usage of the word "new" establish this interpretation. The Hebrew word is *hadash* and it expresses the idea of renewal. Kaiser's comments are clear and helpful:

> But Jeremiah's promise of a "new covenant" (Jer. 31:31–34) appears to many to mean that the program announced to Abraham and David has been superseded, or at least attenuated. However, this confusion results from attaching a modern meaning to the word "new." In Jeremiah's usage, it is meant only to "renew," as can be seen from the use of the same Hebrew word for the "new moon."[24]

The Context Refers to the Ceremonial Law

The immediate context of this section of the epistle to the Hebrews is one that deals with the ceremonial aspects of the law. Whatever interpretation one gives to the words of Jeremiah quoted in Hebrews 8, it must fit the context. While the quotation is concerned with the new-

21. Balthasar Hubmaier, *Balthasar Hubmaier: Theologian of Anabaptism,* trans. H. Wayne Pipkin and John H. Yoder (Scottdale, Pa.: Herald Press, 1989), 188. Hubmaier wrote: "We know that Christ has newly instituted baptism and the Lord's Supper and abolished the ceremonies, figures, and shadows of the Old Testament with his coming, as the epistles to the Colossians and the Hebrews clearly prove, Col. 2:16ff.; Heb. 8:13."

22. The *London Baptist Confession of 1689* affirms: "Believers in Old Testament times were justified in precisely the same way as New Testament believers" (11.6).

23. Further substantiation of this interpretation is found in the writing of John Colquhoun. He writes concerning the old and new covenants in Hebrews 8:6–10: "The design in this epistle to the Hebrew Christians was to show them the preference of the new dispensation of the covenant of grace, which has taken place since the death of Christ to that old dispensation of it, which had been established at Sinai, and had continued until His death. This the writer illustrates not by stating the difference between the covenant of works and the covenant of grace, but by showing the difference between the old dispensation, or *former manner of administration, of the covenant of grace and the new dispensation of the same covenant*" (emphasis added) (*A Treatise on the Law and the Gospel* [reprint, Morgan, Pa.: Soli Deo Gloria, 1999], 69–70). Perhaps the clearest presentation of this distinction between the old and the new administrations of the covenant of grace is seen in the Westminster Confession of Faith, 7.5–6.

24. Kaiser, *Toward Rediscovering the Old Testament,* 25–26.

ness of the new covenant, the surrounding context is concerned with that which was ceremonial, that is, the outward administration of the covenant of grace prior to the new covenant era. The external ceremonies were temporary; they were growing old and were ready to disappear (Heb. 8:13). Whatever was a shadow has been fulfilled by the reality. The types (patterns)[25] are fulfilled by Jesus Christ.

The ceremonial law is also termed the "restorative" or "redemptive" law. The ceremonial laws pointed out, or unto, the manner of redemption. They did not provide redemption themselves; they typified it as well as the Redeemer. The ceremonies prefigured the person and work of the Messiah who was to come. They "illustrated" the way of reconciliation. The ceremonial law was the gospel in figures, the gospel in pictures. Because of their typological function, these laws were necessarily temporary. This fact is beautifully seen in the epistle to the Hebrews. God has taken the priesthood, particularly the high priest, and the work of the priests out of the way, for Jesus is better than Aaron and the Levitical priesthood. Jesus is our high priest who, in the offering of himself, has accomplished redemption (see Heb. 2:17; 3:1; 4:15; 5:5–6; 6:20; 7–10). The ceremonies are no longer to be practiced, yet their meaning is fully established. The Melchizedekian priesthood abides and is better than the Levitical priesthood. We still have a high priest, he still "entered through the . . . tabernacle" (9:11), and we still have a sacrifice. The newness of the new covenant is seen in the "first" one "becoming obsolete and . . . ready to disappear" (8:13). The first covenant is fully described in chapter 9, a chapter that deals extensively with the outward elements, the outward administration, of the covenant of grace prior to the inauguration of the new covenant. It must be understood as referring to the ceremonial aspects of the law, things that are no longer practiced, though their intention is fully validated.[26]

25. In Heb. 8:5, we read that all ceremonial aspects of the law shown to Moses on the mountain were to follow "the pattern." The Greek word for *pattern* is *typos,* from which we get our word *type*.

26. John Calvin wrote, "The ceremonies . . . have been abrogated not in effect but only in use. Christ by his coming has terminated them, but has not deprived them of anything of their sanctity; rather, he has approved and honored it" (*Institutes of the Christian Religion,* ed. John T.

The Ceremonial Law on the Heart?

We have seen that God has written his moral law on the hearts of his people throughout redemptive history, and therefore that that is not new for the people of God.[27] So the words in Hebrews 8 about the writing of the law on the heart, while related, must refer to something else, something that is unique in the new covenant. The context bears this point out. The people of God in the new covenant have a new relationship to the ceremonies of participation in the covenant of grace. What is new is that the ceremonial law is written on the hearts of God's people. Prior to the new covenant, inaugurated by Jesus Christ, the command to obey the ceremonies was not an optional matter for the follower of the Lord. Since the coming of the Lord Jesus Christ, those ceremonies are no longer in effect; any attempt to revert to them is a falling from grace, a severance from Christ (Gal. 5:4).

The Ceremonial Law and Hebrews 8:11

> And they shall not teach everyone his fellow citizen, and everyone his brother, saying, "Know the Lord," for all will know Me, from the least to the greatest of them. (Heb. 8:11)

To assert that the ceremonial law is in view in this passage accords nicely with the immediate context in which it is found in Jeremiah, but how are we to understand the ceremonial law with regard to Hebrews 8:11? Let us first make sure that our basics are in place. First, this verse contains the only negative statement in the quotation, "They shall not." It refers to something that was part of the ceremonial legislation of the old covenant that is going to cease, will no longer be practiced, and will be removed in the new covenant. Second, teaching is involved. The passage addresses something with regard to the

---

McNeill, trans. Ford Lewis Battles [Philadelphia: Westminster, 1960], 2.7.16). Greg L. Bahnsen clearly articulates this idea: "The ceremonial observations no longer apply, but their meaning and intention have been eternally validated" (*Theonomy in Christian Ethics,* rev. ed. [Phillipsburg, N.J.: Presbyterian and Reformed, 1984], 209).

27. Even nonbelievers have "the work of the Law written in their hearts" (Rom. 2:15).

spreading of the knowledge of the Lord that previously occurred among the covenant people of God: "They shall not *teach* . . . saying, 'Know the Lord.'" Third, the ceasing of this teaching and knowledge will be pervasive. It will affect all of those in the covenant: "For all will know Me, from the least to the greatest of them." At the very least, these three basic elements are present in the verse. From them, one can see that Hebrews 8:11 is referring to the removal of the old covenant priesthood and the people and duties associated with it.

The conclusion that the Levitical priesthood and its attendant duties are in view is based on the immediate context and an understanding of the place and function of the priests in the old covenant administration of the covenant of grace. We shall see that the priests occupied a special place as those "known" by the Lord, and that they conveyed, or communicated, the knowledge of the Lord to their fellow citizens. We shall now see how these words in Hebrews 8:11 refer to the priests and the priesthood of the old covenant.

The Priests: Distinctive Class, Distinctive Duties

The Levitical priesthood came from the sons of Aaron. Particularly, the Levites who served as priests were from the households of Kohath, Merari, and Gershon (Num. 4; Ex. 6:16–19; 1 Chron. 23:6), not any others. Service as a priest was not "equal opportunity employment"; it was established by a law of physical descent (Heb. 7:16). The inability to trace one's lineage after the Babylonian exile meant that many Levites had to stop functioning as priests (Neh. 7:64–65). The old covenant priests were a distinctive class.

Much of the distinctiveness of the old covenant priesthood is seen in the unique relationship that priests had with the Lord whom they served. They were the ones who made offerings "before the Lord," who served in his presence, serving in his tabernacle ("dwelling place" in Hebrew). The tribe of Levi knew the Lord in a special sense and was given the privileged duty to teach its fellow citizens:

> Of Levi he said, . . . "They shall teach Your ordinances to Jacob, and Your law to Israel. They shall put incense before You, and whole burnt offerings on Your altar." (Deut. 33:8, 10)

The old covenant priests were in a special relationship before the Lord, whom they represented. In this relationship, they were granted a distinct knowledge of the Lord that others in Israel did not have, and therefore they were the teachers of Israel. In their priestly duties of sacrifice and temple ministrations, they revealed the manner of redemption to the old covenant congregation. These priests, in dealing with the ceremonial aspects of the law, revealed the gospel in pictures and illustrated the way of salvation. Their unique teaching was to cease at the time of the new covenant. Thus, we see that all of the basics are in place. First, this function occurred during the old covenant. Second, this was a teaching function that revealed the knowledge of the Lord. And third, this teaching function, designed by God to eventually cease, affected all of those in the covenant. The Levitical priests had a sort of intimacy, a type of knowing the Lord, that was not common among the Israelites. As Scripture clearly teaches, "The Levites shall be Mine" (Num. 3:12).[28] God established a distinctive relationship with the priests, the Levites. In Malachi, this is referred to as "the covenant of Levi" (Mal. 2:4, 8).[29] Part of the privileged responsibility of this covenant made with Levi was that of teaching and instruction:

28. The Lord speaks of the Levitical priests as "My ministers" and as those "who minister to Me" (Jer. 33:21–22). However, all of Israel is said to belong to the Lord: "I have set you apart from the peoples to be Mine" (Lev. 20:26; see also Isa. 43:1; Ezek. 16:8). All the children of Israel belong to the Lord, and yet, among the Israelites, the Levites (especially?) belong to the Lord.

29. According to Neh. 13:29, we may speak of a covenant of the priesthood. Therefore, we may refer to the priesthood—and all of its attendant, ceremonial elements—as a covenant. This is how we ought to understand the old covenant, as contrasted with the new covenant, in Hebrews. John Calvin understood the ceremonies in this way: "They were only the accidental properties of the covenant, or additions and appendages, and in common parlance, accessories of it. Yet because they were means of administering it, they bear the name 'covenant.' . . . To sum up, then, in this passage 'Old Testament' means the solemn manner of confirming the covenant, comprised in ceremonies and sacrifices" (*Institutes,* 2.11.4).

> True instruction was in his mouth and unrighteousness was not found on his lips; he walked with Me in peace and uprightness, and he turned many back from iniquity. For the lips of a priest should preserve knowledge, and men should seek instruction from his mouth; for he is the messenger of the LORD of hosts. (Mal. 2:6–7)

What About Those Who Were Not Priests?

Those citizens who were not of the priestly caste are described as "laymen" in many of our translations. The Hebrew word for this term can help us understand Hebrews 8 and the newness of the new covenant. The Hebrew word is *zar,* and it is also used to refer to those who are foreigners, outsiders, or strangers. This word can be legitimately translated as "stranger," as one who is an outsider. This fact is clearly seen in passages that refer to the distinctive place and function of the old covenant priests:

> So when the tabernacle is to set out, the Levites shall take it down; and when the tabernacle encamps, the Levites shall set it up. But the *layman* who comes near shall be put to death. (Num. 1:51)

> So you shall appoint Aaron and his sons that they may keep their priesthood, but the *layman* who comes near shall be put to death. (Num. 3:10)

> Now those who were to camp before the tabernacle eastward, before the tent of meeting toward the sunrise, are Moses and Aaron and his sons, performing the duties of the sanctuary for the obligation of the sons of Israel; but the *layman* coming near was to be put to death. (Num. 3:38)

> . . . as a reminder to the sons of Israel that no *layman* who is not of the descendants of Aaron should come near to burn incense before the LORD; so that he will not become like Korah and his company—just as the LORD had spoken to him through Moses. (Num. 16:40)

Those people who were not priests were described as strangers ("laymen"), for they did not know the Lord in the way that the priests did.[30] The Lord is jealous for his glory and for those who represent him in this priestly way. Not everyone could be a priest, and the priestly duties had to be performed with precision—otherwise death could ensue.[31] God required precision in the offerings and for those who offered them because they prefigured the person and work of the Messiah who was to come. Distinctiveness surrounded the Levitical priesthood; the entire office and function of the priesthood was one of distinction. The priests were a distinct class, with distinct duties. Even their garments, the anointing oil, and the incense spoke of their distinctiveness. The role and function of this priesthood was indeed one of distinctive teaching.[32] Therefore, when God removed the priesthood (the persons and the work), the new covenant is precisely described with the words, "I will be their God, and they shall be My people. And . . . all will know Me, from the least to the greatest of them" (Heb. 8:10–11).[33]

The Least to the Greatest of Them

That Hebrews 8:11 refers to the removal of the Levitical priesthood is further substantiated by the words "from the least to the greatest of them." When used of people, this phrase always refers to classes or

30. The Hebrew word *zar* is also used to describe those who did not belong to the nation of Israel (Isa. 1:7; Jer. 5:19; 51:2). The inclusion of the Gentiles, the *goyim,* in significant measure, is also part of the newness of the new covenant. See footnote 32 below.

31. Nadab and Abihu, sons of Aaron, died as a result of disregarding the command of the Lord with respect to their priestly duties (Lev. 10). The distinctiveness of the priests is also illustrated by the fact that the Lord prescribed distinctive anointing oil to be used only when ordaining the priests. If this oil was applied to a layman (stranger), the one who applied it was to be excommunicated—cut off from among the people (Ex. 30:23–33).

32. The law of ceremonies functioned in a tutorial, pedagogical manner (Gal. 3:24).

33. We must also see the removal of the ceremonial distinction between Jew and Gentile as part of the newness of the new covenant. Prior to their inclusion in the new covenant era, the Gentiles were known as "*strangers* to the covenants of promise" (Eph. 2:12). Since Jesus Christ has come, he has reconciled the two groups to God in one body, so that the Gentiles "are no longer strangers and aliens." They "are fellow citizens with the saints, and are of God's household" (Eph. 2:16–19).

ranks of persons.[34] This is true throughout the Old and New Testaments. The old covenant priesthood was a distinct class of people within the covenant community, and the fact that the context is dealing with ceremonial matters further confirms the interpretation.

In Genesis 19:11, God struck with blindness wicked men "both small (*qaton*) and great (*gadol*)," without regard for age or social status. These men were previously described as "the men of the city, the men of Sodom, . . . both young and old, all the people from every quarter" (Gen. 19:4). Another example is found in Deuteronomy 1:17. The judges appointed by Moses were to show no partiality in judgment: "You shall hear the small (*qaton*) and great (*gadol*) alike." Jonah 3:5 records the citywide effect of Jonah's preaching. All persons, from king to subject, were affected: "Then the people of Nineveh believed in God; and they called a fast and put on sackcloth from the greatest (*gadol*) to the least (*qaton*) of them." While additional passages could be cited,[35] these examples show that the phrase is to be understood as referring to all ranks or classes of people.

The Hebrew phrase that is translated "least . . . greatest" (sometimes rendered "great and small") is used seven times in Jeremiah, and each time it refers to classes or ranks of persons. When referring to the least and the greatest, he is consistently referring to all classes of people (6:13; 8:10; 16:6; 31:34; 42:1, 8; 44:12).

The same meaning is also found in the Greek New Testament. The words "the least" and "the greatest" in Hebrews 8:11 are the Greek words *mikros* and *megas*. These words occur together eight times in the New Testament, and they always refer to people of various classes or ranks. Acts 26:22 provides an excellent example. Paul stands before King Agrippa and declares, "I stand to this day testifying both to

34. The Hebrew words for *small* (*qaton*) and *great* (*gadol*), refer to all classes (or ranks) of persons when they are (1) used in connection with each other and (2) refer to people. At other times, the words are used together, but refer to weights and measures (Deut. 25:13–14), cities (Eccl. 9:14), east and west (1 Chron. 12:15), animals in the sea (Ps. 104:25), and houses (Amos 6:11).

35. See also Gen. 27:15; 1 Sam. 5:9; 30:2; Est. 1:5, 20; 1 Chron. 25:8; 2 Chron. 15:13; 18:30; 31:15.

small (*mikros*) and great (*megas*), stating nothing but what the Prophets and Moses said was going to take place." Paul declares that he has spoken to people in Damascus, in Jerusalem, and throughout Judea— "even to the Gentiles" (26:20). He has preached to all ranks and classes of men, from those of "small" rank (*mikros*), including Gentiles, to those of "great" rank (*megas*), including King Agrippa. The remaining New Testament examples confirm this understanding.[36]

Summarizing Hebrews 8:11

Hebrews 8:11 explains that part of the newness of the new covenant is found in the removal of the Levitical priesthood—an office that was especially engaged in teaching and representing the knowledge of the Lord to the people. This function is something that Jeremiah explained would one day no longer occur; it would cease. And this teaching that would cease would have a pervasive effect on all the covenant people. Now that God has removed this way of teaching the knowledge of the Lord and is bringing in the Gentiles in significant measure, it is accurate to say that "all will know Me, from the least to the greatest of them."[37]

36. Along with Heb. 8:11, see Acts 8:11 and Rev. 11:18; 13:6; 19:5, 18; 20:12.

37. It has been asserted that Heb. 8:11 refers to saving knowledge, but it must be recognized that *know* can refer to nonsaving knowledge (Jer. 16:21; Gen. 4:1). As argued throughout this chapter, the context deals with the removal of the ceremonial aspects of the law and refers to the knowledge that is possessed and published by the priests. This is true whether or not they were elect before the foundation of the world. With the author of Hebrews, we must be careful to avoid equating covenant membership with election. This is shown by the warnings of apostasy that are given to new covenant members throughout this epistle—referring to apostasy from the covenant, not apostasy from election (Heb. 3:6–4:6; 6:4–6; 10:26–31; 12:14–17, 25–29). The same examples of old covenant faith*less*ness are applied to members of the new covenant (Heb. 3:7–11). Not all disciples continue with Jesus—in John 6 some "disciples" withdrew from him and followed him no more (John 6:66); they *were* disciples, but they were not elect. Paul went about "strengthening the souls of the disciples, encouraging them *to continue in the faith*" (Acts 14:22). This passage uses the same word for "continue" that is used in Heb. 8:9 to describe those who were covenant breakers under the old covenant. Covenant breaking is a reality in the new covenant as well. Judas was a covenant member who partook of the new covenant meal (Luke 22) and yet, according to the decree of God, he was "the son of perdition" (John 17:12). Judas was a covenant member *and* a covenant breaker. Jesus describes the fruitless branches of John 15 as being "in Me," and yet they are cut off and thrown into the fire (vv. 2, 6). They are not cut off from election, since the elect have been appointed to have fruit that will remain (v. 16). There is one tree in Romans 11: natural branches (Jews) are cut off for unbelief,

The Ceremonies of the Old Covenant and Hebrews 8:12

The ceremonial aspects of the covenant of grace are also in view in Hebrews 8:12. Since God's grace, mercy, and forgiveness are not new in the new covenant, this passage must refer to something else and must accord with the context. Hebrews 8:12 refers to the abrogation of the ceremonies of sacrifice, the priestly duties, of the old covenant. While the sacrifices (the sacrificial system) of the ceremonial law pointed forward to the Redeemer and his work of redemption, they also provided a continual reminder of sin for the people. Redemption was not found in the sacrifices; it was illustrated in the sacrifices, and every illustration presented a reminder of guilt. Hebrews 10:3–4 clearly teaches this:

> But in those sacrifices there is a reminder of sins year by year. For it is impossible for the blood of bulls and goats to take away sins.

God has always been merciful to his people, to their iniquities. Psalm 103 declares that he will separate our sins from us, as far as the east is from the west. He has always offered full pardon, but now, in the new covenant, the continual reminder is removed. God no longer requires the offerings through the priests: "I will remember their sins no more" (Heb. 8:12). Jesus Christ, the High Priest of our confession, has offered himself once for all—the final priest and the final sacrifice. "For by one offering He has perfected for all time those who are sanctified" (Heb. 10:14).

Jeremiah 31 is cited again in Hebrews 10:16–17, in a context concerned with the ceremonial aspects of the old covenant.[38] Admittedly, chapter 10 is dealing with the implied contrasts between the old and the new, the first and the second. Recognizing some of these contrasts between the two administrations of the covenant of grace is helpful:

---

and wild branches (Gentiles) are warned about continuing in faith. All of this is in the new covenant, and so we must avoid equating covenant membership with election.

38. When Rom. 11:27 quotes Jer. 31:34, it refers to the removal of the ceremonial distinction between Jew and Gentile. This distinction is not made in the new covenant (Gal. 3:28).

the impossibility of pardon through the shadows and the assurance of pardon through Jesus Christ, the sacrifices (plural) and *the* Sacrifice, the priests (plural) and *the* Priest, the priests who stand and the *One* who sat down, the priests who serve daily and the *One* whose work is completed. These are contrasts between the ceremonies of the old covenant and the verities of the new. They are the differences between shadow and substance and between pattern and fulfillment.

SUMMARY

The newness of the new covenant pertains to the external aspects, the outward administration, of the covenant of grace. The new covenant is not new in its nature or membership. A single covenant of grace exists, and God's elect have been justified in the same way throughout redemptive history—by grace and through faith. The quotation of Jeremiah 31 in Hebrews 8 does nothing to establish a change in the membership of those who are in the covenant. Children are not excluded in the new covenant; membership still includes believers and their children.[39] The congregation of the people of God has included children throughout redemptive history. Children are still included in the new covenant (Luke 1; Eph. 6).

39. Those who believe that Heb. 8, particularly v. 11, is teaching the exclusion of the children of believers from membership in the new covenant need to observe that the word "least" (*mikros*) in 8:11 is used elsewhere in the New Testament to refer to children (Matt. 18:6, 10, 14; Luke 9:48). This is true also of the Hebrew word for "least," *qaton* (Jer. 6:11–13).

8

Infant Baptism in the New Covenant

RICHARD L. PRATT JR.

[31a]“The time is coming,” declares the LORD,
[b]“when I will make a new covenant
[c]with the house of Israel
[d]and with the house of Judah.

[32a]It will not be like the covenant
[b]I made with their forefathers
[c]when I took them by the hand
[d]to lead them out of Egypt,
[e]because they broke my covenant,
[f]though I was a husband to them,”
[g]declares the LORD.

[33a]“This is the covenant I will make with the house of Israel
[b]after that time,” declares the LORD.
[c]“I will put my law in their minds
[d]and write it on their hearts.

[e]I will be their God,
[f]and they will be my people.

[34a]No longer will a man teach his neighbor,
[b]or a man his brother, saying, 'Know the LORD,'
[c]because they will all know me,
[d]from the least of them to the greatest,"
[e]declares the LORD.
[f]"For I will forgive their wickedness
[g]and will remember their sins no more."
(Jer. 31:31–34)

Many evangelicals appeal to Jeremiah's prophecy of the new covenant in Jeremiah 31:31–34 as a basis for rejecting infant baptism, but a careful examination of this passage in the light of the rest of Scripture reveals that it actually supports the historic Christian practice of infant baptism. Our study will address three main topics: (1) how Jeremiah's prophecy is often used to argue against infant baptism, (2) the original meaning of Jeremiah's prophecy, and (3) the New Testament's outlook on Jeremiah's prophecy. As we will see, Jeremiah's prediction of the new covenant actually encourages Christians to continue the practice of infant baptism until the Lord returns.

HOW IS THE NEW COVENANT USED AGAINST INFANT BAPTISM?

The universally accepted term "New Testament" is based on the phrase "new covenant" in Jeremiah 31:31–34. Accordingly, all evangelicals agree that Jeremiah's prophecy of a new covenant is fulfilled in the New Testament era. Yet, opinions are divided on how Jeremiah's prophecy relates to the practice of infant baptism. Many evangelicals who reject infant baptism believe that this prophecy offers nearly conclusive evidence in favor of their view. We will return to this evidence below, but at this point we should summarize three ways in which Jeremiah's prophecy is often understood in this manner.

In the first place, it is thought that infant baptism is contrary to Jeremiah's prophecy because Jeremiah declared that *the new covenant could not be broken.* As the prophet said in Jeremiah 31:32,

> It will not be like the covenant
>   I made with their forefathers
> when I took them by the hand
>   to lead them out of Egypt,
> because they broke my covenant . . .

In this verse, the prophet declared that the new covenant would "not be like" the old covenant, in that the "forefathers . . . broke" the old covenant. The Old Testament uses the terms "to keep" and "to break" covenant (along with a number of other expressions), to describe, respectively, the obedience and disobedience of God's covenant people to the stipulations or regulations of their covenants. To keep covenant was to offer faithful (albeit imperfect) service in order to receive divine blessing, but to break covenant was to commit unrepentant, flagrant violations, which nullified the offer of blessing and brought divine judgment.

Although Jeremiah's words "to lead them out of Egypt" indicate that he had especially in mind a contrast between the covenant with Moses and the new covenant, the possibility of breaking covenant and incurring divine wrath was a dimension of every major Old Testament covenant. The covenant with Noah (Gen. 6:13–21; 8:20–9:17) focused primarily on God's blessing of natural stability for the human race, but the threat of execution for murderers (Gen. 6:9) and the severe curse on Noah's grandson Canaan (Gen. 9:25–27) indicate that divine judgment may fall on those who rebel against God's covenant requirements. Abraham's covenant (Gen. 15:1–21; 17:1–21) also had much to say about divine blessing, but God explicitly warned about the judgment that would fall on those who broke this covenant (Gen.

17:14). As Jeremiah himself pointed out, the covenant with Moses repeatedly warned of the horrible curses that would come on those who broke that covenant (see also Deut. 28:15–68; 31:16–18). The covenant with David also reflected this basic pattern (Pss. 89; 132:11–18). God stipulated to David that his descendants would sit on his throne "if your sons keep my covenant" (Ps. 132:12; cf. 2 Chron. 6:16; Ps. 89:30–31), but, as Israel's history indicates, they suffered severely for violations of the covenant (2 Sam. 7:14).

Without a doubt, Jeremiah distinguished the new covenant as one that would not be broken, but this aspect of Jeremiah's prophecy poses a serious challenge for infant baptism. As all evangelicals would agree, not everyone baptized in infancy proves to be a covenant keeper. Many people who are baptized into the new covenant as infants turn away from Christ and the salvation he offers. This undeniable reality raises an important question: How can we think that infants are to be baptized into the inviolable new covenant when they often rebel against the new covenant and suffer the judgment of God?

A second feature of Jeremiah's prophecy that is often used to oppose infant baptism is that *the new covenant is fully internalized.* Jeremiah 31:33 speaks plainly in this regard: "I will put my law in their minds and write it on their hearts." This feature of the new covenant demonstrates that God himself will bring about deep internal transformation in his covenant people. The words "mind" and "heart" often denote the inner person, the deeper recesses of personality, or, in contemporary parlance, "the soul." Jeremiah did not see entrance into the new covenant community as entrance into an external environment, but as undergoing a spiritual, inward change.

Jeremiah predicted that this inward change would take place as God intervened in history to inscribe his law deep within the participants of the new covenant. It is apparent that the law of God often regulated the lives of the people of Israel as little more than an external code. Obedience often came reluctantly and resulted from external pressures. But Jeremiah promised that the new covenant would bring this situation to an end. In this regard, Paul echoed Jeremiah's words when he contrasted the old covenant "ministry . . . which was engraved in letters on stone" (2 Cor. 3:7) with the "new covenant . . . ministry of the Spirit . . . that brings righteousness" (2 Cor. 3:6, 8–9).

Jeremiah's emphasis on the inward character of the new covenant also raises significant questions about the practice of infant baptism. It is common for evangelical paedobaptists to speak of baptized children as participating only in the external aspects of the covenant, without inward transformation. Although they may not be regenerated, covenant children are thought to be blessed by the fact that they are part of the visible church or covenant community. In fact, paedobaptists often draw parallels between the condition of baptized children in the visible church today and the condition of children in the nation of Israel during the Old Testament period.

It is not difficult to see why these outlooks raise objections. According to Jeremiah, the law of God is internalized in the participants of the new covenant. They are transformed from within. How then may we baptize people into an external covenant environment apart from regeneration? Does this outlook not deny an essential feature of Jeremiah's prophecy?

A third aspect of Jeremiah 31:31–34 that often leads to objections to infant baptism is that *all participants in the new covenant are eternally redeemed.* Jeremiah was emphatic in this regard:

> No longer will a man teach his neighbor,
>   or a man his brother, saying, "Know the LORD,"
> because they will all know me,
>   from the least of them to the greatest. (v. 34)

In these words, Jeremiah characterized the time of the new covenant as a period in which it would be entirely unnecessary for anyone to encourage other covenant people to "know the Lord." They would already know him "from the least of them to the greatest." The precise connotations of the expression "know the Lord" are difficult to establish. In this context, the word "know" appears to have the connotations of "acknowledge, take recognition of, be rightly and intimately aware of." In this sense, "knowing the Lord" means "properly acknowledging and recognizing him." This is why Jeremiah 31:34 concludes, "For I will forgive their wickedness and will remember their sins no more." In a word, to know God as Jeremiah spoke of it would be to receive eternal salvation. In the covenant of which Jeremiah spoke, salvation would come to each participant. There would be no exceptions.

In light of Jeremiah's stress on the distribution of salvation in the new covenant, it is no wonder that his words are used to oppose infant baptism. Evangelical paedobaptists consistently stress that baptized children are in the new covenant, but that they are not automatically or necessarily saved. In effect, infant baptism introduces unregenerate, unbelieving people into the new covenant community. But this practice appears to contradict Jeremiah's prophecy that salvation will be fully distributed in the new covenant. How can it be right for infants to receive the covenant sign of baptism when they often do not and may never "know the Lord"?

So we have seen at least three ways in which Jeremiah's prophecy of the new covenant has been used to object to the practice of infant baptism. To be sure, other facets of the passage come into view at times, but we have touched on the main ways in which these verses are often employed for this purpose. How can we believe in infant baptism when God himself said that the new covenant would be inviolable, internalized, and include only those who know the Lord?

What Did Jeremiah Mean?

As challenging as the preceding questions may appear, these objections against infant baptism dissipate when we consider the original meaning of Jeremiah 31:31–34. From the reference in Jeremiah 32:1–2 to "the eighteenth year of Nebuchadnezzar," when his armies were "besieging Jerusalem," we can assume that the prophet's words about the new covenant were declared during the years near Jerusalem's fall to

Babylon in 586 B.C. Jeremiah spent much time warning the people of Jerusalem and Judah that massive destruction and exile were imminent, but he also encouraged them not to lose hope that God would one day end their exile and return them to their land. Jeremiah's new covenant prophecy was one of his words of encouragement to a people about to go into exile. We will approach Jeremiah's words about restoration from exile from three vantage points: (1) the structure and content of the passage itself, (2) the surrounding context, and (3) the context of Old Testament prophecy in general.

To grasp what Jeremiah had in mind as he delivered God's promises about the new covenant, we should begin with a more careful analysis of the structure and content of the passage itself. This passage may be outlined as follows:

Negative Announcement of Covenant to Come (31:31–32)
- Declaration (v. 31)
  - "declares the Lord" (v. 31a)
- Denial (v. 32)
  - "declares the Lord" (v. 32g)

Positive Clarification of Covenant to Come (vv. 33–34e)
- Declaration (v. 33a–b)
  - "declares the Lord" (v. 33b)
- Affirmation (vv. 33c–34e)
  - "declares the Lord" (v. 34e)

Explanation of Covenant to Come (v. 34f–g)

As this outline suggests, Jeremiah 31:31–34 can be divided into two main portions, followed by an explanation. The two main portions are marked by the expression "declares the Lord" at the beginning and end of each. The added explanation is marked by the introductory word "for" (*ki*). In effect, the prophet made one announcement of a coming covenant (vv. 31–32), followed it with another announcement of that covenant (vv. 33–34e), and then explained how such a covenant could come about (v. 33f–g).

The first portion of this passage (vv. 31–32) amounts to a declaration that a new covenant was coming to Israel and Judah (v. 31). It would not have been immediately apparent that this was a good thing. After all, the Mosaic covenant had brought God's people under divine judgment. So, in order to present this new covenant as a hopeful event, Jeremiah denied that it would be like the Mosaic covenant (v. 32).

The second portion (vv. 33–34e) announces the coming covenant (v. 33a–b) in language recalling the opening line of verse 31. This time, however, the hopeful character of this covenant is highlighted by positive affirmations of its wondrous nature (vv. 33c–34e).

The third portion (v. 34f–g) explains how it is possible for such a wondrous covenant to be made with Israel. All of this is possible even for those facing exile because the Lord will one day provide radical and unchanging forgiveness of his people's sins (v. 34).

This overview of the structure of the passage allows us to summarize the passage in this way. To begin with, Jeremiah said that the Lord would make a new covenant that could not be broken; it could not fail to bring wondrous blessings from God. When Jeremiah spoke these words, God had already begun to punish his people with foreign oppression and exile. Soon, Jerusalem itself would fall to the Babylonians. What was so remarkable about having another covenant in the future, when the great covenant with Moses had failed to bring eternal salvation? The remarkable thing was that this new covenant would not end in failure.

In the second place, Jeremiah reported positive elaborations on what would happen under the administration of this new covenant (vv. 33–34e). The new covenant would not fail because God would do two things to ensure success. First, he would put his law in the minds and hearts of his people (v. 33c–d). The internalization of the law was God's ideal for his people throughout Old Testament history (e.g., Deut. 6:6; 10:16; 11:18; 30:6; Pss. 37:31; 119:34; Isa. 51:7) and was often obtained (Deut. 30:11–14; 2 Kings 23:25; 2 Chron. 31:21; Pss. 40:8; 119:11). In the new covenant, however, God would touch all his hardened and wayward people to give them hearts that loved and obeyed his law. Second, God would establish the bond of loyalty and intimacy between himself and all his people (Jeremiah 31:33e–34e). Unlike times before, when dross corrupted the covenant community, this covenant bond would extend to every covenant person without exception. This distribution of salvation would also ensure that the new covenant could not fail.

All of these high hopes for the new covenant raised a serious question for Jeremiah and his audience: How could this be? How could such a marvelous, unfailing covenant come to people whose disloyalty had led to the judgment of exile? The explanation (v. 34f–g) is that God would one day forgive their wickedness and sins forever.

With the basic structure and content of the passage in mind, we should look at its immediate context. Our passage is part of a larger section consisting of Jeremiah 31:27–40. This material is separated from the surrounding context by temporal notations at the beginning (31:26) and at the end (32:1).

Jeremiah 31:27–40 is divided into three sections that are introduced by similar expressions: "'The days are coming,' declares the LORD" (v. 27). "'The time is coming,' declares the LORD" (v. 31). "'The days are coming,' declares the LORD" (v. 38). The topic of each section is easily discerned:

- Future planting of God's people in the land (vv. 27–30)
- Future new covenant with God's people (vv. 31–37)
- Future rebuilding and permanence of the holy city (vv. 38–40)

Jeremiah 31:27–30 announces that God will bring his exiled people back to their land. As surely as he watched over them to destroy them, he will watch over them to bring them home. Then Jeremiah 31:31–37 announces that when the people are back in their land, a new covenant will secure the successful reception of divine blessings. This new, unfailing covenant is as sure as the divine decrees that give order to the universe (vv. 35–37). Finally, Jeremiah 31:38–40 announces that once the people have returned and come under the new, unfailing covenant, the entire city of Jerusalem will be restored. The entire city will be made "holy to the LORD . . . never again [to] be uprooted or demolished" (v. 40).

From this overview of the immediate context, we see that Jeremiah's prophecy of the new covenant fits within a threefold scenario for the restoration of Israel after the Exile. Israel would return to the land, a new covenant would be established, and a holy Jerusalem would be permanently erected.

Recognizing this context helps readers to avoid removing Jeremiah's new covenant from the context of his other predictions of the restoration of Israel after the Exile. The new covenant did not stand alone in Jeremiah's thinking. It was not a mere development from failure to success, or from external to internal, or from corruption to purity. The new covenant was part of a scenario that included a full inheritance for God's people and the permanent establishment of the holy city of God. In a word, the fulfillment of the new covenant depended on the fulfillment of the other predictions of chapter 31.

These observations lead to another consideration: How does Jeremiah 31:31–34 fit within the broader context of Old Testament prophecy? What insights may we derive from a panoramic outlook on the prophets? Simply put, we see even more clearly that Jeremiah's concept of a new covenant was part of a set of predictions about the end of Israel's exile.

In the first place, we should note that the term "new covenant" (*berit hadashah*) connects Jeremiah's expectations to a more generic set of predictions. The terminology itself is unique to Jeremiah, but each element ("new" and "covenant") has significant parallels to other prophetic concepts. On the one hand, the term "new" appears elsewhere in the prophetic books as a way of describing the condition of things surrounding the restoration of Israel and Judah after the Exile. Ezekiel spoke of God giving his people "a new spirit" (Ezek. 11:19; 36:26) and "a new heart" (Ezek. 36:26). Isaiah spoke of God's intervention to free his people as "a new thing" (Isa. 43:19; 42:9). He looked forward, after the completion of the restoration from exile, to "new heavens and a new earth" (Isa. 65:17; 66:22). Jeremiah's concept of a "new" covenant fits within this broader portrait of Israel's restoration from exile.

On the other hand, other prophets also associated the concept of "covenant" with Israel's restoration from exile. The expression "covenant of peace" (*berit shelomi*) and similar terminology appear in Isaiah 54:10 and Ezekiel 34:25; 37:26 as descriptions of the period of restoration. These covenant expressions reflected a basic theological outlook that stemmed from the days of Moses: forgiveness, refreshment, renewal, and blessings come to the sinful nation of Israel only as they renew the covenant (e.g., Ex. 24:7–8; 34:10–28; Deut. 29; 31; Josh. 24:1–28; 2 Kings 23:2–3; 2 Chron. 34:30–32). So, it is not surprising at all that Jeremiah spoke of the divine arrangement after exile as a new *covenant*.

The prophets' emphasis on restoration after exile rested on a scenario sketched by Moses in Deuteronomy 4:25–31; 29:1–30:10. Moses wrote that if sin increased to intolerable levels in Israel, God would send his people into exile. But failure and exile would not be the end of God's plan for his people. Instead, he also promised to bring his people back from exile and then bless them more than ever before. Moses recorded God's promise in Deuteronomy 30:4–6:

> Even if you have been banished to the most distant land under the heavens, from there the LORD your God will gather you and bring you back. He will bring you to the land that belonged to your fathers, and you will take possession of it. He will make you more prosperous and numerous than your fathers. The LORD your God will circumcise your hearts and the hearts of your descendants, so that you may love him with all your heart and with all your soul, and live.

Time and again Old Testament prophets reiterated this ancient promise. Even as they threatened exile, they also assured God's people of a wondrous restoration. As we have seen, Jeremiah 31:31–34 fits into this set of expectations.

These broader connections between Jeremiah's new covenant and the hope of restoration from exile alert us to a crucial interpretative perspective: the new covenant is not an isolated item that may be brought into Christian understanding all by itself. Instead, the promised new covenant must be understood as part of a much larger set of hopes for the way things would be after the Exile. Our Christian understanding of the new covenant and its bearing on the question of infant baptism must parallel our understanding of all the other prophecies of restoration.

HOW IS THE NEW COVENANT FULFILLED IN THE CHRISTIAN FAITH?

With the original meaning of Jeremiah 31:31–34 and its prophetic context in mind, we are now in a position to ask how the hope of the new covenant is fulfilled in the New Testament era. Gaining perspective on the New Testament outlook will provide us with significant insight into how infant baptism fits within the new covenant.

At least three New Testament authors explicitly declare that the Christian faith is the fulfillment of Jeremiah's prophecy. Jeremiah 31:31–34 is quoted in whole or in part seven times in the writings of Luke, Paul, and the author of Hebrews. Jesus calls the cup of the Last Supper "the new covenant in my blood" (Luke 22:20), and Paul refers to Christ's words (1 Cor. 11:25). Paul also speaks of himself and his company as "ministers of a new covenant" (2 Cor. 3:6) because they proclaim the gospel of Christ in the power of the Spirit. In several ways, the writer of Hebrews points to the superiority of the Christian faith over Old Testament practices by identifying the Christian faith with Jeremiah's new covenant (Heb. 8:8, 13; 9:15; 12:24). In various ways, these New Testament passages indicate that the new covenant became a reality through the earthly ministry of Christ.

If we were to stop our investigation of the New Testament at this point, we might seem justified in using Jeremiah 31:31–34 to oppose infant baptism. The logic is straightforward. New Testament writers say that the new covenant has come in Christ's first coming; we should not attempt to introduce infants into this covenant through baptism because that would violate Jeremiah's description of the new covenant.

However, these references to Jeremiah 31 do not exhaust the New Testament outlook on what God promised in this portion of Jeremiah. To develop a fuller understanding of the New Testament perspective, we must remember that Jeremiah's new covenant prophecy is inextricably enmeshed with many other promises of Israel's return from exile. It forms one fabric with the many Old Testament expectations of a grand, eternal future for the people of God after the Exile.

It is well known that the New Testament teaches that Old Testament prophecies of the restoration from exile are fulfilled by Christ. But these fulfillments take place in a manner that was unanticipated by the prophets. Instead of happening completely and all at once, the expectations of restoration have been fulfilled and are being fulfilled over a long stretch of time. Jesus explained this process of fulfillment for the kingdom of God in the parable of the mustard seed (Matt. 13:31–32). He explained that the grand kingdom would begin very small, grow slowly, and finally reach full maturity. In the New Testament perspective on the restoration prophecies, accordingly, there are three stages: the *inauguration* of fulfillment in the first coming of Christ, the *continuation* of fulfillment between the first and second comings of Christ, and the *consummation* of fulfillment at the return of Christ (see fig. 2). The New Testament repeatedly explains that Old Testament predictions of the glorious state of blessing after the Exile began to be fulfilled at Christ's first coming, continue to be fulfilled in part today, and will be fully realized when Christ returns.

Because the New Testament does not explicitly apply this threefold fulfillment pattern to Jeremiah's prophecy of the new covenant, the fulfillment of that particular prophecy is often misunderstood. Often interpreters approach this text as if the new covenant was realized in its fullness when Christ first came to earth, but this is a serious error. Christ has not yet completed the restoration, and thus we have not yet obtained the promised blessings in full. The new covenant was inaugurated in Christ's first coming; it progresses in part during the continuation of Christ's kingdom; but it will reach complete fulfillment only when Christ returns in the consummation of all things. We must approach Jeremiah 31:31–34 just as we approach all prophecies regarding the restoration after exile: with the understanding that the restoration of the kingdom and the renewal of the covenant will not be complete until Jesus returns.

FIGURE 2

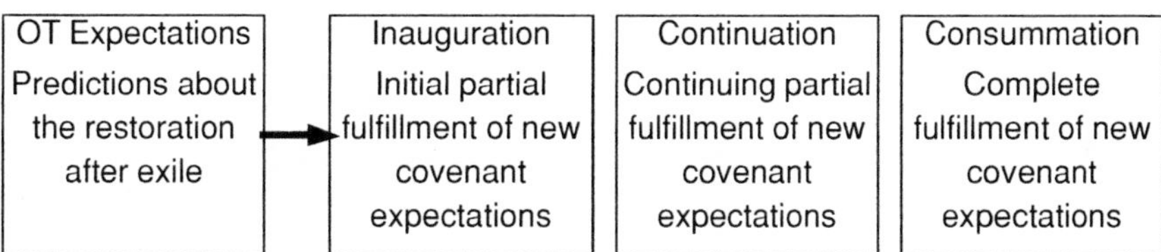

When we apply the basic pattern of New Testament fulfillment to Jeremiah's prophecy of the new covenant, it becomes clear that his expectations provide no basis at all for opposing infant baptism. To illustrate that this is the case, let us return to the three objections that are often raised by Jeremiah 31:31–34.

In the first place, Jeremiah announced that *the new covenant could not be broken.* In the consummation of Christ's kingdom, this prediction will be completely fulfilled. Once Christ returns, it will not be possible to break the new covenant and thereby to enter into another exile. Before that time, however, participants in the new covenant can break the new covenant. In addition to the numerous warnings against apostasy in the New Testament, Hebrews 10:28–31 deserves special attention:

> Anyone who rejected the law of Moses died without mercy on the testimony of two or three witnesses. How much more severely do you think a man deserves to be punished who has trampled the Son of God under foot, who has treated as an unholy thing the blood of the covenant that sanctified him, and who has insulted the Spirit of grace? For we know

> him who said, "It is mine to avenge; I will repay," and again, "The Lord will judge his people." It is a dreadful thing to fall into the hands of the living God.

This passage makes it plain that until Christ returns, it is possible for the new covenant to be broken. The writer of Hebrews acknowledges that covenant breakers under Moses were executed for capital offenses (Heb. 10:28) and then argues, from the lesser to the greater ("how much more" in v. 29), that even more severe punishment is deserved by people who have "trampled the Son of God under foot . . . treated as an unholy thing the blood of the covenant that sanctified [them] . . . and . . . insulted the Spirit of grace" (v. 29). The three objects in focus—the Son of God, the blood of the covenant, and the Spirit of grace—are features of the new covenant. Flagrant violation of these new covenant realities is quite possible and leads to severe punishment.

In fact, the writer of Hebrews applies the warning that "the Lord will judge his people" from Deuteronomy 32:36—a warning to the covenant people under the Mosaic covenant—to this new covenant situation, thus equating the circumstance of the new covenant prior to the return of Christ to the situation that Israel faced under the old covenant. Judgment was and is possible for both the old and the new covenant communities, and judgment flows from covenant breaking, not from covenant keeping. If judgment is a possibility under the new covenant, then so is the covenant breaking that leads to that judgment.

As the New Testament indicates, until Christ returns, it should never be thought that the new covenant cannot be broken. On the contrary, the New Testament expects some participants in the new covenant to break that covenant. Therefore, the rejection of infant baptism on the grounds that infants may prove to be covenant breakers is not well founded.

In the second place, we have seen that *the new covenant is internalized.* This feature of Jeremiah's prophecy may appear to stand against the idea of bringing infants into the outward blessings of the new covenant through baptism. This objection to infant baptism also falls when we think more carefully about how the expectation of internalization is fulfilled.

We can have confidence that after Christ returns in glory, everyone in the new creation will have the law of God written on his or her heart. We will all love and delight in his ways, just as Christ already does (2 Cor. 3:16–18; 1 Thess. 3:11–13). In this sense, we expect Jeremiah's prophecy to find complete fulfillment when Christ returns.

At the present time, however, this expectation is only partially fulfilled. To be sure, the hearts and minds of believers have been renewed by God's grace (Rom. 12:1–2). At the same time, however, we are commanded to be guided by the Scriptures and to watch for corruption in our thinking (e.g., Rom. 1:18–2:29; Eph. 4:17–32; 2 Peter 3:17). The New Testament speaks this way because, while the internalization of the law of God has begun within believers, it has not yet been completed.

For this reason, it should not surprise us to find that even in the New Testament some people are blessed simply to be involved in the more external aspects of the new covenant community. A striking example of this appears in 1 Corinthians 7:14:

> For the unbelieving husband has been sanctified through his wife, and the unbelieving wife has been sanctified through her believing husband. Otherwise your children would be unclean, but as it is, they are holy.

When discussing the responsibilities of believers who are married to unbelievers, Paul makes a remarkable observation. He argues that the unbelievers (*apistos*) are set apart from the world or sanctified (*hagiazō*) by their association with their believing spouses. This language recalls the statement in Hebrews 10:29 that one who turns from Christ "treat[s] as an unholy thing the blood of the covenant that sanctified him." Sanctification in this sense parallels the Old Testament concept of consecration (*qadosh,* "holy"), which is applied both to people and to things as they are set apart from ordinary life for special contact with the presence of God. These people are not necessarily "saved" or "regenerated" (to use common theological categories). The new covenant has not been internalized for them, but they are sanctified by external associations nonetheless. From Paul's use of this language for unbelieving spouses in 1 Corinthians 7:14, we see that prior to the return of Christ, it is appropriate to speak of association with the external aspects of the new covenant. Such association sanctifies even those who have not been transformed by God's grace in their minds and hearts.

Interestingly enough, in 1 Corinthians 7:14 this concept of sanctification is applied, not only to unbelieving spouses, but also to the children of such marriages. As Paul puts it, "Otherwise your children would be unclean, but as it is, they are holy." Again, applying the old covenant designation of "unclean" to indicate unacceptability within the vicinity of the holy presence of God (e.g., Lev. 10:9–10; Num. 5:2–3), Paul asserts that the sanctification of the unbelieving spouse renders even their children holy or consecrated.

Until Christ returns in glory, it is not only permissible and helpful, but also necessary, to speak of certain people as consecrated or sanctified to God by their close associations with the people of God and with the activities of true believers. For this reason, it is quite appropriate to speak of the children of believers as sanctified or consecrated by their involvement in the more external aspects of life in the new covenant, even though they may not be regenerated. So the internalization promised in the new covenant by no means proscribes the baptism of infants.

In the third place, we saw that many evangelicals object to infant baptism because *the new covenant distributes salvation to all of its participants.* As with the previous objections, this point of view is correct insofar as it relates to the complete fulfillment of the new covenant in the consummation. When Christ returns, he will separate the just from the unjust, the sheep from the goats, true believers from unbelievers in the church. The promise that the new covenant will grant salvation to all who participate will be fulfilled by the removal of the unbelievers at the time of judgment. Only true believers will be left, and thus all who remain in the new covenant will be saved.

But prior to the judgment that Christ will render at his return, the new covenant community is not restricted to believers only. If it were, there would be no separation of people at Christ's return. We have already mentioned Hebrews 10:28–31, which speaks of judgment coming against some who have been sanctified by the blood of the covenant. We should add to this passage others that warn the members of church communities (often called "brothers") to be sure to pass the test of perseverance (e.g., 1 Cor. 9:27; 2 Cor. 13:5; 2 Peter 1:10; Rev. 2:7, 11, 17, 26; 3:5, 12, 21; 21:7). The familiar explanation of apostasy found in 1 John 2:19 summarizes the situation well:

> They went out from us, but they did not really belong to us. For if they had belonged to us, they would have remained with us; but their going showed that none of them belonged to us.

As the parable of the ten virgins and the parable of the talents illustrate (Matt. 25:1–30), there are many in the new covenant community who will prove themselves not to be truly regenerate. Consequently, there is no need to withhold baptism from infants on the basis of Jeremiah's new covenant expectations. Until the consummation, the new covenant will continue to be a mixture of true believers and sanctified unbelievers.

As we have seen in this study, Jeremiah's prophecy of the new covenant in Jeremiah 31:31–34 has been the basis of a number of objections to the practice of infant baptism. We have looked at this prophecy in connection with the many other Old Testament expectations of return from exile. Moreover, we have noted how the New Testament understands the fulfillment of these restoration prophecies in three stages. All followers of Christ look forward to the day when this age of sin and death will be entirely replaced by the new world of blessing. At that time, there will be no bearing of children and the question of infant baptism will be moot. Yet, until that day comes, the new covenant will continue to include people who become covenant breakers, who benefit only from the external aspects of the new covenant, and who have never been regenerated. Until that time, we continue to have children in order to multiply and fill the earth. We baptize our children, just as believers circumcised their sons in the Old Testament. We baptize them as the expected heirs of the new covenant, those blessed with a heritage of faith and with special privileges and responsibilities before God.

9

Covenant Transition

Randy Booth

Central to the debate over the proper recipients of baptism is the relationship between the Old and New Testaments, or the old and new covenants. Those who see the new covenant as a *replacement* for the old covenant demand explicit New Testament warrant to *include* the children of believers in the covenant and administer the initial covenant sign to them. Those who comprehend the new covenant as the *extension* of the old covenant, where the children of believers were always included in the covenant, require explicit New Testament warrant to *exclude* their children from the covenant and deny them the initial sign of the covenant. Thus, the degree to which we see either covenant *continuity* or covenant *discontinuity* affects the questions we ask, the standards that must be met, and the answers we will obtain. The first question that must be answered, therefore, has to do with the nature of the transition from the old to the new covenant: Is there a sharp discontinuity, with fundamental and essential changes that usher in a brand new program, or is there a smooth and organic continuity that leads to a renewed and expanded version of essentially the same covenant?

Four areas of inquiry will help us to discern the nature of the transition between the old and new covenants and the unity of God's redemptive plan throughout history: (1) How does the New Testament view the Old Testament? (2) What role does the covenant household play in the redemptive work of the old and new covenants? (3) Are there connecting links between the two covenants? (4) Is Christ the Mediator of both the old and the new covenant? If the unity of the two covenants is established, then answering the questions about covenant membership and the proper recipients of their signs becomes a much simpler task.

How Does the New Testament View the Old?

The New Testament opens with John the Baptist announcing, not a brand new program for God's people, but rather a call to repentance and a return to the original intent of the covenant revealed to Abraham. The Pharisees and Sadducees were falsely relying on their physical descent from Abraham (Matt. 3:9), but John warned them that such reliance was a false hope—it had always been a false hope. God had always required faith and obedience like that of Abraham. Anything less was a violation of his covenant and would receive God's judgment (Matt. 3:10), rather than his blessing. The message of the new covenant was first proclaimed to "the lost sheep of the house of Israel" (Matt. 10:6), "to the Jew first and also to the Greek" (Rom. 2:10). The long-promised Messiah had finally arrived.

The demand for a converted heart was certainly not a new element in the new covenant, but had always been the standard of covenant faithfulness. Before the new covenant's call for repentance, God warned Israel repeatedly that circumcision had to be far more than simply an outward or physical rite; rather, it had to be an outward sign of an inward truth. For example, he warned through the prophet Jeremiah, "Circumcise yourselves to the LORD, and take away the foreskins of your hearts, you men of Judah and inhabitants of Jerusalem, lest My fury come forth like fire, and burn so that no one can quench it, because of the evil of your doings" (Jer. 4:4). And again, "'Behold, the days are coming,' says the LORD, 'that I will punish all those who are circumcised with the uncircumcised—Egypt, Judah, Edom, the people of Ammon, Moab, and all who are in the farthest corners, who dwell in the wilderness. For all these nations are uncircumcised, and all the house of Israel are uncircumcised in the heart'" (Jer. 9:25–26). Formalism (i.e., form without substance) has always been an abomination to the Lord; it always invites his judgment.

God's redemptive plan was initially revealed after mankind's fall into sin (Gen. 3:15), and it was further unfolded through the various administrations of his covenant. Each new administration of his redemptive plan displayed additional dimensions of his glorious work of salvation, all of which had Christ in view *from the beginning*. This covenant work of God culminated magnificently in the new covenant of Jesus Christ. The covenant people of God swerved and stumbled along the way, with periods of faithfulness and unfaithfulness, but *our covenant-keeping God never altered his plan or failed to keep his promises.* Indeed, Abraham's children's children continued to be the recipients of all God's covenant promises. It is no wonder, then, that Abraham saw Christ's day and rejoiced (John 8:56).

Being a physical descendant of Abraham—i.e., one of Abraham's children or his children's children—did make one a part of the covenant people of God, for God had promised Abraham, "And I will establish My covenant between Me and you and your descendants after you in their generations, for an everlasting covenant, to be God to you and your descendants after you" (Gen. 17:7). This promise is made to every covenant household, but it was first made to Abraham and by extension to the nation of Israel.[1] When someone outside of Abraham's extended household (i.e., outside Israel) embraced Abraham's God, they too entered the same covenant with the same promises and obligations.

The covenant relationship transcended the physical relationship.[2] Moreover, entering the covenant by birth or by conversion was never

1. One of the common names in Scripture for God's covenant people is "the *children* of Israel."

2. Otherwise, Ruth the Moabitess (or any other woman) would not have been considered part of Israel. This illustrates the problem of reducing the sign of circumcision to a national badge.

the end of the story. Covenant faithfulness was always a condition for receiving covenant blessings, rather than covenant curses. "And God said to Abraham: 'As for you, you shall keep My covenant, you and your descendants after you throughout their generations'" (Gen. 17:9). Faith and obedience have always been the conditions for covenant blessings. The Bible does not divide the people of God into the "physical seed" and the "spiritual seed" of Abraham, as though God has two separate and distinct people. In both the Old and the New Testaments, the physical people are considered the true seed of Abraham only by faith alone. Nowhere in Scripture do we see God approving of or accepting any, except those who are faithful to the covenant (i.e., true believers). Paul explains in Romans 9:6–8 that faith in the promises of God, not physical birth, was and is the essence of the people of God:

> But it is not that the word of God has taken no effect. For they are not all Israel who are of Israel, nor are they all children because they are the seed of Abraham; but, "In Isaac your seed shall be called." That is, those who are the children of the flesh, these are not the children of God; but the children of the promise are counted as the seed.

According to the New Testament, the new covenant is the fulfillment of what was revealed in the old covenant—an extension of what went before. The New Testament persistently reveals its connection with the Old Testament. It tells us that "the blessing of Abraham" came "upon the Gentiles in Christ Jesus" (Gal. 3:14). A large part of the blessing of Abraham included Abraham's household—his children and his children's children—and that blessing is now ours in Christ. The Abrahamic covenant, along with all its promises, had Christ and the new covenant in view. The New Testament reveals: "Now to Abraham and his Seed were the promises made. He does not say, 'And to seeds,' as of many, but as of one, 'And to your Seed,' who is Christ" (Gal. 3:16). Galatians 3:29 even refers to those of us who belong to Christ as "Abraham's offspring, heirs according to promise" (NASB). When Mary receives the news of the child she is carrying, she rejoices and declares: "He has helped His servant Israel, in remembrance of His mercy, as He spoke to our fathers, to Abraham and to his seed forever" (Luke 1:54–55). And likewise Zacharias, the father of John the Baptist, rejoiced, saying:

> Blessed is the Lord God of Israel, for He has visited and redeemed His people, and has raised up a horn of salvation for us in the house of His servant David, as He spoke by the mouth of His holy prophets, who have been since the world began, that we should be saved from our enemies and from the hand of all who hate us, to perform the mercy promised to our fathers and to remember His holy covenant, the oath which He swore to our father Abraham: to grant us that we, being delivered from the hand of our enemies, might serve Him without fear, in holiness and righteousness before Him all the days of our life. (Luke 1:68–75)

Those who insist that the new covenant is a brand-new covenant (which replaces the old covenant), as opposed to a renewed covenant (which expands the former covenant), end up requiring more than the New Testament will allow. According to their view, only those things that are stated or repeated in the New Testament have any validity or authority for the new covenant believer.[3] The Old Testament, being "old," has been set aside and invalidated, having being abrogated by the New Testament. But the writers of the New Testament do not adopt this dispensational approach to biblical interpretation.[4] Many places in the New Testament recognize the complete unity and continuity between the old and new covenants. Here are a few examples:

3. Compare 1 John 2:7–8 with Lev. 19:18 to see an example of how a commandment can be both new and not new. The newness is found in Jesus (John 13:34).

4. Several people have objected to my alleged characterization of Baptists as "dispensationalists." I have always recognized that many Baptists are not self-consciously dispensational and do not willingly wear that theological label. Nevertheless, to the degree that one separates Israel from the church or distinguishes sharply between the old and new covenants, one is dispensational. Latent dispensationalism is still dispensationalism.

> Yes, and all the prophets, from Samuel and those who follow, as many as have spoken, have also foretold these days. (Acts 3:24)

> Of this salvation the prophets have inquired and searched diligently, who prophesied of the grace that would come to you, searching what, or what manner of time, the Spirit of Christ who was in them was indicating when He testified beforehand the sufferings of Christ and the glories that would follow. To them it was revealed that, not to themselves, but to us they were ministering the things which now have been reported to you through those who have preached the gospel to you by the Holy Spirit sent from heaven—things which angels desire to look into. (1 Peter 1:10–12)

> Now I say that Jesus Christ has become a servant to the circumcision for the truth of God, to confirm the promises made to the fathers. (Rom. 15:8)

> Therefore remember that you, once Gentiles in the flesh—who are called Uncircumcision by what is called the Circumcision made in the flesh by hands—that at that time you were without Christ, being aliens from the commonwealth of Israel and strangers from the covenants of promise, having no hope and without God in the world. But now in Christ Jesus you who once were far off have been made near by the blood of Christ. (Eph. 2:11–13)

> For if you were cut out of the olive tree which is wild by nature, and were grafted contrary to nature into a good olive tree, how much more will these, who are the natural branches, be grafted into their own olive tree? (Rom. 11:24)

The New Testament offers a greater revelation of God and his redemptive work, but it does not abruptly do away with the Old Testament and start all over. We even find explicit admonition in the New Testament for believers to rely on the authority of the Old Testament.

When Jesus said, "Man shall not live by bread alone, but by every word that proceeds from the mouth of God" (Matt. 4:4), he was quoting from and referring to the Old Testament. Jesus was unequivocal about the fact that his ministry did not abolish the Old Testament. He asserted in Matthew 5:17–19:

> Do not think that I came to abolish the Law or the Prophets; I did not come to abolish, but to fulfill. For truly I say to you, until heaven and earth pass away, not the smallest letter or stroke shall pass away from the Law, until all is accomplished. Whoever then annuls one of the least of these commandments, and so teaches others, shall be called least in the kingdom of heaven; but whoever keeps and teaches them, he shall be called great in the kingdom of heaven. (NASB)

The Bereans were commended for "examining the Scriptures [Old Testament] daily, to see whether these things were so" (Acts 17:11 NASB). Even the apostle Paul's teaching had to withstand the scrutiny of the Old Testament. He refers to the Old Testament when he says in Romans 15:4, "For whatever was written in earlier times [in the Old Testament] was written for our instruction" (NASB). In 1 Corinthians 10:11, we are told, "Now these things happened to them as an example, and they were written [in the Old Testament] for our instruction, upon whom the ends of the ages have come" (NASB). And again we read approvingly of the new covenant use of the Old Testament Scriptures in 2 Timothy 3:15–17:

> From childhood you have known the sacred writings [Old Testament] which are able to give you the wisdom that leads to salvation through faith which is in Christ Jesus. All Scripture [Old Testament] is inspired by God and profitable for teaching, for reproof, for correction, for training in righteousness; that the man of God may be adequate, equipped for every good work. (NASB)

Besides these passages, Christ and the writers of the New Testament repeatedly quote from and apply the Old Testament Scriptures to New Testament believers.[5] The New Testament does not set aside the Old Testament. It relies on and emphasizes the continued validity of the Old Testament for God's people under the new covenant. It is important to reiterate that those who claim that the new covenant is brand-new (i.e., that it replaces the old covenant) may not legitimately make authoritative use of the Old Testament, since it has been made invalid by the new covenant. *Yet the New Testament clearly, repeatedly, and emphatically makes authoritative use of the Old Testament, applying it to the members of the new covenant.*[6]

God alone may exercise the prerogative to amend his Word. In other words, Christians may not arbitrarily declare any portion of God's Word void, including any portion of the Old Testament. Any claim of change between the old covenant and the new covenant must be validated by further revelation of God as found in the Scriptures themselves. We have one Bible, not two. Both the Old and the New Testaments are to direct the belief and practice of the new covenant believer. We might as well sever a tree from its roots and expect it to survive, as to sever the old covenant from the new. The Old and New Testaments are tied together and are interdependent. The Old Testament needs the New Testament, and the New Testament needs the Old Testament, to be properly interpreted and understood.

The doctrines of the New Testament and the roots of the new covenant are revealed in the Old Testament, or old covenant. When we read in Galatians 3:29 that we are "Abraham's offspring" and "heirs according to promise" (NASB), we are immediately driven to Genesis to gain understanding. When we read in Philippians 3:3 that "we are the true circumcision" (NASB), we must go to the Old Testament to discover what circumcision was and what function it performed. When

5. E.g., 2 Cor. 6:16–18; Rom. 8:36; 9:25–26; 10:6–8, 11, 13, 15; Gal. 4:27; Heb. 8:8–12; 10:30; 13:5; 1 Peter 2:10.

6. I realize that many who assert that the new covenant is brand-new do still use the Old Testament as a source of authority. But their use of the Old Testament, as anything other than a historical record, is inconsistent with their professed view of the nature of the new covenant.

we read in Romans 15:8 that Christ came "to confirm the promises given to the fathers" (NASB), or in Ephesians 2:12 that the Gentiles were "excluded from the commonwealth of Israel, and strangers to the covenants of promise" (NASB), it is only in the Old Testament that we discover the foundation for these teachings.

How did the Jews understand the baptism of John in John 3:25?[7] What were the various baptisms of Hebrews 9:10? Why was circumcision of the heart in Colossians 2:11–12 represented by baptism? What represented circumcision of the heart in the Old Testament? It would be useless to try to answer these basic questions without turning to the Old Testament—the old covenant. The New Testament similarly drives us immediately to the Old when we try to understand the doctrines of creation, sin, redemption, the sacrifice of Christ, the Atonement, the priesthood, the eldership, church discipline, the Lord's Supper, marriage, divorce, households, covenants, judgment, heaven, and much more.

Given the unchangeable character of God, there can be no question about the principle of unity and continuity in his revelation (the Bible). *Unity and continuity should be presumed over discontinuity.* Who but God alone has the prerogative to change what God has said? When it comes to Scripture, only God is permitted to say what is in fact new about the new covenant. This basic unity of God and his revelation is seen in the fact that God has, from the beginning, dealt with humanity in terms of redemptive covenants. God has had one plan from the start to redeem sinners. He has pursued and brought that plan to pass in a smooth and unbroken fashion. God has continuously unfolded, through more and more revelation, his redemptive plan for man and the world. Only God may determine who is and who is not to be included in, or excluded from, his covenant people. In the old covenant, the children of believers were included among his covenant people and received his covenant sign. In the new covenant—an expansion

7. Consider John the Baptist's declaration with regard to Jesus, "Behold, the Lamb of God who takes away the sin of the world!" (John 1:29 NASB). Such a statement makes no sense apart from the Old Testament.

of the old covenant—God nowhere reveals a new restriction on covenant membership or covenant blessings. God still loves believers, their children, and their children's children for a thousand generations of those who love him and keep his commandments.

COVENANT HOUSEHOLDS IN THE OLD AND NEW COVENANTS

In our modern era, overly individualistic concepts of God's redemptive work have blinded many Christians to the centrality of the corporate nature of God's dealings with men. Federalism, or covenant headship, has been the biblical standard from Adam to the new covenant. That is, some men have represented other men before God. There is no place where this is more apparent and central than in the covenant household—the family. It was not only Adam, but Adam's children and his children's children, who suffered the consequences of his sin. As the Westminster Shorter Catechism puts it in question 16: "The covenant being made with Adam, not only for himself, but for his posterity; all mankind, descending from him by ordinary generation, sinned in him, and fell with him, in his first transgression." Families fell in Adam, and it is families that God will redeem from the Fall.

Redemptively, the household is not marginal or incidental in Scripture. It plays a central role in both the old and new covenants. Old Testament society was ordered by God and was dominated by the household and tribal structure (the tribe was the extended family).[8] In fact, we do not find God making covenants with people without including their households. For example, "I will pour water on him who is thirsty, and floods on the dry ground; I will pour My Spirit on your descendants, and My blessing on your offspring" (Isa. 44:3).[9] We find,

8. It is important that we read and understand Scripture in its historical context. Familial and tribal concepts of society were dominant until recently. They are also the biblical point of view. A focus on the individual has been emphasized in American culture and is a key assumption in Baptist theology.

9. See also Isa. 59:21; 66:22.

after Adam, an ocean of evidence in Scripture of this essential aspect of redemption. For example, Noah, who "found grace in the eyes of the Lord," went into the ark with "all [his] household" (Gen. 6:8; 7:1).[10] The Lord "plagued Pharaoh and his house" (Gen. 12:17). "All" who were "born in [Abraham's] house" or who were "bought with his money" were to be circumcised (Gen. 17:12–13, 23, 27). The Lord "closed fast all the wombs of the household of Abimelech" because of his sin (Gen. 20:17–18 NASB). As a result of the sin of Simeon and Levi, Jacob said, "I shall be destroyed, I and my household" (Gen. 34:30 NASB). Entire households were spared death where the blood of the Passover lamb was applied to their doorposts (Ex. 12:27). The Levites were numbered according to their household membership (Num. 3:15). Joshua spoke for his entire household when he declared, "As for me and my house, we will serve the Lord" (Josh. 24:15). God judged the house of Eli because of the sins of his sons (1 Sam. 3:12–14). David brought God's judgment upon his household because of his sinful conduct with Bathsheba (2 Sam. 12:10).

The household of our father Abraham ("the father of all those who believe," Rom. 4:11) was the pattern for this covenant household. God had promised Abraham "to be God to you and your descendants after you" (Gen. 17:7). God would make him "a great and mighty nation," and "all the nations of the earth shall be blessed in him" (18:18). But the condition of familial faithfulness was central. Abraham had to personally keep covenant with God, and his descendants would also have to keep covenant with God. Abraham would have to command his children and household to keep the way of the Lord:[11] "For I have known him, in order that he may command his children and his household after him, that they keep the way of the Lord, to do righteous-

10. Notice that Gen. 7:1 says, "For *you alone* I have seen to be righteous before Me in this time" (NASB). This righteousness characterizes Noah, not necessarily his family. Nevertheless, Noah's family receives the benefit of God's covenant grace because they are his family.

11. Although these were the conditions of the covenant, God's covenant blessings were still given as an act of his free grace. Meeting the covenant conditions was not meritorious; it did not earn God's blessings. Nevertheless, the conditions of covenant faithfulness (in both the Old and the New Testaments) had to be met in order to receive the gracious gift (i.e., undeserved favor) of God.

ness and justice, that the LORD may bring to Abraham what He has spoken to him" (18:19).

The Old Testament emphasis on the covenant household continues in the New Testament. An elder "must be one who manages [governs] his own household well, keeping his children under control with all dignity" (1 Tim. 3:4 NASB). Likewise, deacons must be "good managers [governors] of their children and their own households" (1 Tim. 3:12 NASB). In Philippians 4:22, we are told of the saints who were "of Caesar's household." These saints were probably Caesar's slaves, yet they were considered a part of his household. When Matthew describes Jesus feeding the multitude with the loaves and fishes, he numbers the crowd by households: "Now those who ate were four thousand men, besides women and children" (Matt. 15:38). This was not a put-down of women and children. It was normal to think in terms of covenantal family units. Of the nine people who are mentioned by name in the New Testament as being baptized, two were unmarried, two are of unknown marital status, and five were heads of households. In every single case where a known head of a household believed and was baptized, we are told that the entire household was also baptized. Finally, on the day when the new covenant was inaugurated, as Peter spoke to the "men of Israel" (Acts 2:22) and they asked what they should do, he spoke to them using the familiar formula of the Abrahamic covenant: "For the promise is to you and to your children, and to all who are afar off, as many as the Lord our God will call" (v. 39).[12]

THE CONNECTING LINKS BETWEEN THE TWO COVENANTS

The unity of God, of his Word, of his covenants, and of his people is revealed from Genesis to Revelation. The New Testament opens without missing a beat from the Old Testament: "The book of the ge-

12. God made his covenant promise in Gen. 17 and 18 to Abraham, to his children, and to the nations. Thus, when Peter spoke to the men of Israel, saying that "the promise is to you and to your children, and to all who are afar off" (Acts 2:39), this was not a brand-new concept, but rather a familiar formula.

nealogy of Jesus Christ, the Son of David, the Son of Abraham" (Matt. 1:1). The new covenant is what the Old Testament was all about. Speaking of the Old Testament, Jesus declared, "You search the Scriptures, for in them you think you have eternal life; and these are they which testify of Me" (John 5:39). It was the Old Testament that was used when Paul "as his custom was, went in to them, and for three Sabbaths reasoned with them from the Scriptures, explaining and demonstrating that the Christ had to suffer and rise again from the dead, and saying, 'This Jesus whom I preach to you is the Christ'" (Acts 17:2–3).[13]

One of the primary places where the unity of, and continuity between, the old and new covenants is seen is in the prophecies about the new covenant that are recorded in the Old Testament and in the New Testament's owning of those prophecies. The Old Testament prophets, along with Moses and Abraham, were well aware of the fact that Christ and the new covenant were the ultimate objects of their labors:[14]

> Yes, and all the prophets, from Samuel and those who follow, as many as have spoken, have also foretold these days. You are sons of the prophets, and of the covenant which God made with our fathers, saying to Abraham, "And in your seed all the families of the earth shall be blessed." To you first, God, having raised up His Servant Jesus, sent Him to bless you, in turning away every one of you from your iniquities. (Acts 3:24–26)

Old Testament prophets expected the coming new covenant. They spoke of this glorious day in the context of covenantal history. They did not view the new covenant as something divorced from God's past redemptive dealings with his people. In fact, it was "the Spirit of Christ within them" (1 Peter 1:11 NASB) who was predicting what was to

13. Examples of this unity can be multiplied. E.g., Luke 16:27–31; 24:25–27; Eph. 2:11–13; 2 Tim. 3:14–16.

14. Cf. John 8:56; 1 Cor. 10:1–4; Acts 3:17, 24; 1 Peter 1:10–12.

come. This covenant unity and continuity was to be expected because God's covenant promises were everlasting:[15] "My covenant I will not violate, nor will I alter the utterance of My lips" (Ps. 89:34 NASB).[16]

The old covenant laid the foundation for the new covenant. In Jeremiah's prophecy, we see the relationship of the new covenant with earlier covenants: "'Behold, days are coming,' declares the LORD, 'when I will make a new covenant with the house of Israel and with the house of Judah'" (Jer. 31:31 NASB). Notice that it is "with the house of Israel" and "with the house of Judah" that the new covenant is made.[17] Ezekiel likewise connects the Abrahamic, Mosaic, and Davidic covenants with the new covenant when he says:

> And My servant David will be king over them [Davidic], and they will all have one shepherd; and they will walk in My ordinances, and keep My statutes, and observe them [Mosaic]. And they shall live on the land that I gave to Jacob My servant, in which your fathers lived [Abrahamic]; and they will live on it, they, and their sons, and their son's sons, forever; and David My servant shall be their prince forever [Davidic]. And I will make a covenant of peace with them; it will be an everlasting covenant with them [new]. And I will place them and multiply them, and will set My sanctuary in their midst forever. (Ezek. 37:24–26 NASB)

Similarly, in the New Testament we find new covenant unity and continuity with preceding covenants. Romans 16:20 looks back to the Adamic covenant. Peter draws a parallel with the Noahic covenant in 1 Peter 3:5–7. The new covenant is founded on the Abrahamic in Romans 4:16. The validity of the Mosaic is revealed in Romans 3:31. Romans 15:12 sees the new covenant as based on the Davidic covenant.

15. Gen. 17:7 speaks of "an everlasting covenant"; Heb. 13:20 refers to "the everlasting covenant." (Some of the particular promises of certain covenants find greater fulfillment in the new covenant. For example, possession of the land of Canaan becomes possession of the whole earth.)

16. See also 1 Chron. 16:15–17.

17. The relationship between Jer. 31 and Heb. 8 is dealt with in more detail elsewhere in this book.

Basic unity and progressive development are demonstrated in all the divine covenants.

The Old Testament looked forward to the new covenant as the climax and culmination of God's covenant purpose. God's people could always depend on his promises to them, to their children, and to their children's children—to all who were covenant keepers. The Old Testament was not a failed experiment that had to be replaced by a new plan; rather, the old and new covenants are a unified part of God's one, perfect plan of redemption.

The promised Seed of Abraham was the fulfillment of the prophecy of Isaiah, who, in covenantal language, said, "'The virgin shall be with child, and shall bear a Son, and they shall call His name Immanuel,' which translated means, 'God with us'" (Matt. 1:23 NASB). Christ would "shepherd" God's "people Israel" (Matt. 2:6). As Mary rejoiced over her coming child, she recalled God's promise to all faithful generations (Luke 1:50) and the fulfillment of the promises to Abraham and the fathers (Luke 1:54–55). Zacharias, the father of John the Baptist, declared that the Savior had come "to show mercy toward our fathers, and to remember His holy covenant, the oath which He swore to Abraham our father" (Luke 1:72–73 NASB). Instead of doing away with those previous covenants, the birth of Jesus Christ validated and confirmed them, "for I say that Christ has become a servant to the circumcision on behalf of the truth of God to confirm the promises given to the fathers" (Rom. 15:8 NASB).

The advent of Christ was not the beginning of something brand new; rather, it was the culmination and climax of God's ancient plan to save his people. The Old Testament was not passing away,[18] it was expanding. The everlasting covenants of the fathers were indeed everlasting, and the birth of the Redeemer proved that God never turns from his promises. The Great Commission (Matt. 28:16–20) is rooted

18. Hebrews 8:13 says, "In that He says, 'A new covenant,' He has made the first obsolete. Now what is becoming obsolete and growing old is ready to vanish away." In the context of the argument being made in Hebrews, this is a reference to the old covenant ceremonial law that became obsolete as a result of the finished work of Christ, the High Priest and perfect sacrifice.

in the promise made to Abraham that he and his seed would be a blessing to the nations. Acts 2 implements that promise. John 4:21–23 tells us that "salvation is from the Jews."

The prophecy of Malachi and the gospel of Luke form a hinge between the old and the new covenants. Just prior to the coming of Christ and the inauguration of the final, expansive, and glorious new covenant, God's covenant people had once again become woefully negligent of their covenant obligations and were in jeopardy of receiving God's chastisement and judgment for their rebellion against him. They had forgotten, corrupted, and neglected the worship of God. In addition, their households were in serious trouble, as men forsook their wives and abandoned their responsibilities for their children. From the beginning of God's establishment of his covenant with Abraham, blessing for the people of God was conditioned upon fidelity to God and family. "For I have known him [Abraham], in order that he may command his children and his household after him, that they keep the way of the LORD, to do righteousness and justice, that the LORD may bring to Abraham what He has spoken to him" (Gen. 18:19). "As for you, you shall keep My covenant, you and your descendants after you throughout their generations" (Gen. 17:9).

At the close of the Old Testament, the prophet Malachi comes to God's covenant people with an indictment and a warning. His people have broken their covenant with God. His message calls them back to the *original intent* of God's gracious covenant with Abraham and points to the coming Messiah as the climax of God's redemptive plan. Central to this plan, in both the Old and New Testaments, is the covenant household. One of the primary indictments of the people was that of covenant unfaithfulness in the family. Husbands were being unfaithful to their wives: "The Lord has been witness between you and the wife of your youth, with whom you have dealt treacherously; yet she is your companion and your wife by covenant" (Mal. 2:14). As a result, one of the main purposes for the covenant household was being corrupted: "But did He not make them one, having a remnant of the Spirit? And why one? He seeks godly offspring. Therefore take heed to your spirit, and let none deal treacherously with the wife of his youth" (v. 15). Other details of covenant unfaithfulness in the household are dealt with in this short book. God then warns his people:

> Behold, I send My messenger, and he will prepare the way before Me. And the Lord, whom you seek, will suddenly come to His temple, even the Messenger [Mediator] of the covenant. . . . But who can endure the day of His coming? And who can stand when He appears? For He is like a refiner's fire and like fuller's soap. (Mal. 3:1–2)

God will not tolerate covenant breaking in the covenant household. As Ecclesiastes 5:5 says, "It is better not to vow than to vow and not pay." God's covenant blessings are conditioned on covenant faithfulness. He insists upon our households producing godly offspring, or else we will not enjoy his covenant blessings. Instead, we will know covenant curses—misery, rather than joy.

As we have seen, God's covenant with Abraham (and all subsequent developments of the covenant) was conditioned upon covenant faithfulness. Abraham was instructed to "command his children and his household after him, that they keep the way of the LORD, to do righteousness and justice" (Gen. 18:19). Under Moses, God's people were required to diligently instruct their children in the commands of God:

> Hear, O Israel: The LORD our God, the LORD is one! You shall love the LORD your God with all your heart, with all your soul, and with all your might. And these words which I command you today shall be in your heart; you shall teach them diligently to your children, and shall talk of them when you sit in your house, when you walk by the way, when you lie down, and when you rise up. You shall bind them as a sign on your hand, and they shall be as frontlets between your eyes. You shall write them on the doorposts of your house and on your gates. (Deut. 6:4–9)

Throughout redemptive history, we see either God's covenant blessings or his covenant curses coming upon his people, depending on the faithfulness (faith and obedience) or unfaithfulness (unbelief and disobedience) of fathers toward their children and children toward their fathers. If there is not repentance for this covenant breaking, God promises swift and severe judgment—curses on the individuals and upon the land. The coming judgment will leave them "neither root nor branch" (Mal. 4:1). The people are warned to repent, "lest I come and smite the land with a curse" (v. 6 NASB).

Notice also that the specific requirement was: "Remember the law of Moses My servant, even the statutes and ordinances which I commanded him in Horeb for all Israel" (v. 4 NASB). As Abraham was to command his household to do what was just and righteous as a condition of covenant blessing, so also we must understand that the law is the perfect expression of that very justice and righteousness. Love for God is expressed by keeping his law, as Jesus said: "If you love Me, keep My commandments" (John 14:15).[19] It is not some vague or sentimental standard that God requires when it comes to covenant households; it is his Word, and his Word alone, that is to provide the instruction:

> But as for you, continue in the things which you have learned and been assured of, knowing from whom you have learned them, and that from childhood [infancy] you have known the Holy Scriptures, which are able to make you wise for salvation through faith which is in Christ Jesus. All Scripture is given by inspiration of God, and is profitable for doctrine, for reproof, for correction, for instruction in righteousness, that the man of God may be complete, thoroughly equipped for every good work. (2 Tim. 3:14–17)

At the opening of the New Testament, we read of the fulfilling of the promise that God made at the close of the Old Testament. This is the other half of the hinge between the old and new covenants:

19. Law keeping is not the basis for justification (that would be the sin of legalism), but it is the fruit of justification, which is by faith. Cf. Eph. 2:8–10.

> And it is he who will go as a forerunner before Him in the spirit and power of Elijah, to turn the hearts of the fathers back to the children, and the disobedient to the attitude of the righteous; so as to make ready a people prepared for the Lord. (Luke 1:17)[20]

At the very heart of God's redemptive covenant (the covenant of grace) is the relationship between fathers and their children. This is not a footnote to God's plan for his people. It is not only central to the immediate work of God in the lives of individuals and families, but vital to the long-term perpetuation of the kingdom of God from generation to generation and vital to a godly and healthy society.

The promise of the new covenant, the gospel of Christ, is to begin or renew this gracious work of familial affection. It is true that Jesus said, "Do not think that I came to bring peace on the earth; I did not come to bring peace, but a sword. For I came to set a man against his father, and a daughter against her mother, and a daughter-in-law against her mother-in-law; and a man's enemies will be the members of his household" (Matt. 10:34–36 NASB). The initial saving work of God often brings division to unbelieving and unfaithful households. This is the sanctifying work of the Spirit—the "setting apart." Yet the next generation should witness a major turning of the hearts of the new, sanctified household toward one another. You marry only "in the Lord." You begin a new household built by the Lord and raise up the next generation in "the fear and admonition of the Lord."

20. Some, consistent with a dispensational hermeneutic, insist that Luke 1:17 (alluding to Mal. 3) is referring to the pre–new covenant era and is therefore irrelevant to the new covenant. Our argument, however, is that there is a smooth transition between the old and the new covenant. John the Baptist is the messenger who prepares the way for the Messenger of the new covenant (i.e., Christ). John's work is to prepare the way before Christ by calling Israel to repentance and by removing the deadwood. Christ, like the refiner's fire and the fuller's soap (Mal. 3:2), will finish the clean-up work. However, as John 15, Romans 11, and Matthew 7 reveal, Jesus continues to remove those who are unfaithful and unfruitful, even in the new covenant era. Both the blessing of covenant keepers and the cursing of covenant breakers continue from the old to the new covenant. See also Rev. 2–3: Ephesus—the warning of the removal of the lampstand (2:5); Pergamum—does the Lord war against them all or just the Nicolaitans (2:16)? Laodicea—neither cold nor hot and will be spit forth (3:16); churches called to repentance: Ephesus, Pergamum, Thyatira, Sardis, Laodicea (five out of seven).

God anointed an infant in the womb to be the forerunner of Christ's kingdom and the new covenant (Luke 1:15). Some argue that John's ministry interjected a radical new element into God's redemptive plan—shifting from the corporate, external, and physical emphasis of the older covenants to the individual, internal, and spiritual emphasis of the new covenant. Yet a closer look at John's ministry reveals that instead of calling people to a new redemptive reality, he called them back to the original demands that God had placed on his covenant people. His first objective was to mark out a faithful remnant of God's covenant people, and his second was to call on the unfaithful Jew to repent and be counted among the covenant faithful.

John's ministry was to the people of Israel, many of whom had forgotten their true faith and exchanged it for mere externalism and a false reliance on their physical relationship to Abraham. But God never intended for Israel to rely on anything other than the true faith of their father Abraham—faith in a promised Redeemer. Therefore, God sent John forth with this express purpose:

> He will turn back many of the sons of Israel to the Lord their God. And it is he who will go as a forerunner before Him in the spirit and power of Elijah, to turn the hearts of the fathers back to the children, and the disobedient to the attitude of the righteous; so as to make ready a people prepared for the Lord. (Luke 1:16–17 NASB)

John called on the nominal Jews to repent of their sins and return to the faith of their fathers. His baptism was a sign of their renewal and cleansing. Moreover, John was not remiss in warning the unrepentant Jews (who knew better to start with) that they could expect judgment (covenant curses) for their covenant unfaithfulness (Matt. 3:1–9; Luke 3:7–9). When the Pharisees and Sadducees came to him for baptism, John warned them that their reliance on a physical relationship to Abraham was not sufficient and that, because of their unfaithfulness, they could expect to be cut off:

> Do not suppose that you can say to yourselves, "We have Abraham for our father"; for I say to you, that God is able from these stones to raise up children to Abraham. And the axe is already laid at the root of the trees; every tree therefore that does not bear good fruit is cut down and thrown into the fire. (Matt. 3:9–10 NASB)

The Lord was pruning the dead branches from the olive tree (Rom. 11:16–24) in preparation for the new covenant of Jesus Christ. Only those who were faithful to the covenant would enjoy the promises made to the fathers. One of God's promises to Abraham was that he would be God to his children.

CHRIST, THE MEDIATOR OF BOTH OLD AND NEW COVENANTS

The old and new covenants are essentially one. The Redeemer of God's elect, Jesus Christ, is the object of each. The apostle Paul gave assurance to the Gentile Christians concerning their relationship to Jewish believers when he said, "There is . . . one Lord, one faith, one baptism, one God and Father of all who is over all and through all and in all" (Eph. 4:4–6 NASB). This is the same God who said, "My covenant I will not violate, nor will I alter the utterance of My lips" (Ps. 89:34 NASB). Paul informs us, "For there is one God and one Mediator between God and men, the Man Christ Jesus" (1 Tim. 2:5). This means that Jesus Christ is the Mediator of the covenant in both the Old and New Testaments. He is the Mediator for Abraham, for Moses, for David, and every other covenant member—past, present, and future.

Part of the work of a mediator (i.e., one who stands between two parties), is that of being a messenger. For example, Elihu, in speaking to Job regarding God's mercies, says, "If there is a messenger for him, a mediator, one among a thousand, to show man His uprightness, then He is gracious to him" (Job 33:23–24). In the book of Malachi, God declares:

> Behold, I send My messenger, and he will prepare the way before Me. And the Lord, whom you seek, will suddenly come to His temple, even the Messenger [Mediator] of the covenant. . . . But who can endure the day of His coming? And who can stand when He appears? For He is like a refiner's fire and like fuller's soap. (Mal. 3:1–2)

The "Messenger" or Mediator of the covenant is Jesus Christ. Part of his covenant mediation will be to bring a message of judgment from God against all those who have profaned his covenant. As the Mediator or Messenger between God and man, Jesus is going to clean house. His mediation will bring a message of blessing to those who are covenant keepers and a message of cursing to those who are covenant breakers. Consider the closing chapter of the Old Testament:

> "For behold, the day is coming, burning like an oven, and all the proud, yes, all who do wickedly will be stubble. And the day which is coming shall burn them up," says the LORD of hosts, "that will leave them neither root nor branch. But to you who fear My name the Sun of Righteousness shall arise with healing in His wings; and you shall go out and grow fat like stall-fed calves. You shall trample the wicked, for they shall be ashes under the soles of your feet on the day that I do this," says the LORD of hosts. "Remember the law of Moses My servant, even the statutes and ordinances which I commanded him in Horeb for all Israel. Behold, I am going to send you Elijah the prophet before the coming of the great and terrible day of the LORD. And he will restore the hearts of the fathers to their children, and the hearts of the children to their fathers, lest I come and smite the land with a curse." (Mal. 4:1–3 NKJV, 4–6 NASB)

Here are the promised covenant blessings and curses associated with the mediation of the coming Christ—the Messenger of the covenant. The message will be good news for some and terrifying news for others. This two-edged message from the covenant Mediator finds expression in the New Testament when Jesus warns:

> I am the true vine, and My Father is the vinedresser. Every branch in Me that does not bear fruit He takes away; and every branch that bears fruit He prunes, that it may bear more fruit. You are already clean because of the word which I have spoken to you. Abide in Me, and I in you. As the branch cannot bear fruit of itself, unless it abides in the vine, neither can you, unless you abide in Me. I am the vine, you are the branches. He who abides in Me, and I in him, bears much fruit; for without Me you can do nothing. If anyone does not abide in Me, he is cast out as a branch and is withered; and they gather them and throw them into the fire, and they are burned. If you abide in Me, and My words abide in you, you will ask what you desire, and it shall be done for you. By this My Father is glorified, that you bear much fruit; so you will be My disciples. (John 15:1–8)

Unfruitful covenant members in the old covenant were cut off, and unfruitful covenant members in the new covenant are likewise cut off.[21] Like an unfaithful husband or wife who is divorced by his or her spouse—a covenant was entered into, and then the covenant was broken—the covenant relationship was then severed. Romans 11:16–24 affirms that covenant breakers in the new covenant receive the same judgment as covenant breakers in the old covenant:

> For if the firstfruit is holy, the lump is also holy; and if the root is holy, so are the branches. And if some of the branches were broken off, and you, being a wild olive tree, were grafted in among them, and with them became a partaker of the root and fatness of the olive tree, do not boast against the branches. But if you do boast, remember that you do not support the root, but the root supports you. You will say then, "Branches were broken off that I might be grafted in." Well said. Because of unbelief they were broken off, and you stand by faith. Do not be haughty, but fear. For if God did not spare the natural branches, He may not

21. Only the elect are eternally secure. This is why the apostle Peter admonished covenant members to "make your calling and election sure" (2 Peter 1:10), and the apostle Paul instructed covenant members to "examine yourselves as to whether you are in the faith" (2 Cor. 13:5).

> spare you either. Therefore consider the goodness and severity of God: on those who fell, severity; but toward you, goodness, if you continue in His goodness. Otherwise you also will be cut off. And they also, if they do not continue in unbelief, will be grafted in, for God is able to graft them in again. For if you were cut out of the olive tree which is wild by nature, and were grafted contrary to nature into a good olive tree, how much more will these, who are natural branches, be grafted into their own olive tree?

There is one olive tree that represents God's covenant people in both the old and new covenants. The fruitful branches will remain attached to the root (i.e., Christ); the unfruitful branches will be broken off and burned.

How could Jesus mediate wrath upon those for whom he intercedes? Certainly judgment is appropriate and expected for those who are not covenant members. But how could this judgment and wrath come upon those who are *in* the covenant? The answer is that not all who are in the covenant are elect.[22] Jesus, as the Mediator or Messenger of the covenant, intercedes for his elect. Jesus, as the Mediator or Messenger of the covenant, executes judgment upon all those who have profaned their circumcision or their baptism. "Of how much worse punishment, do you suppose, will he be thought worthy who has trampled the Son of God underfoot, counted the blood of the covenant by which he was sanctified a common thing, and insulted the Spirit of grace?" (Heb. 10:29).[23] This mediatorial work of blessing and cursing is part of both the old and the new covenants. We must not forget

22. Not all husbands are faithful husbands. There are many husbands who have entered the covenant of marriage and been unfaithful, covenant-breaking husbands. The fact that they are unfaithful husbands does not mean that they are not in covenant with their wives. It may mean that their unfaithfulness will lead to them being cut off from the covenant via divorce. At that point they are no longer husbands, but ex-husbands.

23. Some contend that the words "by which he was sanctified" refer to Jesus (see John 17:19). Such an interpretation cannot be sufficiently supported. Moreover, even if they did refer to Jesus, it must be admitted that the word "sanctify" is used in a different way than it is earlier in Heb. 10:14. Surely the sanctification experience of Jesus is far different from that which we experience.

that Christ is also the Mediator for those who lived under the old covenant as well. Did he not intercede for Abraham, Moses, and David?[24] Did he not judge all those who had uncircumcised hearts?[25]

Peter tells us, "For the time has come for judgment to begin at the house of God; and if it begins with us first, what will be the end of those who do not obey the gospel of God?" (1 Peter 4:17). We should recall that the high priest entered the Holy Place wearing a breastpiece of judgment and the names of the tribes of Israel upon stones (Ex. 28). Further, consider the judgment that came upon Ananias and Sapphira for lying to the Holy Spirit (Acts 8), or the judgment (death and illness) that came upon those who sinfully participated in the covenant meal (1 Cor. 11). The epistle to the Hebrews declares that "the Lord will judge His people" (10:30). Finally, the mediatorial work of Christ is clearly connected to judgment in this warning: "Jesus, the mediator of a new covenant. . . . See to it that you do not refuse Him who is speaking" (Heb. 12:24–25 NASB). "For not even the Father judges any one, but He has given all judgment to the Son" (John 5:22 NASB).

Summary

The transition from the old covenant to the new covenant is a smooth unfolding of God's redemptive plan, because the two covenants are organically connected—they are essentially one covenant of grace. The New Testament, by the words of Christ and his apostles, affirms the covenants of the Old Testament and applies them to members of the new covenant.[26] The family unit, or covenant household, is central to God's work of redemption in both the old and the new covenants as he continues to set apart believers and their children.[27] The New Testament is totally dependent upon the revelation of the Old Testament, appealing to its authority.[28] Without

24. Cf. 1 Tim. 2:5.
25. Cf. Jer. 9:25–26.
26. Cf. Matt. 5:17–19; Eph. 2:11–13; Rom. 15:8–9.
27. Cf. Gen. 17:9–14; Acts 2:39; 1 Cor. 7:14.
28. Cf. Acts 17:11; 1 Cor. 10:11; 2 Tim. 3:15–17.

question, Christ is the object, the Messenger, and the Mediator, of both the old and the new covenants.[29] The unity and continuity of the two covenants is established.

Therefore, the questions about covenant membership and the proper recipients of its signs are easy to answer. Believers and their children have always been members of God's gracious covenant and recipients of his covenant promises and signs. God has nowhere changed those terms or excluded anyone who was included in the past. Believers and their children are still the recipients of God's covenant promises and signs.

29. Cf. Mal. 3:1–2; 1 Tim. 2:5.

10

Covenant Theology and Baptism

CORNELIS P. VENEMA

Benjamin Breckinridge Warfield, the great Presbyterian theologian in the tradition of the old Princeton Theological Seminary, was not known for his terse or pithy writing style. However, in his polemics with the Reformed Baptist theologian Augustus Hopkins Strong on the subject of infant baptism, he was uncharacteristically brief, even blunt:

> The argument in a nutshell is simply this: God established His church in the days of Abraham and put children into it. They must remain there until He puts them out. He has nowhere put them out. They are still then members of His Church and as such entitled to its ordinances.[1]

According to Warfield, the whole issue concerning the proper recipients of the sacrament of baptism comes down to this question: Who belongs to the church or covenant community of God's people?

1. Benjamin Breckinridge Warfield, "The Polemics of Infant Baptism," in *Studies in Theology* (1932; reprint, Grand Rapids: Baker, 1981), 9.408.

Baptism, as a sign and seal of God's covenant promise, must be administered to all those with whom God covenants. Since God covenants with believers and their children, they are entitled to the divinely appointed ordinances that administer the covenant. The baptism of the children of believing parents, therefore, is an act performed in obedience to the divine institution of the sacrament as a sign and seal of the covenant of grace. Because God covenants with believers *and their children,* the church baptizes them on the ground of their membership in the church and the covenant people of God.

No doubt Warfield's uncharacteristically blunt conclusion to his debate with Strong aptly identifies the central matter in the long-standing debate between paedobaptists and Baptists.[2] This debate can be reduced to one principal question: Does the covenant of grace in its New Testament administration embrace the children of believing parents just as it did in its Old Testament administration? However complex and diverse the arguments, pro and con, on the subject of infant baptism may be, this remains the overriding issue.

Precisely because the debate between paedobaptists and Baptists centers on the doctrine of the covenant of grace, particularly the similarity and dissimilarity of the covenant in its Old and New Testament administrations, it can hardly be resolved merely by appealing to specific biblical texts. Typically, in the polemics on paedobaptism, Reformed authors appeal to texts that *imply* a continuation of the Old Testament practice of including the children of believers within the covenant community. Baptist authors counter by pointing out that no single text in the New Testament *expressly* teaches that any children ought to be baptized. Both sides in the debate, ironically, employ a kind of argument from silence to make their case. Paedobaptists argue that the silence of the New Testament confirms the continuation of Old Testament practice. After all, if the children of believing parents had been excluded from the new covenant, surely this would have be-

2. Throughout this chapter, I will use the term *Baptists* to designate those who reject the baptism of the children of believing parents and insist upon the exclusive practice of believer's baptism.

come a bone of contention in the early church, which was at first comprised largely of Jewish Christians. Baptists respond by pointing out the connection often made between faith and baptism, arguing that faith is ordinarily required in the New Testament prior to the administration of baptism.

It will not be my purpose in this chapter to enter into these polemics or exegete the most pertinent biblical passages. Other chapters in this volume address these issues more directly. Rather, I will set forth the main lines of covenant theology that undergird the paedobaptist position. The Reformed practice of baptizing believers and their children, as Warfield rightly maintained, is largely based on an understanding of the biblical doctrine of the covenant of grace. In the principal writings of the Reformers of the sixteenth century,[3] and in the great confessional symbols of the Reformed tradition,[4] the one argument for paedobaptism that repeatedly stands out is the argument based on the covenant. Children, like adult believers, are to be baptized because they belong to the covenant community in Christ. In order to summarize the covenant theology that supports the paedobaptist position, we will proceed in a series of steps, moving from the more general and basic elements of covenant theology to the specific implications of this theology for the question of the proper subjects of Christian baptism. Thus, in what follows we will begin with an extended treatment of the doctrine of the covenant of grace. What

3. E.g., John Calvin, *Institutes of the Christian Religion*, ed. John T. McNeill, trans. Ford Lewis Battles (Philadelphia: Westminster, 1960), 4.16.

4. For a summary of the Reformed confessions' teaching, see Cornelis Venema, "The Doctrine of the Sacraments and Baptism according to the Reformed Confessions," *Mid-America Journal of Theology* 11 (2000): 21–86, esp. pp. 80–82. The Heidelberg Catechism represents well the consensus of these confessions, when it answers question 74, "Are infants also to be baptized?" as follows: "Yes; for since they, as well as adults, are included in the covenant and Church of God, and since both redemption from sin and the Holy Spirit, the Author of faith, are through the blood of Christ promised to them no less than to adults, they must also by baptism, as a sign of the covenant, be ingrafted into the Christian Church, and distinguished from the children of unbelievers, as was done in the old covenant or testament by circumcision, instead of which baptism was instituted in the new covenant." The quotations from the Reformed confessions throughout this chapter are taken from *Ecumenical and Reformed Creeds and Confessions*, classroom edition (Dyer, Ind.: Mid-America Reformed Seminary, 1991).

do we mean by the covenant of grace, and do the various administrations of this covenant represent one unitary covenant or several disparate covenants? After treating the doctrine of the covenant of grace, we will take up more briefly the particular issue of the role and use of sacraments in the administration of the covenant. Who appoints the sacraments of the covenant at various stages in its administration, and for what purpose? Within the more immediate context of the doctrine of the sacraments, we will then turn to the sacrament of baptism, its relation to the rite of circumcision in the Old Testament, and its peculiar significance in the new covenant. Only after having laid a foundation in the doctrine of the covenant and its sacraments, will we be in position to address the particular question in dispute: Who ought to be baptized? Anticipating possible Baptist objections to the argument, the chapter will conclude with a brief consideration of two common Baptist criticisms of Reformed covenant theology.

THE COVENANT OF GRACE

To summarize the biblical and Reformed doctrine of the covenant of grace is a daunting task. The history of Reformed theology since the Reformation of the sixteenth century is, in some respects, a history of the development and articulation of the theology of the covenant. Just as the Reformed tradition is known for its emphasis on the doctrine of sovereign and gracious election, so it is known also for its emphasis on the communication of God's grace in Christ to his people by means of covenant.

One of the best summaries of covenant theology is the classic statement in the Westminster Confession of Faith. Although the other Reformed symbols assume the doctrine of the covenant, only the Westminster Confession gives formal and thorough expression to it. In chapter 7, "Of God's Covenant with Man," the Confession offers the following key affirmations:

I. The distance between God and the creature is so great, that although reasonable creatures do owe obedience unto him as their Creator, yet they could never have any fruition of him as their blessedness and reward, but by some voluntary condescension on God's part, which he hath been pleased to express by way of covenant.

II. The first covenant made with man was a covenant of works, wherein life was promised to Adam; and in him to his posterity, upon condition of perfect and personal obedience.

III. Man, by his fall, having made himself uncapable of life by that covenant, the Lord was pleased to make a second, commonly called the covenant of grace; wherein he freely offereth unto sinners life and salvation by Jesus Christ; requiring of them faith in him, that they may be saved, and promising to give unto all those that are ordained unto eternal life his Holy Spirit, to make them willing, and able to believe. . . .

V. This covenant was differently administered in the time of the law, and in the time of the gospel: under the law, it was administered by promises, prophecies, sacrifices, circumcision, the paschal lamb, and other types and ordinances delivered to the people of the Jews, all foresignifying Christ to come; which were, for that time, sufficient and efficacious, through the operation of the Spirit, to instruct and build up the elect in faith in the promised Messiah, by whom they had full remission of sins, and eternal salvation; and is called the old testament.

VI. Under the gospel, when Christ, the substance, was exhibited, the ordinances in which this covenant is dispensed are the preaching of the Word, and the administration of the sacraments of Baptism and the Lord's Supper: which, though fewer in number, and administered with more simplicity, and less outward glory, yet, in them, it is held forth in more fulness, evidence and spiritual efficacy, to all nations, both Jews and Gentiles; and is called the new testament. There are not therefore two covenants of grace, differing in substance, but one and the same, under various dispensations.

According to this summary statement of the biblical doctrine of the covenant, in order to enjoy a life-relationship or fellowship with man, his image bearer, the triune God voluntarily condescends to enter into covenant with him. This was already true prior to the fall into sin, when God as Creator covenanted to grant Adam life and eternal blessedness upon the condition of his perfect obedience.[5] However, after the fall into sin, which ruptured the communion of life between the triune Creator and his covenant creature, the covenant of grace was initiated and established by the triune Redeemer to restore fallen man to saving fellowship with him. The God of the Scriptures is a covenant God, and the creature who bears his image is a covenant creature. The union and communion with God that comprise man's peculiar life and blessedness are covenantal in nature. The triune God enters into and maintains fellowship with his people by means of covenant.

The covenant of grace, accordingly, is the means instituted by God's grace and mercy to restore fallen sinners to communion with him. Having forfeited through sinful rebellion any claim upon God's favor or right to his blessing, sinners lie under the curse of death and separation from God. Only by virtue of God's gracious initiatives, in coming to his people and restoring them to communion with him, do fallen sinners find salvation and life. These initiatives, according to scriptural revelation, are always covenantal in nature.

The Nature of the Covenant

In the history of Reformed theology, there has been considerable debate and even divergence of opinion regarding the precise nature of the covenant relationship. In the older writings, the tendency was to treat the covenant as a kind of compact or agreement between two

5. For a treatment of the prelapsarian "covenant of works," see Charles Hodge, *Systematic Theology* (1871; reprint, Grand Rapids: Eerdmans, 1952), 2.115–22; Herman Bavinck, *In the Beginning: Foundations of Creation Theology,* ed. John Bolt, trans. John Vriend (Grand Rapids: Baker, 1999), 197–216; L. Berkhof, *Systematic Theology* (Grand Rapids: Eerdmans, 1939), 211–18; Cornelis Venema, "Recent Criticisms of the 'Covenant of Works' in the Westminster Confession of Faith," *Mid-America Journal of Theology* 9 (1993): 165–98.

parties.[6] Francis Turretin, for example, defined the covenant of grace as "a gratuitous pact entered into in Christ between God offended and man the offender. In it God promises remission of sins and salvation to man freely on account of Christ; man, however, relying on the same grace promises faith and obedience."[7] However, in more recent discussions of the covenant of grace, the sovereign and unilateral initiative of God in graciously covenanting with his people has received greater prominence. Although it was clearly recognized by the older writers that God alone effectively and graciously brings the covenant relationship to bear fruit through the mediation of Christ and the working of the Holy Spirit, recent writers have especially emphasized this feature of the covenant relationship.[8] The covenant relationship is, in its origin and administration, an initiative and work of God's undeserved grace and mercy.

The covenant relationship is marked by communion and friendship between God and his people. This relationship involves mutual promises and obligations. God makes promises and stipulates obligations, and so binds himself to his people as a husband to his wife, as a bridegroom to his bride, or as a father to his children.[9] For their part, the covenant people of God are invited to embrace the covenant promises by faith and to acknowledge their corresponding obligations. However, this mutuality and fellowship, which mark the union and communion of the covenant relationship, do not imply an equal standing between God and his people in the covenant. God takes the initiative in establishing the covenant. He graciously administers and sus-

6. See John Murray, *The Covenant of Grace: A Biblico-Theological Study* (London: Tyndale Press, 1953), 5–7.

7. Francis Turretin, *Institutes of Elenctic Theology,* ed. James T. Dennison Jr., trans. George Musgrave Giger (Phillipsburg, N.J.: P&R, 1992–97), 2:175.

8. See, e.g., Murray, *The Covenant of Grace;* O. Palmer Robertson, *The Christ of the Covenants* (Phillipsburg, N.J.: Presbyterian and Reformed, 1980); Meredith G. Kline, *By Oath Consigned* (Grand Rapids: Eerdmans, 1968). Robertson's biblical-theological study is an outstanding survey of the biblical history and diverse administration of the covenant of grace.

9. These are some of the main metaphors utilized in the Scriptures to describe God's relationship with his people. See, e.g., Ps. 103:13–14; Mal. 3:17; Jer. 3:6–10; 31:20–22; Hos. 1:14–23; Luke 3:28; Eph. 5:21–33.

tains it. And he ensures its fruitfulness. The triune God begins, maintains, and finally realizes his covenant purpose of establishing a relationship of saving communion with his people.

The Covenant Promise

Because the covenant of grace is a sovereign initiative of God's undeserved grace, the basis and source of the covenant's blessings are found in the covenant promise. In Genesis 3:15, often called the protevangelium or "first gospel" promise, the Lord God comes to Adam and Eve after the fall into sin and pledges to provide a seed of the woman who will crush the head of the serpent. Although little is told about the covenant of grace in this passage, it does reveal God's gracious purpose to redeem a people for communion with him and to provide a Savior, born of the woman, who would destroy the tempter and his work. This passage anticipates God's covenant with Noah and his family (Gen. 9:9) and the formal establishment of the covenant of grace in Genesis 12, 15, and especially 17.

In the accounts of the establishment of the covenant of grace in Genesis, the Lord comes to Abram and promises to make of him a great nation and to bless all the families of the earth through him (Gen. 12:2–3). The Lord also promises to give Abram a son and through him descendants more numerous than the stars of the heavens (Gen. 15:4–5). When Abram believes this promise, God reckons this to him as righteousness (15:5; cf. Rom. 4; Gal. 3:8) and, by means of a self-maledictory oath ceremony, confirms his pledge to do as he has promised. Then, in the great account of the establishment of the covenant of grace in Genesis 17, the Lord God comes once more to Abram and reaffirms his promise: "As for Me, behold, My covenant is with you, and you will be the father of a multitude of nations. . . . I will establish My covenant between Me and you and your descendants after you throughout their generations for an everlasting covenant, to be God to you and to your descendants after you" (vv. 4, 7).

Any tracing of the way in which God graciously deals with his covenant people throughout the course of the history of redemption, beginning with Abraham, Isaac, and Jacob and finally fulfilled in the person and work of Jesus Christ, will quickly reveal that it is a story of God's covenant faithfulness through and through. What sustains this history is not the faithfulness or perseverance of God's people, but rather the extraordinary and undeserved faithfulness and perseverance of God. However many promises the Lord God makes to Israel, these all find their yes and amen in Christ (2 Cor. 1:20). The prophecies of the Old Testament find their fulfillment in the coming and work of Christ (Luke 24:44). The covenant of grace, therefore, is ultimately rooted in God's gracious promise to provide life and salvation for his people through Jesus Christ.

Although the covenant of grace, throughout its administrations from Noah to Abraham to Moses to Christ, includes a great number of promises, some specific to Israel and others more basic and enduring, the one great promise is the promise of salvation in communion with God through Christ.[10] This promise includes such blessings as the forgiveness of sins and acceptance with God (free justification), the renewal of life in obedience by the working of the Spirit, and the final glorification of life in unbroken fellowship with God. These promises are sure and certain of fulfillment, for they are as immutable as God himself, who extends them and secures their realization by the work of Christ through his Spirit. As the Westminster Confession of Faith puts its, in the covenant of grace God "freely offereth unto sinners life and salvation by Jesus Christ . . . promising to give unto all those that are ordained unto eternal life his Holy Spirit, to make them willing, and able to believe" (7.3).

The Covenant Obligation

Although the covenant of grace is initiated and maintained by God's undeserved favor toward his people, it nonetheless obligates those to whom its promises are extended to embrace them by faith. Because the covenant involves mutual promises and commitments, those with whom God graciously covenants are obligated to respond to him in

10. For a summary of the biblical evidence for this claim, see Berkhof, *Systematic Theology,* 277.

faith and obedience. For this reason, the Westminster Confession of Faith speaks of God's "requiring of them [sinners] faith in him [Christ], that they may be saved." Just as God graciously commits himself in covenant to his people, so his people are called to live before him in love and devotion. God's covenant faithfulness summons his people to a corresponding faithfulness, even as a husband who loves his wife invites her thereby to love and be subject to him. In this way, there is mutuality in the covenant relationship in which those whom God loves must in turn love God and others with him (Ex. 20; Deut. 6:5; Matt. 12:30–31).

Just as the biblical record of the administration of the covenant of grace records various promises and pledges of God's grace to his people, so it records various demands and obligations that correspond to the particular dispensations of the covenant. When God first entered into a covenant relationship with Abraham, he demanded among other things that Abraham walk before him and be blameless (Gen. 17:2). When God subsequently covenanted with the children of Israel under Moses at Sinai, he gave them the Ten Commandments (Ex. 20) together with an elaborate system of ceremonial and civil law. Likewise, with the coming of Christ and the preaching of the gospel of God's grace under the new covenant, the covenant people of God are called to faith in Christ and obedience to his law ("the law of Christ," Gal. 6:2). The promised blessings of covenant life and fellowship with God require faith and repentance.

One of the more difficult questions that arise at this point in the formulation of covenant theology is whether the covenant is conditional or unconditional. On the one hand, it would seem that the covenant of grace is unconditional. God sovereignly and unilaterally establishes the covenant. He maintains and fulfills immutably the promises that he makes to his people. As we shall see more fully below when we consider the place of Christ as the Mediator of the covenant of grace, God the Father secures the covenant's blessings for his people by sending his Son to accomplish their redemption by his atoning sacrifice and the outpouring of his Spirit. *Everything that God demands of his people in the covenant of grace he graciously grants them in Christ.* Not only are the covenant's obligations preceded by God's gracious promise, but these obligations are fulfilled for and in believers by the triune God—Father, Son, and Holy Spirit—in their respective operations. God's demands are born of grace and fulfilled in us by grace. In these respects, the covenant of grace is unconditional, excluding every possible form of merit, whereby the faith and obedience of God's people would be the basis for their obtaining life and salvation.

However, when the covenant is viewed from the point of view of the work of Christ and the manner of its administration, it is conditional. The blessings of the covenant are contingent, for example, upon the work of Christ in fulfilling the conditions of obedience first set down in the pre-Fall covenant of works (Rom. 5:12–21). The curse due to the covenant breaker who violates the law in one particular, was borne by Christ upon the cross (Gal. 3:13). In these and other respects, the work of Christ procures the blessings that God promises to those with whom he covenants (Eph. 1:3). Furthermore, the obligations of faith and obedience, though not meritorious conditions, are necessary responses to the covenant's promises and are, as such, instrumental to the enjoyment of the covenant's blessings. Faith and obedience, of course, are themselves the fruits of God's grace. They are God's gifts, for salvation is of grace alone, not of works, lest anyone should boast (Eph. 2:6–10).[11] Yet they are also the response of God's people to the summons of his grace, and thus are indispensable to the receiving and enjoying of what the covenant communicates. Without faith and repentance, the sinner may have no expectation of God's favor or blessing.

11. For a classic Reformed treatment of the way in which salvation, including the benefits of free justification and sanctification, is graciously granted to us by the triune God—Father, Son, and Holy Spirit—see John Calvin, *Institutes,* 3.1–11. The covenant's obligations are fulfilled in us, according to Calvin, by the Spirit, who grants faith to the believer and simultaneously renews him in holiness. For a study of Calvin's view, see Cornelis Venema, *The Twofold Nature of the Gospel in Calvin's Theology* (Ann Arbor, Mich.: University Microfilms, 1985), esp. pp. 189–280.

The Covenant Parties

The question whether the covenant of grace is conditional or unconditional raises another difficult question: With whom does God covenant in the covenant of grace? Does God covenant with the elect only, or does he covenant with believers and their children, not all of whom are elect? Throughout the history of theological reflection on the covenant of grace, Reformed theologians have answered this question with one or another of these two answers. Some have also attempted to address this question by speaking of the "dual aspect" of the covenant.

The first of these answers—that God covenants with the elect only in the covenant of grace—is suggested by the Westminster Confession of Faith (7.3), which says that God promises in this covenant "to give unto *all those that are ordained unto eternal life* by his Spirit, to make them willing, and able to believe" (emphasis added). The Westminster Larger Catechism, question 31, suggests this answer more clearly when it states that "the covenant of grace was made with Christ as the second Adam, and in him with all the elect as his seed."[12] In the strictest sense of the covenant as a saving communion with God, the parties of the covenant of grace are the triune God and his elect people.

The grounds often given for this answer, which is the opinion of many Reformed theologians,[13] are several. First, when the covenant of grace is viewed from the vantage point of God's sovereign counsel and purpose, it is seen in terms of God's electing intention to give his Son as the representative Head of his people, whose salvation he accomplishes and guarantees. Because the covenant of grace is the historical means by which the triune God effects his saving purposes for his elect people, the covenant is, strictly speaking, designed for and ef-

12. The Westminster standards, however, clearly teach that the covenant of grace, in its concrete administration, also includes in a more general way some who are not elect (Larger Catechism, Q. 162 and Q. 166). This is evident from the distinction drawn between the "visible" and the "invisible" church in the Westminster Confession of Faith, chap. 25, and the way in which the recipients of baptism are described in chap. 28.

13. Berkhof, *Systematic Theology*, 273, claims that the "great majority" of Reformed theologians take this view. However, he also acknowledges that, among these theologians, most also admit that there is another and broader sense in which God covenants with some who are not elect in the particular sense of God's "purpose of election" (cf. Rom. 9:6–13).

fectual in securing the salvation of all those whom the Father elects, for whom the Son atones, and in whom the Spirit effectively works faith and repentance.[14] Second, the covenant of grace is made with those who are "in Christ," that is, with those for whom Christ's mediation is the sure basis of their salvation. Not all those who are Abraham's seed are in Christ in this sense (cf. Gen. 21:12; Rom. 9:8; Gal. 3:16, 29; 4:28), and therefore a distinction has to be made between those who are "children of the promise" in the strict sense and those who are not. The promise of salvation is effectual and fruitful in the case of those who are called according to God's purpose of election, but not all of Abraham's seed are recipients of the promise in this way. Some, like Esau, are not full heirs of the promise of salvation made to Abraham. Third, because the salvation of those with whom God covenants is the fruit of God's sovereign design and working, it cannot depend on the uncertain obedience or faithfulness of sinners. If the salvation of those with whom God covenants were finally to rest upon the basis of covenant obedience or faithfulness, it would no longer be salvation by grace, nor would it bring any assurance or certainty of the covenant's blessing. Salvation may not be explained merely by the fact that certain covenant members are faithful. This would be a form of Arminianism, which makes election contingent upon covenant faithfulness. And fourth, if the covenant is viewed not merely as a means to an end, but as an end in itself, then what it promises must be a reality in the experience of those with whom God covenants. Since the covenant relationship expresses the fullness of friendship and fellowship with God, it is not possible that the nonelect could be members of it.

14. For this reason, Reformed theologians historically have spoken of a "covenant of redemption" or *pactum salutis.* This "covenant of redemption" represents the pretemporal counsel of the Father, the Son, and the Holy Spirit to provide redemption for the elect by means of their respective work in the covenant of grace. Accordingly, the Father purposes to send his Son to make atonement for the elect, and, together with the Son, purposes to bestow the Spirit to apply the benefits of Christ's atonement to the elect. For representative treatments of this covenant of redemption, see Hodge, *Systematic Theology,* 2:357–62; Geerhardus Vos, "Doctrine of the Covenant in Reformed Theology," in *Redemptive History and Biblical Interpretation: The Shorter Writings of Geerhardus Vos,* ed. Richard J. Gaffin Jr. (Phillipsburg, N.J.: Presbyterian and Reformed, 1980), 245–52; Berkhof, *Systematic Theology,* 265–72.

Despite these substantial reasons for affirming that the covenant of grace is made with the elect only, many Reformed theologians have maintained that the covenant embraces all believers and their children, not all of whom are elect in the strict sense. These theologians, while acknowledging that the life and salvation promised in the covenant of grace are inherited only by the elect, argue that the covenant promise, together with its accompanying obligation, is extended to Abraham and his seed. In the administration of the covenant of grace throughout the course of redemptive history, there are many in the covenant community who *break covenant with God and become liable to his covenant wrath.* In the Old and New Testaments, members of the covenant community are warned against the danger of unbelief and impenitence. Such unbelief and disobedience among the people with whom God covenants carry the fearful prospect of God's judgment. The blessings promised in the covenant belong to those who believe and obey. However, the curses of the covenant will undoubtedly fall upon those who despise their covenant birthright and refuse the gracious promise and invitation extended to them (Hebrews; 1 Peter 4:17). The only way to avoid the false presumption that all those with whom God covenants are guaranteed salvation (because they are presumably elect) is to recognize that there may be covenant breakers who ought to be cut off from the number of God's people. Such covenant breaking and its consequence, though it may contradict the saving purpose for which the covenant of grace was instituted by God, reminds us that the circle of the covenant is in this respect wider than the circle of election.

In order to resolve this question, Reformed theologians have sought to distinguish in a variety of ways between all those with whom God covenants (believers and their children) *in the wider sense of the covenant's administration* and those in whom the covenant comes to fruition (the elect) *in the narrower sense of the covenant's communion of life.*[15] This distinction aims to acknowledge that the covenant embraces all believers

15. For a discussion of this "dual aspect" of the covenant, see Vos, "Doctrine of the Covenant in Reformed Theology," 258–67; John Murray, *Christian Baptism* (Philadelphia: Presbyterian and Reformed, 1962), 51–53; Berkhof, *Systematic Theology,* 284–89.

and their children as recipients of the gospel promise and obligation, on the one hand, while simultaneously acknowledging that some fall away in unbelief and disobedience, on the other hand. Although the unbelief and disobedience of some with whom God covenants are anomalous—they prevent the covenant breaker from entering into that life and salvation which the covenant aims to impart—they are nonetheless real and undeniable. There are nonelect persons in the covenant who do not respond to the promise in the way of faith and obedience. The presence of such persons "under" the covenant, however, should not be viewed as evidence of failure on God's part in communicating his grace to his own. For it is through the covenant that God grants life and salvation to those whom he has elected to save.

The Covenant Mediator

All the blessings promised by God to believers and their children in the covenant of grace find their basis and surety in Christ. This was as true of the old covenant believer as it is of the new. The central figure in the story of redemption related in the Scriptures is Jesus Christ, the son of Abraham, the son of David (Matt. 1:1). He is the focus and content of all the promises of God in Scripture, from the "mother promise" of Genesis 3:15 to the promise of the consummation of the covenant in Revelation 21–22. He also obtains for his people the life and salvation offered through the covenant of grace (Matt. 1:28). He is the promised "seed" through whom the blessings of the covenant are extended to all the families of the earth (Gal. 3:16). He is the one who crushes the head of the serpent and brings salvation to his people in fulfillment of the covenant promises first made to Abraham (Luke 1:72). All the ceremonies and prophecies of the Old Testament find their goal and fruition in Christ, of whom they spoke and toward whose coming they looked (Luke 24:44; 2 Cor. 1:20; Heb. 1:1–2; 2 Peter 1:19).

The Unity of the Covenant

A critical theme in the theology of the covenant, as this has been articulated historically in the Reformed tradition, is the insistence that there is *one* covenant of grace throughout the course of the history of redemption. To use the well-known language of John Calvin, the covenant of grace is one in substance and diverse in mode of administration.[16] However diverse and particular may be the various dispensations or administrations of the covenant of grace—so that we may even speak of "covenants" in the plural (Rom. 9:4)—they do not differ as to substance.

There are a number of biblical arguments that support this claim. First, the covenant promise of life and salvation is described in the same way throughout the Scriptures. When God first entered into an everlasting covenant with Abraham, he promised to be God to him and to his seed after him (Gen. 17:7). This language is used of the covenant made at Sinai under Moses (Ex. 19:5; 20:1), of the covenant made on the Plains of Moab (Deut. 29:13), of the covenant with David (2 Sam. 7:14), and of the new covenant in Christ (Jer. 31:33; Heb. 8:10). In the description of the consummate state in Revelation 21:1–8, this language is also employed to describe the unbroken communion that God will enjoy with his people in the new heaven and new earth. All the blessings of life and fellowship with the triune God in the Old and New Testaments are summed up in the covenantal promise of union and communion with God.

Second, the Mediator of the covenant is the same in every dispensation or administration of the covenant of grace. Jesus Christ, according to the writer of Hebrews, is "the same yesterday and today and forever" (13:8). When Abraham, the father of all believers, trusted God, he placed his trust in Jesus Christ (Gal. 3:16; cf. John 8:56). All those who are heirs with Abraham of the promises of the covenant are heirs through faith in Jesus Christ (Gal. 3:16–29). The one mediatorship of Christ is reflected in the language of Revelation, which speaks of those whose names have been "written from the foundation of the world in the book of life of the Lamb who has been slain" (Rev.

16. Calvin, *Institutes,* 2.10.1: "The covenant made with all the patriarchs is so much like ours in substance and reality that the two are actually one and the same. Yet they differ in the mode of administration."

13:8). It is also reflected in the book of Hebrews, which speaks of "the blood of the eternal covenant" (Heb. 13:20). Christ is the one through whom all believers receive every spiritual blessing in the heavenlies (Eph. 1:3). He is the only mediator between God and man (1 Tim. 2:5), and his is the only name given among men whereby they can be saved (Acts 4:12).

Third, the gospel preached in the old covenant is the same as the gospel preached in the new covenant. As the apostle Paul states in Galatians 3:8, "The Scripture, foreseeing that God would justify the Gentiles by faith, preached the gospel beforehand to Abraham, saying, 'All the nations will be blessed in you.'" This gospel was already declared at the beginning of the history of redemption to Adam (Gen. 3:15). It was reaffirmed in God's covenant with Abraham, and it finds its fulfillment in the birth and ministry of Jesus Christ in the fullness of time.

Fourth, the obligation of the covenant of grace is essentially the same throughout the course of its various and successive administrations. Abraham, the father of all believers, believed God, and it was reckoned to him for righteousness. In so doing, he set an example of faith for all believers who receive the promise, not by works performed in obedience to the law, but by faith in Christ. Jews and Gentiles alike obtain salvation by faith alone, not by works (Rom. 4:9–25; Gal. 3:7–9, 17–18). The gracious promise of the covenant precedes the giving of the law, thereby teaching us that salvation is by grace alone through faith alone, and not on account of the righteousness of works.

For these reasons, the covenant of grace, throughout its successive and diverse administrations, is essentially one and the same covenant. Although Old Testament believers embraced Christ by faith under the veil of the shadows and ceremonies of the law, they embraced the same Mediator by the work of the same Spirit, and thereby enjoyed the same fundamental blessings of salvation—favor with God and renewal of life in consecration to his will.

THE SACRAMENTS OF THE COVENANT

In the administration of the covenant of grace, God has appointed the sacraments as a means of confirming to his people the covenant promise and its corresponding obligation. These sacraments are visible signs and seals of the covenant; God has ordained them to attest to his people the life and salvation promised in the gospel.

In order to guide us in our summary of the nature and function of the sacraments of the covenant, we will once again use the Westminster Confession of Faith as a standard statement of the Reformed view. The following articles from chapter 27, "Of the Sacraments," and chapter 28, "Of Baptism," are especially important to our purpose:

> I. Sacraments are holy signs and seals of the covenant of grace, immediately instituted by God, to represent Christ, and his benefits; and to confirm our interest in him: as also, to put a visible difference between those that belong unto the church, and the rest of the world; and solemnly to engage them to the service of Christ, according to his Word. (chap. 27)

> I. Baptism is a sacrament of the new testament, ordained by Jesus Christ, not only for the solemn admission of the party baptized into the visible church; but also, to be unto him a sign and seal of the covenant of grace, of his ingrafting into Christ, of regeneration, of remission of sins, and of his giving up unto God, through Jesus Christ, to walk in newness of life. Which sacrament is, by God's own appointment, to be continued in his church until the end of the world. . . .
>
> III. The grace which is exhibited in or by the sacraments rightly used, is not conferred by any power in them; neither doth the efficacy of a sacrament depend upon the piety or intention of him that doth administer it: but upon the work of the Spirit, and the word of institution, which contains, together with a precept authorizing the use thereof, a promise of benefit to worthy receivers.

IV. Not only those that do actually profess faith in and obedience unto Christ, but also the infants of one, or both, believing parents, are to be baptized. . . .

VI. The efficacy of Baptism is not tied to that moment of time wherein it is administered; yet, notwithstanding, by the right use of this ordinance, the grace promised is not only offered, but really exhibited, and conferred, by the Holy Ghost, to such (whether of age or infants) as that grace belongeth unto, according to the counsel of God's own will, in his appointed time. (chap. 28)

The Nature and Function of Sacraments

The starting point for an appreciation of the nature and function of the sacraments is their divine authorship or appointment. God appoints sacraments, in addition to the communication of the gospel of salvation in Christ through the preaching and teaching of the Word, as a means of grace. The sacraments are not human inventions, primarily serving to confirm the faith and profession of those who are members of the covenant community or church. They are not "badges" of a Christian profession before God, but "tokens" of God's grace to his people. They are God-ordained instruments to communicate the grace of the covenant to its members. In the Old and New Testaments, the sacraments were instituted by the covenant Lord as an integral part of his administration of the covenant of grace.

What distinguishes the sacraments from the preaching and teaching of the Word is their use of visible signs and seals. In the sacraments, God consecrates the sacramental elements to a holy use, employing them as visible confirmations of the invisible grace of the covenant. The sacraments visibly *represent* the gospel promise of life and salvation in Christ. There is a correspondence in the sacraments between the visible signs and the grace to which they point. The water of baptism, for example, points to or signifies the washing away of sin through the blood of Christ and the regenerating Spirit. The bread of the Lord's Supper visibly speaks of the body of Christ given for the remission of sins. Furthermore, the sacraments are seals that confirm or attest the truth of the gospel promise. They are not only signs that visibly represent, but also seals that authenticate and assure believers of the truth of the promise of the covenant. In the sacraments, believers are provided a more open display and evident confirmation of the veracity of the Word and the promise of the covenant.

The Westminster Confession emphasizes that the efficacy of the sacraments depends upon the Spirit's working in and through them to confirm the gospel promise. Just as the Spirit uses the preaching of the gospel to create and nourish the faith of believers, so the Spirit uses the visible word of the sacrament to nourish and confirm the faith of believers. However, the Spirit does not work through the sacraments because of any intrinsic power in them. The sacraments depend upon the Spirit's power and remain instrumental to the communication of the grace of God in Christ. They require the same response as does the Word, namely, faith in Christ and consecration to God. The sacraments do not *by themselves* work regeneration and faith in their recipients. Nor are they administered on the basis of the presumed regeneration of their recipients, as if they were an attestation of the state of grace of their recipients.

Circumcision and Baptism

In the dispute between paedobaptists and Baptists regarding the proper recipients of the sacrament of baptism, one of the more crucial questions has to do with the similarity and dissimilarity of the sacraments of Old Testament circumcision and New Testament baptism. Baptist authors typically argue that these sacraments are radically different in their meaning and significance. Because circumcision and baptism are so different in meaning, they say, no conclusions about the proper recipients of baptism may be drawn from the practice of circumcising the male infants of covenant members. But Reformed authors note that these sacraments have considerably more in common than what distinguishes them. Just as the sacrament of circumcision in the Old Testament signified and sealed incorporation into the covenant community, so the rite of baptism in the New Testament is an initiation into the community of Christ and his people. The similarities between the two sacraments are far more weighty than their dissimilarities.[17]

Although Baptists often argue, for instance, that the sacrament of circumcision was only a sign of outward membership in the nation of Israel and not a sign of a spiritual blessing, this is clearly contradicted by the Bible. In the passage that records its appointment as a sacrament of the old covenant, circumcision is virtually identified with the covenant relationship itself, which is a relationship of communion and fellowship between the Lord and his people (Gen. 17:11). Circumcision, like the covenant which it signifies and seals to believers and their children, was a sacrament that in its deepest meaning stood for fellowship with God. As a visible sign and token of an invisible grace, circumcision specifically reminded the children of Israel of their need to remove the defilement and corruption of sin (cf. Deut. 10:16; 30:6; Jer. 4:4). The sacrament of circumcision was a bloody sign of the need for the removal of sin, the guilt and corruption of which constituted an insuperable obstacle to fellowship with a holy God. Moreover, the apostle Paul teaches in Romans that circumcision was for Abraham a sign and seal of the righteousness of faith (4:11). Abraham's circumcision was not merely a sign that he would be the father of the Jewish nation, but also a seal of his justification through faith alone, apart from works. In this, Abraham became, says the apostle, "the father of *all* who believe without being circumcised." Circumcision, therefore, was a sign and seal of the most basic and glorious spiritual blessings: covenant communion and fellowship with God, the need to remove the defilement of sin as an obstacle to favor with a holy God, and the righteousness of faith whereby believers become acceptable to God.

Because these spiritual blessings belong to the covenant that circumcision signified and sealed to Old Testament believers, it is not surprising to find the apostle Paul treating baptism as the new covenant

17. For a discussion of the relationship between circumcision and baptism, see Pierre Ch. Marcel, *The Biblical Doctrine of Infant Baptism,* trans. Philip Edgcumbe Hughes (London: James Clarke, 1953), 82–95.

counterpart to circumcision (Col. 2:11–13). In the new covenant, circumcision no longer serves as a sign and seal of fellowship with God (Gal. 2:3). Baptism now serves, by the Lord's appointment, as a sign and seal of fellowship with the triune God and incorporation into the church of Jesus Christ (Matt. 28:16–20). Baptism now represents the spiritual circumcision "made without hands, in the removal of the body of the flesh" (Col. 2:11). The spiritual blessings represented by circumcision in the old covenant are now represented by baptism in the new covenant. Through baptism, believers receive a sign and seal of their communion with Christ and of their having put off their sin-dominated nature or flesh. This spiritual circumcision occurs through union with Christ, which is signified and sealed by the sacrament of baptism. What was formerly confirmed through the sacrament of circumcision is presently confirmed through the sacrament of baptism: the forgiveness of sins (Mark 1:4; Acts 2:38; Heb. 10:22), the washing away of sin through fellowship with Christ (Rom. 6:2–10; 1 Cor. 6:11; Eph. 5:26; Col. 2:12), regeneration, and fellowship with Christ and his body (Acts 2:40–41; 1 Cor. 12:13).

THE PROMISE IS TO YOUR CHILDREN

Now that we have considered several of the key elements of covenant theology, including the nature and function of the sacraments as God-appointed media to signify and seal the covenant promise in Christ, we are in a position to draw the conclusion to which this theology inevitably compels us.

We know from the biblical history of the covenant of grace that, in the Old Testament administration, God promised communion and fellowship with himself to Abraham and his seed. Believers and their children were embraced within the covenant promise and favor of God. In this way, the faithfulness of Israel's covenant-keeping God was extended from generation to generation, as an everlasting covenant whose blessings would ultimately extend to all the families of the earth. These covenanted blessings, however, placed believers and their children under corresponding obligations of faith and obedience. The covenant love of God was promised to a thousand generations of those who loved him and kept his commandments. In order to attest and confirm this covenant relationship, its promises as well as its obligations, God gave his people the sacrament of circumcision. This sacrament was a sign and seal of God's promise, and of the obligations of covenant fellowship with him. It was a sacrament of inclusion or initiation into the covenant relationship, with all of its promises and obligations.

But what about the new covenant in Christ? According to the biblical revelation, this covenant *fulfills* the promises of the old: Christ is the one in whom all the promises of God have their yes and amen. The seed promised under the old covenant, the one through whom the blessings of the covenant would extend to all the peoples, is none other than Christ himself (Matt. 1:1–17; Gal. 3:16). Those who believe in Christ are heirs of the covenant, children of Abraham who are reckoned righteous by faith, even as he was. In this new covenant administration, the covenant promise of communion and fellowship with the living God is fulfilled by the work of Christ, the Mediator, and the ministry of the Spirit whom he poured out at Pentecost. The covenant promise of life and salvation is now offered to sinners who are called by means of the gospel to faith and repentance. However much greater and richer the new covenant administration in Christ may be, it does not abrogate or displace the old covenant. Rather, the new covenant in Christ's blood is the fulfillment of all that the old covenant promised and foreshadowed. In this new covenant administration, furthermore, God has appointed a sacrament to signify and seal to his people the promises and obligations of the gospel. Through baptism, believers are initiated into the fellowship of the triune God and his people, separated from the world of unbelief and sin, and incorporated into the body of Christ. By means of this sign and seal of spiritual circumcision, God represents and attests the life and salvation that come through the work of Christ.

The question now arises: How does the new covenant administration differ from the old, so far as its subjects or recipients are concerned? The promise and the obligation remain the same. The Mediator is the same. The same gospel is preached. However, the sacramental rite of inclusion among the people of God differs. Formerly, believers and their children were circumcised, but now baptism is the sacramental means of signifying and sealing the covenant promise and its obligation. But is there a further difference? Must we conclude that, whereas children were formerly recipients of the promise, they are no longer? Is the new covenant administration, so far as its proper recipients are concerned, *more restricted, less encompassing in its reach,* than had been the case previously?

The answer to this question is provided for us in the apostle Peter's sermon at Pentecost. Although Baptists often quote Peter's words calling his listeners to repent and be baptized, insisting that they illustrate the necessity of faith and repentance as prerequisites to baptism, they tend to gloss over his words immediately following—"For the promise is for you *and your children and for all who are far off, as many as the Lord our God will call to Himself*" (Acts 2:39). Here, at this critical turning point in the history of redemption, on the day of the Spirit's outpouring at Pentecost, Peter reaffirms the Old Testament covenant promise. In the first sermon preached in the epoch of the founding of the church after Pentecost, the apostle embraces the old covenant promise, which includes the children of believing parents and also all the families of the earth to whom the promise of life and salvation in Christ will be extended.

Far from there being any hint of restriction on the covenant's reach—as though children are now being excluded, whereas previously they were included—the apostle Peter clearly announces the greater embrace and richer extension of God's promise than had previously been the case. The promise is not only for believers, but also for the children of believers. And it is not only for the children of believers, but also for all those among the families and peoples of the earth whom God will reach with the promise of salvation in Christ.

Although this may not be the "proof text" that Baptists are looking for—it does not state that the children of believing parents are to be baptized, nor does it give an account of the baptism of such children—it provides strong evidence nonetheless. The language of this text has no apparent significance apart from what it assumes, namely, that God's grace was always extended to believers and their children, from generation to generation, incorporating them into his household and numbering them among his beloved children. Wrested from its natural home within the context of the biblical theology of the covenant of grace, this passage would be an inexplicable "bolt out of the blue." However, when it is read against the background of the old covenant administration, it makes perfectly good sense. The Lord is now fulfilling his promise to Abraham and his descendants after him; the promise of salvation in Christ comes to believers, their children, and all the families or peoples of the earth. A more compelling testimony than this is hard to imagine, that the new covenant in Christ continues to embrace believers *and their children.* Only now the promise is more clearly revealed to embrace all whom the Lord God is calling into fellowship with himself through Christ.

Answering Two Common Objections

In the history of the debate between paedobaptists and Baptists, many different kinds of arguments have been employed. Advocates of one or the other position have adduced a variety of exegetical, historical, and theological considerations to support their position. Many of these considerations are addressed more fully in other contributions to this volume. However, two common Baptist objections to the paedobaptist position are particularly relevant to the subject of this chapter: covenant theology and the baptism of believers' children. So to conclude our summary of covenant theology and baptism, we will briefly note these objections and the covenantal or paedobaptist response to them.

Paedobaptism and Nominalism

One of the most frequent objections to paedobaptism is the claim that it encourages nominalism and complacency on the part of those who are baptized. The children of believing parents are at the time of their baptism incapable of the kind of faith and repentance required for receiving the gospel promise and its corresponding obligation. Their incorporation into Christ and the fellowship of his body, therefore, occurs without their believing reception of the gospel promise or consent to its obligations. As a practical matter, this means that unbelieving and impenitent persons are admitted to the church, the body of Christ, without having experienced the regenerating work of the Holy Spirit evidenced in conversion. Churches that practice infant baptism, for this reason, cannot avoid including a whole class of persons in the church who are Christians in name only, and not in truth. The historical problem of what is sometimes called a "halfway covenant" illustrates the undesirable consequences of this practice. In this arrangement, nominal members of the church, who have given no visible confirmation of the regenerating work of the Holy Spirit, are permitted to present their children for baptism. And even though Reformed churches expressly repudiate the idea of sacramental regeneration, as though the sacrament worked salvation *ex opere operato* ("by virtue of the work performed"), the practice of paedobaptism invariably encourages the notion that the children are automatically saved. When the rite of Christian baptism is administered to children, nominalism and complacency are never far behind.

There are several points that need to be made in reply to this objection. First, there is a difference between the proper use of the sacrament of baptism and its improper use. Unless it can be demonstrated that nominalism is a necessary and inherent feature of the paedobaptist view, this objection only addresses the improper practice of many churches that baptize the children of believing parents, but fail to emphasize the obligations of baptism. However, nothing that we have seen in the covenant theology undergirding the practice of paedobaptism encourages nominalism. The sacramental sign and seal of incorporation into the fellowship of Christ always demands the response of faith and repentance from believers and their children. The privileges of covenant membership do not diminish, but rather accentuate, the responsibilities of the covenant. The sacrament of baptism, whether administered to adult believers or to the children of believers, places all of its recipients under the same gracious promise and corresponding obligations. Admittedly, the term *infant baptism* may inappropriately suggest that the sacrament of baptism, when administered to the children of believing parents, has a different meaning than when it is administered to adult believers. However, it cannot be too strongly emphasized that baptism signifies and seals the same promises to, and places the same demands upon, the children of adult believers as it does upon adult believers.

Second, the argument that infant baptism encourages nominalism could equally well be used against the Old Testament practice of circumcision. If baptizing the children of believing parents in the new covenant encourages a complacent and nominal view of covenant membership, then the circumcising of the children of believing parents in the old covenant would likewise have encouraged the same complacency and nominalism. However, as we have seen in our consideration of the respective significance of circumcision and baptism, these sacraments equally emphasize the privileges and responsibilities of the covenant relationship.

And third, the practice of believer's baptism does not ensure against nominalism. Insisting that faith and repentance, as subjective attestations of the regenerating work of the Holy Spirit, are prerequisite to baptism does not protect the church from baptizing those whose faith and repentance are counterfeit. All the true marks of regeneration, including faith and repentance, can be counterfeited, and no church or believer has the capacity, which alone belongs to God, to discriminate infallibly between the true and the untrue. There is nothing, therefore, in the Baptist position that provides a hedge against the sacrament of baptism being administered to nonregenerate persons. There is no lack of historical evidence that Baptist churches often tolerate nominalism on the part of their baptized church members. Baptist churches do not prevent nominalism by practicing believer's baptism any more than Reformed churches encourage nominalism by practicing paedobaptism.

Paedobaptism and Baptismal Regeneration

One of the great difficulties in the dispute between paedobaptists and Baptists is the difficulty of mutual understanding. The paedobaptist position is, as we have argued, the fruit of a broadly covenantal understanding of the Scriptures. It is framed by a coherent set of convictions regarding the substantial unity of the covenant of grace throughout the course of the history of redemption, and the nature of the sacraments as God-appointed signs and seals of the covenant promise. The Baptist position, by contrast, is the fruit of a quite different set of convictions about the covenant of grace in its diverse administrations. Within the framework of the Baptist position, the old and new covenants substantially diverge in their promises and demands. They also substantially diverge in their sacraments. Furthermore, the Baptist view of the sacraments insists that they are primarily means to attest the faith and repentance of their recipients. They are means of confirming the subjective spiritual state of believers. By means of the sacraments, *believers address God and others.* This is quite far removed from the paedobaptist conviction that, in the sacraments, *God addresses his people*—believers and their children and as many as he calls to himself.

It is essential to bear this in mind, when considering another common Baptist objection to paedobaptism, namely, that it implies a doctrine of baptismal regeneration. According to this objection, the chief reason why paedobaptism encourages nominalism is that it presumes the regeneration of the children of believing parents, apart from their conscious and subjective response to the call of the gospel. Despite the paedobaptist insistence that the sacraments do not work *ex opere operato,* and despite the Reformed churches' insistence that baptized children must respond to their baptism in faith and repentance, the Baptist suspects the paedobaptist of harboring a doctrine of baptismal regeneration. The Reformed practice of infant baptism, in their view, betrays a continuing commitment to the kind of sacramentalism that is taught by the Roman Catholic and Lutheran churches. However many disclaimers the paedobaptist might make to this objection, the Baptist regards the paedobaptist position as a veiled form of baptismal regeneration.

The problem with this objection is that it reflects a fundamentally different view of the sacraments of the covenant of grace than that taught within the framework of covenant theology. Because the Baptist views the sacrament of baptism as an attestation of the regeneration and conversion of the person who is baptized, he assumes that the paedobaptist regards the baptism of an infant as an attestation of the child's regeneration. However, this represents a fundamental misapprehension of the covenantal view. The doctrine of the covenant, so far as it undergirds the practice of infant baptism, teaches that *the only ground for administering the sacrament is that of covenant membership.* Adult believers and their children are baptized for the same reason—because the Lord is pleased to signify and seal to them that they belong to him and his people, are recipients of his gracious promise in Christ, and are under the obligations of love and fidelity toward him. When we ask whether a person should be baptized, the question is not whether he is truly regenerate (which only God knows), but whether he is one to whom God addresses the promise and demand of the covenant.

Warfield, therefore, put it correctly, as well as succinctly, when he summarized the covenantal argument for paedobaptism: "God established His church in the days of Abraham and put children into it. They must remain there until He puts them out. He has nowhere put them out. They are still then members of His Church and as such entitled to its ordinances."

11

Infant Baptism in the Reformed Confessions

LYLE D. BIERMA

The case for covenantal infant baptism cannot be made with an appeal to the Reformed confessions alone. For one thing, confessions are ecclesiastical interpretations of Scripture, not Scripture itself. Although they carry authority in the denominations that subscribe to them, one may never "consider human writings . . . equal to the divine writings" or put anything "above the truth of God" as found in the "infallible rule" of Holy Scripture (Belgic Confession, art. 7). Furthermore, confessions contain only brief summaries, not detailed expositions, of the major themes of Scripture. A teaching as complex and disputed as infant baptism requires much more in the way of exegetical and theological analysis than confessions can provide.

Nevertheless, the Reformed confessions of the sixteenth and seventeenth centuries *support* the case for covenantal infant baptism in at least three ways. First, as statements of faith adopted by Reformed and Presbyterian communities around the world, they provide reliable summaries of what tens of millions of Christians have believed about infant baptism for centuries. Second, as relatively brief surveys of biblical teaching, they help one to see the connections between covenantal baptism and other major themes of the Christian faith. With confessions, one is less prone than with longer theological works to miss the forest because of the trees. Finally, as responses in part to Anabaptist criticism of paedobaptism in the sixteenth century, these confessions offer instruction in how to meet similar challenges to this doctrine in our own time.

An overview of baptismal teaching in all the Reformed confessions would take us far beyond the space allotted. Even partial collections of these documents fill entire books.[1] What we shall do in this chapter, therefore, is examine five of the most prominent of these confessions, representing different national families of Reformed Protestantism in the sixteenth and seventeenth centuries: the Belgic Confession (Low Countries, 1561), the Heidelberg Catechism (Germany, 1563), the Second Helvetic Confession (Switzerland, 1566), and the Westminster Confession of Faith and Larger Catechism (England and Scotland, 1647, 1648).[2] After quoting and briefly commenting on the paragraphs that discuss infant baptism in each confession, we shall look at some of the common themes running through these texts and then at the broader theological contexts in which they are located.

TEXTS AND HISTORICAL NOTES

Belgic Confession, Article 34

> . . . For that reason we detest the error of the Anabaptists, who are not content with a single baptism once received and also condemn the baptism of the children of believers. We believe our children ought to be baptized and sealed with the sign of the covenant, as little children were

1. One such partial collection, E. F. K. Müller's *Die Bekenntnisschriften der reformierten Kirche* (Leipzig: Deichert, 1903), is 976 pages long.

2. For an introduction to the different Reformed families, see Jan Rohls, *Reformed Confessions: Theology from Zurich to Barmen*, trans. John Hoffmeyer, Columbia Series in Reformed Theology (Louisville: Westminster John Knox, 1997), 9–28.

> circumcised in Israel on the basis of the same promises made to our children.
>
> And truly, Christ has shed his blood no less for washing the little children of believers than he did for adults. Therefore, they ought to receive the sign and sacrament of what Christ has done for them, just as the Lord commanded in the law that by offering a lamb for them the sacrament of the suffering and death of Christ would be granted them shortly after their birth. This was the sacrament of Jesus Christ.[3]
>
> Furthermore, baptism does for our children what circumcision did for the Jewish people. That is why Paul calls baptism the "circumcision of Christ" (Colossians 2:12).[4]

The Belgic Confession (BC) was composed in 1559 and published in 1561 by Guido de Brès (1522–1567), a Reformed pastor from the French-speaking part of the Low Countries (today's southern Belgium). At the time, Lowlands Protestants were experiencing intense persecution at the hands of their Roman Catholic ruler, Philip II of Spain, and de Brès himself was imprisoned and hanged for his role in the Protestant cause. Much of the BC was patterned after the French Gallican Confession (1559), whose primary author, John Calvin, had once been de Brès's teacher in Geneva. Not long after its publication and translation from French into Dutch, the BC was formally recognized by several synods as a confessional standard for the Reformed churches in the Low Countries.

The term "Anabaptists" (literally, "rebaptizers") in the excerpt above was applied pejoratively in the sixteenth century to a variety of individuals and groups who sought a more radical reform of the church than the Lutherans and Zwinglians had undertaken. In renouncing the Anabaptist rejection of paedobaptism, de Brès was defending what

3. The allusion here is to Lev. 12:6. Cf. Luke 2:22–24.

4. This translation of a 1619 French text of the Belgic Confession was made by the Christian Reformed Church in North America and adopted by the CRC Synod of 1985. It can be found in *Ecumenical Creeds and Reformed Confessions* (Grand Rapids: CRC Publications, 1988), 78–120 (quotation, pp. 113–14).

he considered an important biblical truth. At the same time, he was trying to convince the Roman Catholic authorities that Reformed Protestants should not be identified with Anabaptists, who in that day were commonly (though often unfairly) considered as threats to the existing social and political order.

Heidelberg Catechism, Question 74

Q. Should infants, too, be baptized?

A. Yes. For they as well as adults belong to God's covenant and community (Genesis 17:7) and no less than adults are promised forgiveness of sin through Christ's blood (Matthew 19:14) and the Holy Spirit, who produces faith (Psalm 22:10; Isaiah 44:1–3; Luke 1:15; Acts 2:39–39; 16:31).

Therefore, they, too, ought to be incorporated into the Christian church by baptism, the sign of the covenant, and distinguished from the children of unbelievers (Acts 10:47; 1 Corinthians 7:14). This was done in the Old Testament by circumcision (Genesis 17:9–14), in whose place baptism was instituted in the New Testament (Colossians 2:11–13).[5]

The Heidelberg Catechism (HC) was named after the capital city of the Palatinate, one of the major territories of the German Empire. The catechism was commissioned by the ruler of the Palatinate, Frederick III, was very likely composed by Heidelberg professor Zacharias Ursinus (1534–1583) in cooperation with a committee of theologians and churchmen, and was adopted as a confessional standard and teaching guide by a Palatinate synod in 1563. It was soon translated from German into Dutch, and was recognized by various Dutch synods as a confession also for the Reformed churches in the Netherlands. Eventually it became the most widely translated and circulated Reformation confession in the world.

5. This translation of the German text of the Heidelberg Catechism was made by the Christian Reformed Church in North America and adopted by the CRC Synod of 1975. It can be found in *Ecumenical Creeds and Reformed Confessions,* 12–77 (quotation, p. 44). I have made a few alterations to the translation of answer 74, based on my own reading of the German text.

Although usually characterized as a Reformed catechism, the HC represented an attempt by Frederick III to build a theological consensus in his territory by blending certain Reformed emphases with the doctrinal tradition of the Lutheran Augsburg Confession. His discomfort with theological labels is reflected in question 74, quoted above, which strongly suggests, but never states, that it is addressing the Anabaptist view of baptism.

Second Helvetic Confession, Chapter 20

> 6. We condemn the Anabaptists, who deny that young infants, born of faithful parents, are to be baptized. For, according to the doctrine of the gospel, "for of such is the kingdom of God" (Luke 18:16), and they are written in the covenant of God (Acts 3:25). Why, then, should not the sign of the covenant of God be given to them? Why should they not be consecrated by holy baptism, who are God's peculiar people and are in the Church of God? We condemn also the Anabaptists in the rest of those peculiar opinions which they hold against the Word of God. We therefore are not Anabaptists, neither do we agree with them in any point that is theirs.[6]

Of the five confessions before us, this one certainly contains the strongest polemic against the Anabaptists. That is hardly surprising when one considers that both the Anabaptists and the Second Helvetic Confession (SHC) had their roots in the northern Swiss Reformation. The Anabaptists were an offshoot of the Zwinglian reform party in Zurich, breaking with Zwingli in the mid-1520s over the issue of paedobaptism and then spreading to other parts of Europe during the ensuing Protestant persecution. The SHC was composed originally in 1562 as a personal confession by Heinrich Bullinger (1504–75), Zwingli's successor at the helm of the Zurich Reformation. A revision of the confession was adopted four years later by sev-

6. Joel R. Beeke and Sinclair B. Ferguson, eds., *Reformed Confessions Harmonized* (Grand Rapids: Baker, 1999), 218.

eral northern Swiss churches and subsequently by Reformed communities in other parts of the continent.

Westminster Confession of Faith, Chapter 28

4. Not only those that do actually profess faith in and obedience unto Christ (Mark 16:15–16), but also the infants of one, or both believing parents, are to be baptized (Genesis 17:7, 9; Galatians 3:9, 14; Colossians 2:11–12; Acts 2:38–39; Romans 4:11–12; 1 Corinthians 7:14; Matthew 28:19; Mark 10:13–16; Luke 18:15). . . .

6. The efficacy of baptism is not tied to that moment of time wherein it is administered (John 3:5, 8); yet, notwithstanding, by the right use of this ordinance, the grace promised is not only offered, but really exhibited, and conferred, by the Holy Ghost, to such (whether of age or infants) as that grace belongeth unto, according to the counsel of God's own will, in His appointed time (Galatians 3:27; Titus 3:5; Ephesians 5:25–26; Acts 2:38, 41).

Westminster Larger Catechism, Question 166

Q. Unto whom is baptism to be administered?

A. Baptism is not to be administered to any that are out of the visible church, and so strangers from the covenant of promise, till they profess their faith in Christ, and obedience to Him (Acts 8:36–38), but infants descending from parents, either both, or but one of them, professing faith in Christ, and obedience to Him, are in that respect within the covenant, and to be baptized (Genesis 17:7, 9; Galatians 3:9, 14; Colossians 2:11–12; Acts 2:38–39; Romans 4:11–12; 1 Corinthians 7:14; Matthew 28:19; Mark 10:13–16; Luke 18:15; Romans 11:16).[7]

Anabaptists are not named here, and much of the anti-Anabaptist polemic of a century before is gone, but the presence of these lines in the Westminster standards bears witness to the abiding impact of the Anabaptists and the more recent challenge of the English Baptists.

7. Ibid., 217, 219.

The Westminster Confession (WC) and Westminster Larger Catechism (WLC), along with the Westminster Shorter Catechism of 1647, were produced by a gathering of 121 churchmen known as the Westminster Assembly (1643–1648), named for its meeting place at Westminster Abbey in London, England. These men, mostly Presbyterians, were called together by the Puritan-controlled Parliament during the English Civil War to draft proposals for reforming the Church of England. The Westminster standards turned out to have a greater influence in the Church of Scotland, however, and subsequently in Presbyterianism the world over.

COMMON THEMES

As we have seen, the treatment of infant baptism in the Reformed confessions was shaped in large part by the Anabaptist challenge to this doctrine and practice during the Reformation. Two themes in particular in the confessions quoted above are best understood against the background of this challenge: the covenantal unity of the Old and New Testaments, and the unique status of the children of believers. First, the confessions suggest that the Anabaptist and Reformed views of paedobaptism are rooted in fundamentally different approaches to the interpretation of Scripture, especially the relationship between the testaments. All parties of the Reformation, Anabaptists included, held to the principle of *sola Scriptura* ("by Scripture alone"), that is, that Scripture is the ultimate authority in matters of doctrine and life and thus the premier guide for reform of the church. When it came to the application of this principle, however, the parties divided. The Anabaptists perceived a basic disjunction between the Old and New Testaments and a displacement of much of the Old by the New. The primary authority for the church's belief and practice after Christ was the apostolic teaching of the New Testament. The Old Testament remained normative only insofar as its teachings were corroborated by the New. Therefore, since there is clear testimony in the New Testament to adult baptism and none to the baptism of infants, it is obvious what the practice of the Christian church should be.[8]

This line of argument was set forth as early as 1524 in a well-known letter to Thomas Müntzer by Conrad Grebel and his Anabaptist followers in Zurich. The problem with the Lutheran and Zwinglian reformers, the letter states, is that they are still caught up to some extent in Roman Catholic doctrine and ritual. This amounts to a "hiding of the divine word, and the mixing of it with the human."[9] Müntzer (a radical reformer from Germany) should "esteem as good and right only what may be found in pure and clear Scripture. . . . Whatever we are not taught by clear passages or examples must be regarded as forbidden."[10]

When the letter applies this principle to specific issues, however, it is the "divine word" of the New Testament that quickly comes to the fore. Müntzer should abolish the German Mass and the use of German hymns in worship because neither can be found in the New Testament. Instead, he should "act in all things only according to the word, and bring forth and establish by the word *the usages of the apostles*."[11] On the basis of the word, he should establish a Christian church "with the help of Christ and His rule, as we find it instituted in Matthew 18:15–18 and applied in the epistles."[12] Furthermore, Müntzer and his comrades ought not to use the sword for protection or ever engage in war "since all killing has ceased with [true Christian believers]—unless, indeed, we would still be of the old law [i.e., Old Testament]."[13] Finally, baptism as instituted by Christ and described in the New Testament is to be administered to believers only. There are no accounts in the New Testament of children being baptized, and

8. For more on this Anabaptist hermeneutic, see the chapter on Pilgrim Marpeck in David C. Steinmetz, *Reformers in the Wings* (Philadelphia: Fortress, 1971), 219–30.

9. Hans J. Hillerbrand, ed., *The Protestant Reformation* (New York: Harper & Row, 1968), 123–24.

10. Ibid., 124.

11. Ibid., 124–26 (quotation, p. 126; emphasis added).

12. Ibid., 127.

13. Ibid.

thus "infant baptism is a senseless, blasphemous abomination, contrary to all Scripture."[14]

The Reformed confessions, however, take a much different approach to the relationship between the testaments and to the normativity of the Old Testament for the church after Pentecost. Whereas the Anabaptists saw a basic disjunction between the Old and New Testaments, the confessions recognize a substantial unity between them, on the basis of which Old Testament teachings and practices are regarded as normative unless rescinded, replaced, or fulfilled in the New Testament.

This unity of Scripture and continuity within the history of redemption is alluded to in the confessions, even before their treatment of baptism. The church of Christ, for example, is not just a New Testament phenomenon, but "has existed from the beginning of the world and will last to the end" (BC, 27; cf. HC, 54; SHC, 17.1). The gospel, too, is not just good news on the lips of Jesus and the apostles in the New Testament. God revealed it already in Paradise after the Fall, proclaimed it by the patriarchs and prophets of the Old Testament, and even "portrayed it by the sacrifices and other ceremonies of the law" (HC, 19).

When it comes to the doctrine of baptism, all five confessions find evidence of the unity of Scripture in an eternal, trans-testamental covenant established by God with Abraham and his descendants in Genesis 17. Right from the beginning, children were included in the covenant community (HC, SHC) and received the sign of the covenant promises (BC, HC). The covenant sign has changed from circumcision to baptism in the New Testament age (BC, HC), but the covenant community is still intact and the promises remain the same (WLC, BC, HC). Hence, "our children ought to be baptized and sealed with the sign of the covenant, as little children were circumcised in Israel on the basis of the same promises made to our children" (BC).

The implication here is that one cannot deny infant baptism on the basis of the silence of the New Testament. The Old Testament is un-

14. Ibid., 127–28 (quotation, p. 128).

mistakable in its command to apply the sign of the covenant to infants, and that command has never been rescinded. From this perspective, therefore, it is not first of all the responsibility of the confessions to show where in the New Testament infant baptism is commanded; it is the responsibility of the Anabaptists to show where in the New Testament the fundamental covenant structures established in the Old Testament were overturned.[15]

The first common theme running through these confessional texts, then, is the covenantal basis for infant baptism. The second is the unique status that baptized covenant infants enjoy. When de Brès states at the end of BC, 34 that "baptism does for our children what circumcision did for the Jewish people," one of the things he likely has in mind is his assertion at the beginning of the article that "by [baptism] we are received into God's church and set apart from all other people and alien religions, that we may be dedicated entirely to him, bearing his mark and sign." The HC declares that infants, who like adults "belong to God's covenant and community . . . ought [also] to be incorporated into the Christian church by baptism, the sign of the covenant, and distinguished from the children of unbelievers." The SHC speaks of covenant infants, "who are God's peculiar people and are in the Church of God," being "consecrated," or set apart, by baptism. Finally, the WLC asserts that children of professing believers are not among those outside the visible church or "strangers from the covenant of promise."

All of the confessions except the BC state explicitly that children of believing parents are part of the covenant community even before their baptism. They also speak with one voice about baptism as a formal consecration, or setting apart, of covenant children from unbe-

15. Cf. John Murray, *Christian Baptism* (Philadelphia: OPC Committee on Christian Education, 1952), 52–53: "Has [the OT covenant relation] been discontinued? Our answer to these questions must be that we find no evidence of revocation. In view of the Abrahamic covenant, in view of the basic identity of meaning attaching to circumcision and baptism, in view of the unity and continuity of the covenant [of] grace administered in both dispensations, we can affirm with confidence, that evidence of revocation or repeal is mandatory if the practice or principle has been discontinued under the New Testament."

lievers outside the community. The only apparent difference among these confessions has to do with *when* covenant children become members of the institutional church. Two of them indicate that such children are "received" (BC) or "incorporated" (HC) into the Christian church at the time of their baptism, and a third defines the purpose of baptism as in part "the solemn admission of the party baptized into the visible Church" (WC, 28.1). The SHC, too, states that "to be baptized in the name of Christ is to be enrolled, entered, and received into the covenant and family . . . of the sons of God" (20.2), but it then goes on to claim that covenant children are "in the Church of God" even before their baptism (20.6). Similarly, the WLC declares that by baptism one is "solemnly admitted into the visible church" (165), and yet implies that the infants of at least one believing parent may be baptized because they are already inside the visible church (166). How is this discrepancy to be understood? Most likely, the SHC and WLC are using "covenant" and "visible church" in more than one sense here, that is, sometimes to mean the church as an institution and at other times the church as the organic people of God. Thus, one could be officially admitted to the visible church as an institution while already a part of the community of God's people (WLC). One could be formally enrolled in the institutional covenant community by baptism, while already a member of the covenant people of God by virtue of being born to believing parents (SHC).

In any case, at first glance this language of being set apart from other people, distinguished from unbelievers, specially marked, and peculiar, may seem somewhat self-serving and conceited. But when viewed against the background of the Anabaptist challenge to paedobaptism, the reason for such language becomes clearer. It reflects a concern on the part of the Reformed about the implications of the Anabaptist doctrine of the church. If, as the Anabaptists claimed, the church is a voluntary association of believers, and membership in the church is restricted to those who have been baptized following a profession of repentance and faith, what then is the status of the children of these believers? Does not Anabaptist teaching imply that they are outside of the church? If so, are they then to be reckoned as unbelievers and pagans? Or do they belong to some third category alongside of believers and unbelievers? These are the troubling questions that the confessional language of distinction, consecration, and peculiarity was intending to address. This language reflects a conviction that nowhere in Scripture, Old or New Testament, are children considered as anything other than full members of the covenant community. They are not the same as children of unbelievers or those outside of the visible church. Rather, by their baptism they are formally recognized as members of a peculiar people, a special community in which God has promised to work graciously through the corporate relationships in which his people exist and to extend his salvation through the generations.[16]

THEOLOGICAL CONTEXT

To understand the doctrine of infant baptism in the Reformed confessions, we need to look not only at the articles or questions that deal specifically with this doctrine, but also at the contexts in the confessions in which these articles and questions appear. The first thing to notice is that the treatment of infant baptism in each confession forms a relatively small part of a section on baptism in general. In the English translation that we are using of the BC, for example, the subject of infant baptism takes up just twenty-seven lines of a ninety-two-line article on baptism. The HC treats it in only one of six questions and answers devoted to baptism, and the WLC in only one of three. In the SHC, finally, just one of six subsections in the chapter on baptism is devoted to paedobaptism, and in the WC, one of seven (along with a passing reference in another). Except in the Westminster standards, infant baptism is not mentioned until the very end of the article or section on the general doctrine of Christian baptism.

16. Cf. Peter Y. De Jong, *The Church's Witness to the World* (Pella, Ia.: Pella Publishing, 1960–62), 2:367–69, and G. C. Berkouwer, *The Sacraments,* trans. Hugo Bekker (Grand Rapids: Eerdmans, 1969), 173–74.

When we take into account the controversy surrounding paedobaptism during the Reformation and the complex biblical and theological issues it raises, it might seem surprising that the confessions actually devote so little space to this doctrine. But the proportion of space is significant. It suggests that from the perspective of the confessions, there is no such thing as a separate doctrine of infant baptism, only a doctrine of baptism—a baptism of which adults and infants alike are the legitimate recipients. Whether one is an adult being baptized after conversion or an infant being baptized before conversion, the situation is basically the same. "Christ has shed his blood no less for washing the little children of believers than he did for adults" (BC). As the HC says, both "belong to God's covenant and community and . . . are promised forgiveness of sin . . . and the Holy Spirit, who produces faith." Both are called to embrace those promises by faith, the adult immediately and the infant as he or she grows older. Both are saved, not by their baptism, but by God's grace as they live in faith and obedience as members of the covenant community. The confessions speak of only one doctrine of baptism, therefore, because there is only one covenant, one people of God, one promise, one set of conditions, and one covenantal sign—for adults and children alike.

In all these confessions, then, the doctrine of infant baptism is presented in the context of baptism in general. Baptism, in turn, is treated in the context of the doctrine of the sacraments. To gain a greater appreciation for the Reformed doctrine of paedobaptism, therefore, one must understand something of the broader confessional teaching on the sacraments in general.

The sacramental teaching of the confessions is often misunderstood, even by some in the Reformed tradition itself. For example, in *Infant Baptism and the Covenant of Grace,* Baptist theologian Paul Jewett presents a caricature of the Reformed view of the sacraments in an attempt to show the differences between the Reformed and the Lutheran doctrines of baptism. Using as his authority a Lutheran doctrinal statement from 1592, Jewett portrays the sacraments in the Reformed view as simply outward signs and seals of the inward grace to which they point. Hence, "baptism merely signifies inward ablution; . . . it does not work regeneration, faith, and grace, but only signifies and seals them; . . . [and] salvation does not depend on baptism, so that when a minister of the church is not available, the infant should be permitted to die without baptism."[17]

What Jewett fails to take into account is that the position of the Reformed confessions is more nuanced than that. One is not limited to the options of mere signification and sealing, on the one hand, and guaranteed conferral of grace, on the other. According to the confessions, the sacraments are means of grace, "visible signs and seals," as the BC puts it, "of something internal and invisible, *by means of which God works in us* through the power of the Holy Spirit. So they are not empty and hollow signs" (BC, 33; emphasis added). By the working of the Holy Spirit and the blessing of Christ, the sacraments "become effectual means of salvation" (WLC, 161).

Of course, the signs and seals are not to be confused with the spiritual reality that they convey. The outward washing of baptism, for example, does not itself wash away sins; only Jesus' blood and the Holy Spirit do that (HC, 72). Nor do the sacraments automatically confer grace upon all who receive them (BC; WC, 28.5). In the case of baptism, once again, we are not given a guarantee of what has happened or will happen to a particular individual, but only of what God has done and will do for his covenant people as a community. Nor, finally, is the efficacy of baptism necessarily tied to the moment when it is administered. The regeneration of elect covenant infants that is signified and sealed in baptism can take place before or after their baptism without detracting from its efficacy. Nevertheless, the relationship between the signs of the sacraments and the reality they signify is such that they do serve as occasions on which God has chosen to offer, exhibit, and, in his own time, bestow his promised grace (WC). There may be exceptional circumstances in which God performs this gracious work apart from these means (cf. WC, 10.3), but Christ has instituted them

17. Paul K. Jewett, *Infant Baptism and the Covenant of Grace* (Grand Rapids: Eerdmans, 1978), 77–80 (quotation, pp. 79–80).

for our use, and deliberately to neglect them can only be construed as "a great sin" (WC, 28.5).[18]

The sacraments as means of grace, however, can only be understood as part of the broader doctrine of the church in the Reformed confessions. The BC, for example, stresses the importance of distinguishing the true church from the false church (BC, 29), because the true church is "the gathering of those who are saved and there is no salvation apart from it" (BC, 28; cf. WC, 25.2). The primary operations of divine grace take place in the church, or covenant community, through the word and sacrament. That is why the BC lists the pure preaching of the word and the pure administration of the sacraments as the first two "marks" by which the true church is identified. The true church, as the gathering of the saved, is distinguished first and foremost by the right use of the means that God has chosen to form this community. To withdraw from this church, therefore, or not to join it in the first place, is not simply an act of disobedience; it places in jeopardy one's very salvation (BC, 28).

If the confessions place the doctrine of infant baptism in the context of baptism in general, and place baptism in general in the context of the sacraments, and place the sacraments in the context of the church, then they locate the doctrine of the church in the larger context of God's sovereign work of salvation. According to HC, 54, "The Son of God, through his Spirit and word, gathers, protects, and preserves for himself a community elected for eternal life." In this view, the church is not a voluntary association of baptized believers, but a divinely established community of those whom the Father has elected from eternity, the Son has atoned for in his death, and the Spirit irresistibly regenerates and leads to faith. It is in and through the church and her means of grace that this divine plan of salvation is implemented.

The baptism of infants is fully in keeping with this emphasis in the Reformed confessions on the sovereignty of grace in salvation. Divine election, the ultimate ground of our salvation, is unconditional; that

18. Cf. Cornelis Venema, "Sacraments and Baptism in the Reformed Confessions," *Mid-America Journal of Theology* 11 (2000): 72–78.

is, it is not conditioned upon any merits or acts or claims of human beings. Likewise, it is only at God's initiative that the covenant community of the saved is called into being and continues to exist. It is fitting, then, that baptism—as a sign and seal of God's promises of salvation and of his placement of the baptized into the arena where he brings these promises to fruition—be viewed first of all as something that God does. Baptism is primarily God's speaking to us, not our speaking to him. It is there that *he* signifies and seals an operation of grace that *he* performs in the context of a community that *he* has established. How can this salvation *sola gratia* ("by grace alone") be any more graphically demonstrated than in the baptism of a tiny covenant child—helpless, uncomprehending, and wholly incapable of any meritorious work? Infant baptism sets before the church in sacramental shorthand the entire doctrine of God's sovereignty in the salvation of the elect.[19]

In conclusion, the defense of infant baptism in the Reformed confessions and the rejection of the Anabaptist view do not rest on the interpretation of a few disputed biblical texts. Rather, they are based on a comprehensive perspective on the flow of redemptive history, on an emphasis on the communal dimensions of God's gracious dealings with his people, and on a web of interconnected doctrines relating to divine election, the church, the sacraments, and the meaning of baptism. From the viewpoint of the confessions, infant baptism is not, in the last analysis, simply a doctrine about baptism. It is about God's work of salvation by grace alone as it comes to expression in the midst of his covenant community.

19. For an extended discussion of the doctrine of baptism in the context of God's sovereign work of salvation, see Geoffrey W. Bromiley, *Children of the Promise: The Case for Baptizing Infants* (Grand Rapids: Eerdmans, 1979), 38–51, and Richard A. Muller, "How Many Points?" *Calvin Theological Journal* 28 (1993): 425–33.

12

Infant Baptism in History: An Unfinished Tragicomedy

PETER J. LEITHART

Written early in the third century, Tertullian's homily *On Baptism* provides the first undisputed evidence for infant baptism.[1] It is ironic that this evidence comes from Tertullian (born ca. 160), since he cautioned against infant baptism, just as he urged the unmarried to delay baptism until they had developed habits of continence. To be sure, Tertullian believed that infants were validly baptized, but he thought that the practice was unnecessary and dangerous. Infants have no need of baptism, for "why should innocent infancy hurry to the remission of sins?" Besides, baptizing infants burdens them with duties that they cannot keep and places them in

1. All the evidence prior to Tertullian is disputed, and there is no agreement on the implications of Tertullian's statements. Key contributions to the debate include Oscar Cullmann, *Baptism in the New Testament,* trans. J. K. S. Reid (London: SCM, 1950); Kurt Aland, *Did the Early Church Baptize Infants?* trans. G. R. Beasley-Murray (London: SCM, 1963); Joachim Jeremias, *Infant Baptism in the First Four Centuries,* trans. David Cairns (London: SCM, 1960); Joachim Jeremias, *The Origins of Infant Baptism: A Further Study in Reply to Kurt Aland,* trans. Dorothea M. Barton (London: SCM, 1963).

grave danger: "If [people] understand the obligations of baptism, they will fear more receiving than delaying it."[2]

After Tertullian, references to infant baptism occur regularly. Origen (185–251) claimed that the practice was handed down from the apostles, and he occasionally made comments that anticipated the later Augustinian rationale for infant baptism:

> The little ones are baptized for the forgiveness of sins. Which sins? Or at what time have they sinned? Or how can there be the slightest reason for the baptism of little children, unless it is to be found in the passage: "No one is free from taint, not even he whose life upon earth lasts but a day"? Even little children are baptized. Because the taint which we have from the moment of birth is removed in the sacrament of baptism.[3]

Cyprian (200–258), who served as bishop of Carthage during the last decade of his life, argued strenuously in favor of paedobaptism. Summarizing the decision of a synod held at Carthage in the mid-third century, he wrote:

> In respect of the case of the infants, which you say ought not to be baptized within the second or third day after their birth, and that the law of ancient circumcision should be regarded, so that you think that one who is just born should not be baptized and sanctified within the eighth day, we all thought very differently in our council. For in this course which you thought was to be taken, no one agreed; but we all rather judge that the mercy and grace of God is not to be refused to any one born of man. . . . And therefore, dearest brother, this was our opinion in council, that by us no one ought to be hindered from baptism and from the grace of God, who is merciful and kind and loving to all. Which, since it is to be observed and maintained in respect of all, we think is

2. Tertullian, *On Baptism,* 18, in *Tertullian's Homily on Baptism,* ed. Ernest Evans (London: SPCK, 1964).

3. Quoted in Burkhard Neunheuser, *Baptism and Confirmation* (Montreal: Palm, 1964), 70–71. Origen's claim that infant baptism was apostolic may be found in his homilies on Romans (5.9) and Leviticus (8.3).

> to be even more observed in respect of infants and newly-born persons, who on this very account deserve more from our help and from the divine mercy, that immediately, on the very beginning of their birth, lamenting and weeping, they do nothing else but entreat.[4]

Cyprian's logic is intriguing, and points to some of the wider issues in the debate concerning infant baptism. For Cyprian, baptism is extended to infants because the grace of God embraces all. Infant baptism is justified by an appeal to the universal grace found in the gospel and by the fact that the church embraces all who are "born of man." The community of the reborn is as wide as the community of the born.

Despite these testimonies, Tertullian's cautions reflect a widespread resistance to infant baptism, and "believers' baptism must have been frequent well into the fourth century." Many of the church fathers, including some (like Augustine) who had Christian parents, "were not baptized until the end of their student days."[5] Still, by the time of Augustine's fifth-century disputes with Pelagius, infant baptism was sufficiently well-established that Augustine could base his arguments on the fact of a commonly accepted practice. And in the sixth century, Justinian made infant baptism mandatory within the Christian empire. In the East, paedobaptism has remained the rule to the present day. Detractors of infant baptism reappeared periodically in the medieval West, and again in the Reformation, but throughout most of church history most of the church has accepted infant baptism.

That, in brief compass, is the shape of the story. Identifying the genre of the story, however, depends on one's assumptions about God's will for Christian baptism.[6] For Baptists, the story is definitely a tragedy.

4. Cyprian, "Epistle LVIII," in *The Ante-Nicene Fathers,* ed. Alexander Roberts and James Donaldson, vol. 5 (reprint, Grand Rapids: Eerdmans, 1971), 353–54.

5. Everett Ferguson, "Baptism," in *Encyclopedia of Early Christianity,* ed. Everett Ferguson (New York: Garland, 1980), 133. Ferguson lists Basil, Gregory of Nyssa, Gregory of Nazianzus, John Chrysostom, Ephraim the Syrian, Jerome, Rufinus, and Augustine as examples of delayed baptism.

6. Wider questions are implicit here, since the genre of the story of patristic Christianity turns on the question of infant baptism: Did the church "fall" into paedobaptism and proto-

Infant baptism became established because of "alien influences" in the church, which transformed baptism into either a magical ritual or a "mere sign," and in either case baptism and the gospel were diminished.[7] Infant baptism is a "wound" in the body of Christ, a "hole" in baptismal practice, an arbitrary and despotic rite.[8] Paedobaptists, by contrast, normally tell the story as one of straightforward continuity: The apostolic practice of infant baptism, reflected in various ways in the New Testament, continued undisturbed throughout two silent centuries, after which the apostolic practice became more openly discussed and more firmly grounded. According to this story line, opponents of infant baptism, such as Tertullian, were aberrations, and the story is pure comedy. Samuel Miller expressed this view with remarkable rhetorical force: "I can assure you, my friends, with the utmost candour and confidence, after much inquiry on the subject, that, for more than fifteen hundred years after the birth of Christ, there was not a single society on earth, who opposed infant baptism on any thing like the grounds which distinguish our Baptist brethren."[9]

Perhaps additional evidence will one day turn up to clarify the practice of the church between the apostles and Tertullian. Given the evidence that we currently have, however, neither the comic nor the tragic version of the story makes sense. The Baptist story of tragedy cannot account for the opening chapters of the story—namely, the biblical evidence in favor of paedobaptism. A sudden shift from inclusion of infants in Israel to exclusion of infants from the new Israel would have left identifiable skid marks on the historical record. There are none. Paedobaptists, on the other hand, have not fully acknowledged the weight of the evidence against the universality of infant bap-

---

Catholicism at the end of the patristic age, or was the establishment of medieval Christendom (liturgically founded on the baptism of infants) a fulfillment of the gospel?

7. See, for example, G. R. Beasley-Murray, *Baptism in the New Testament* (Grand Rapids: Eerdmans, 1962), chap. 6, esp. pp. 352–92.

8. Karl Barth, *The Teaching of the Church regarding Baptism,* trans. Ernest A. Payne (London: SCM, 1969), 41.

9. Samuel Miller, *Infant Baptism Scriptural and Reasonable* (Philadelphia: Presbyterian Board of Publication, 1834), reprinted as appendix A in Robert R. Booth, *Children of the Promise: The Biblical Case for Infant Baptism* (Phillipsburg, N.J.: P&R, 1995), 167–80.

tism. If the story is one of pure continuity, how does one explain the practice of delaying baptism, which was (apparently) widespread well into the fourth century? How are the early postapostolic liturgies, which clearly assume believer's baptism, to be explained? And, if the church practiced infant baptism virtually without contest, why was confirmation the key to initiation in the medieval church?

Even Miller's confident statement is less than it seems; he does not claim that paedobaptism was universally practiced, but only that those who opposed infant baptism did not oppose it on the same grounds as modern Baptists. And even this is inaccurate. Gregory of Nazianzus, who, like Tertullian, encouraged people to delay baptism, granted that it is permissible to baptize children, provided that they can "take in something of the mystery, and answer . . . , and even if they do not yet understand fully, can nevertheless retain some impression."[10] That sounds a lot like a modern Baptist argument.

In place of the tragic "fall from original purity" (seen by Baptists) and the comic "continuity of practice from the apostles" (seen by paedobaptists), I propose the following story: Paedobaptism was, as the other essays in this volume indicate, the practice of the apostolic church. Due to "alien influences," the biblical and covenantal rationale was soon lost and the practice was vitiated. Even when infant baptism was eventually established as the universal practice, it was often detached from its biblical and covenantal moorings, so that the historical practice of the church often floated free, full of tensions and internal contradictions. As a result, the practice of the Western churches at least has not been fully paedobaptist for many centuries. My story is still a comedy, but a tragicomedy, a story of tragedy narrowly averted. More precisely, it is an unfinished tragicomedy, since the whole church has not yet embraced the biblical and apostolic practice that included infants in the race of the Last Adam. There are several reasons to prefer this rendition of the story: tragicomedy makes better sense of the evidence, it makes for a better story, and it makes us part of the story.

10. Quoted in Jeremias, *Infant Baptism in the First Four Centuries,* 96.

As indicated in the previous paragraph, one thread of the argument here is that the "alien influences" that affected baptismal practice in the patristic church created pressure *against* rather than in favor of paedobaptism. If, as some Baptists argue, the church succumbed to these influences, one would have expected a Baptist outcome. That paedobaptism triumphed is one of the chief oddities of the story.

Paedobaptism is a classic case of the axiom that "the law of prayer is the law of faith" (*lex orandi, lex credendi*). A practice in search of a justification, infant baptism was the rule long before there was much of a coherent theology to explain why it was done. Evaluating the practice of baptism in the patristic church is thus just as important as summarizing its theology. Accordingly, I will first examine some of the earliest baptismal liturgies to show that they were constructed on something like Baptist assumptions, even when children were included. From that point, I will offer suggestions about the sources of these "alien influences" and conclude by indicating that even the establishment of the paedobaptistic norm was not motivated by fully biblical assumptions.

The prevalence of certain liturgical forms in the early church (such as Easter and Pentecost baptisms) has been greatly exaggerated,[11] but evidence from various locations indicates that adult baptism very early became the model for Christian initiation. The *Apostolic Tradition* is the oldest extant Western liturgical text and was probably written by Hippolytus of Rome (died *ca.* 236) in the late second or early third century. It requires that catechumens be instructed for three years before proceeding to baptism, though for the "zealous" the time period may be waived and replaced by "conversion alone." At the end of the catechumenate, the catechumens pray, are examined with regard to character and acts of mercy, and then move into preparation for the baptism proper. The baptismal rite itself begins with a fast and vigil, and includes verbal renunciation of Satan and confession. Officiants are then instructed, "First baptize the children," and parents and other family mem-

11. For a careful consideration of the evidence, see Paul F. Bradshaw, *The Search for the Origins of Christian Worship: Sources and Methods for the Study of Early Liturgy* (New York: Oxford University Press, 1992).

bers are allowed to speak for children who are "unable to speak for themselves."[12] Although children are included in this ritual, it is clearly designed with adults in mind. It cannot be applied to infants without considerable modifications. Children appear to be included as something of an afterthought, and a surprising afterthought at that.

Syrian evidence points in the same direction. The *Didache* is a second-century Syrian document, and it contains the earliest extrabiblical evidence of early Christian worship. It hints that baptism was normally applied to adults, or at least to children rather than infants.[13] Much of the *Didache* is taken up with an exposition of the "two ways" that are set before the baptized, and most of this ethical instruction assumes that the candidates are adults. One section, for example, gives instruction regarding proper conduct in social relations—husbands with wives, masters with slaves, and the like. Advice is given to parents concerning their conduct toward children, but no instruction is directed to children, a striking omission that is hard to explain if children were expected to hear the instruction (chap. 4).[14] Little is said concerning the baptismal rite itself, but a fast is enjoined: "Thou shalt order the baptized to fast one or two days before" (chap. 7). Clearly, this rite and its preparation were not designed for infants.

Baptismal liturgies in the following centuries remained ill-suited for infants. Although he agrees that infant baptism was practiced throughout the fourth century, Edward Yarnold concludes from his study of the fourth-century baptismal homilies of Cyril (died 387), Ambrose (339–397), and Chrysostom (347–407) that "the impression is inescapable that adult baptism was normal, almost unvariable even, in Jerusalem, Milan, and Antioch." Many details are unclear, but these homilies indicate that catechetical instruction, fasts and vigils, self-examinations, and recitation of creeds and prayers were stan-

12. Hippolytus, *Apostolic Tradition,* 17–20, in Thomas M. Finn, *Early Christian Baptism and the Catechumenate: Italy, North Africa, and Egypt* (Collegeville, Minn.: Liturgical Press, 1992), 47–51.

13. The complete text is found in "The Teaching of the Twelve Apostles," in *The Ante-Nicene Fathers,* ed. Alexander Roberts and James Donaldson, vol. 7 (reprint, Grand Rapids: Eerdmans, 1970), 377–82.

14. Compare Paul's inclusion of exhortations to children in Eph. 6:1–3 and Col. 3:20.

dard elements of preparation for, and performance of, baptism.[15] Cyril of Jerusalem reminds his hearers of the renunciation of Satan and the confession of faith they made at baptism:

> You began by entering the outer room of the baptistery. You faced westward, heard a voice commanding you to stretch out your hand, and renounced Satan to his face. . . . You are told to stretch out your hand, and to address the devil as if he were before you: *I renounce you, Satan. . . .* When you turned from west to east, the region of light, you symbolized this change of allegiance. Then you were told to say: *I believe in the Father, the Son and the Holy Spirit, and in one baptism of repentance.*[16]

Chrysostom describes a similar scene from Antioch:

> Now consider once again the posture of captivity. The priests who introduce you first of all tell you to kneel down and pray with your hands raised to heaven, and by this attitude of body recall to your mind the one from whom you have been delivered and the other whom you are about to join. After that the priest approaches each in turn and demands your contracts and confessions and instructs each one to pronounce those fearful and awesome words: *I renounce you, Satan.*[17]

Elsewhere, Chrysostom makes it clear that children were also initiated into the church at Antioch. In his Easter sermon, he explains that the church baptizes infants "even though they have no sins, that they might gain righteousness, filiation, inheritance, and the grace of being brothers and sisters and members of Christ and the grace of being the dwelling-place of the Holy Spirit."[18] Yet again, it is clear that the rite was designed with adults in mind.

15. Edward Yarnold, *The Awe-Inspiring Rites of Initiation: The Origins of the R.I.C.A.* (Edinburgh: T & T Clark, 1994), 1–54.

16. See text in Yarnold, *Awe-Inspiring Rites of Initiation,* 70–75.

17. Ibid., 158.

18. Quoted in Mark Searle, "Infant Baptism Reconsidered," in *Alternative Futures for Worship,* vol. 2, *Baptism and Confirmation,* ed. Mark Searle (Collegeville, Minn.: Liturgical Press, 1987), 45–46.

In the West, the situation was similar, and it continued into the early medieval period. In Spain, Isidore of Seville (died 636) described a baptismal liturgy that included a catechumen stage for "those who come fresh from gentile surroundings with the wish to believe in Christ" and a renunciation of the devil, adding that "because children are not able to make renunciation themselves, this rite is performed through the hearts and mouths of those who carry them."[19] Many other medieval baptismal orders required parents to renounce Satan and confess faith on behalf of their children, and some medieval liturgies even included instructions for introducing infants into the status of a catechumen, though they were incapable of receiving the kind of instruction originally expected of catechumens.[20] As Peter Cramer says, "One of the great questions raised by the history of baptism" is "how it was that even after the habit of infant baptism had become widespread in the churches of Latin Christendom, the *form of* adult baptism . . . continued largely to prevail."[21]

Inevitably, this disjunction raised questions about the character of infant baptism: Since an infant cannot fast and keep vigil, and cannot renounce Satan and confess his faith, has he really and fully been baptized? The practice of parental confession on behalf of the child (which has no apparent biblical justification) raised the question of whether one can be baptized on the basis of another person's confession. Many of the theological issues that have plagued infant baptism arise from the mixed signals of a baptismal liturgy attempting to apply an adult form to infants. Liturgically, these questions were addressed by shifting much of the significance of baptism to other rites. The early history of confirmation and its association with first communion is somewhat sketchy (see below), but it seems reasonable to see it as a corrective to a defective baptismal practice. The practice of the me-

19. Isidore, *Concerning Ecclesiastical Office,* in *Documents of the Baptismal Liturgy,* by E. C. Whitaker (London: SPCK, 1970), 109–10.

20. For example, see the Sarum Rite, published in Whitaker, *Documents of the Baptismal Liturgy,* 231–53.

21. Peter Cramer, *Baptism and Change in the Early Middle Ages, c. 200–c. 1150* (Cambridge: Cambridge University Press, 1993), 3.

dieval church suggests that the infant, though baptized, was not really initiated into the church until he received catechetical training as a teenager, underwent the "strengthening" or "perfecting" rite of confirmation, and was admitted to the Lord's Table.

If covenantal baptism was practiced by the apostolic church, then this evidence of a departure from, or modification of, apostolic practice must be accounted for. The *Apostolic Tradition* and the *Didache* are very early documents, and their apparent emphasis on adult baptism is therefore difficult to explain. If the apostles advocated the baptism of infants, how did a different model so quickly become the norm? Several possibilities may be suggested. Because of the Jewish persecution of believers, many biblically informed Christians were killed in the period between the resurrection and the destruction of Jerusalem in A.D. 70. Meanwhile, as the church moved out of Palestine into the Greco-Roman world, the gospel, though thoroughly Jewish in origin, was embraced by people with very different fundamental assumptions about the world. Theologically, the difference between Paul and Justin Martyr or Ignatius is evident and striking. Nonbiblical assumptions penetrated the worship of the church.

The "alien influences" on fourth-century baptismal liturgies are easier to identify. Indisputably, one factor was the effect of mystery religions on the theology and vocabulary of Christian initiation. The church fathers expounded the meaning of baptism largely through biblical typology. For Origen, baptism was an exodus through the sea and deliverance from Egypt, a betrothal of the church to Christ that mimics the betrothals of the patriarchs who found their wives "beside the waters," and a cleansing from uncleanness like the cleansing of Naaman the Syrian in the Jordan River.[22] Although these typologies continued to be common currency in the fourth century, another vocabulary came alongside. Beginning with Athanasius (300–373), the language of the mystery religions began to be applied to Christian sacraments.[23] Cyril of Jerusalem used the loaded term *mystagogia* as

22. See Neunheuser, *Baptism and Confirmation*, 67–77.

23. Ibid., 96. Earlier writers had used *mystērion* in a variety of ways, but, according to Neunheuser, Athanasius was apparently the first to apply it to "liturgical actions."

a title for his catechetical homilies. When Chrysostom spoke of the "awesome mysteries" and the "awesome rite of initiation," he was employing phrases that "formed part of the vocabulary of the pagan mystery-religions." And his notion that the sacraments are "mysteries about which it is forbidden to speak" is likewise influenced by the secrecy that attended mystery rites.[24]

It was not only the vocabulary that changed. The elaborate and highly evocative baptismal liturgies evident in the catechetical lectures of the fourth century show striking similarities to initiation rites in the mystery cults. Thomas Finn outlines the stages of initiation into mystery cults in a way that highlights the parallels with Christian liturgies:

> Initiation into the mysteries was not just an isolated happening. The rites demanded attentive preparation, part of which was purificatory (*katharsis*) and part formative. Entry into the group of devotees (*systasis*) was graded. The ancient Eleusinian mysteries, for instance, consisted of two parts. The "Lesser Mysteries," which assembled the candidates for instruction and a test of their worthiness, were celebrated in the spring and involved ritual purification and public sacrifice. The goal of these lesser mystery rites was to prepare the candidates by purification and form the candidates for initiation into the "Greater Mysteries," a ten-day festival held in the fall and consummated in the sacred precincts of Demeter's sanctuary at Eleusis.[25]

Christian initiations of course differed in many details, but there are similarities in the underlying structure of preparation leading to dramatic and secret rites of passage. By contrast, Tertullian had insisted on the "simplicity" of Christian baptism, "without display, without innovative contrivances," in contrast to pagan mysteries that build prestige by their solemnity and secrecy.[26] All this is consistent with Jeremias's claim that a movement toward the postponement of baptism

24. Yarnold, *Awe-Inspiring Rites of Initiation*, 59–66.

25. Thomas M. Finn, *From Death to Rebirth: Ritual and Conversion in Antiquity* (Mahwah, N.J.: Paulist, 1997), 70.

26. Tertullian, *On Baptism*, 2.

made significant headway during the fourth century, and his conclusion that those who delayed baptism were "influenced by a magical understanding of baptism." With the influx of former pagans into the church following Constantine's conversion at the beginning of the fourth century, it is not surprising to find evidence of "superstitious conceptions of baptism which many of these pagans brought with them."[27]

One of the points to note here is that the influence of mystery religions pushed in the direction of believer's baptism, rather than paedobaptism. Entry into the mysteries was based on a conversion, a consciously chosen change in the direction of one's life and beliefs. The influence of mystery religions on Christian baptism thus reinforced earlier liturgical pressure to make adult baptism the norm.

Verbal and ritual echoes of the mystery religions are part of a larger movement toward what Alexander Schmemann calls "mysteriological piety." In mysteriological piety, worship is attached to a myth, but the worshiper places his faith in the worship or liturgy itself, rather than the myth. The worshiper ritually reenacts the myth, and as he moves through the mythical sequence in a ritual form, he is inducted into the salvation that the myth describes. In the New Testament, by contrast, priority is given to the story; Paul never preaches faith in baptism, but faith in Christ and the gospel. Worship and sacraments function as ecclesiastical realizations of events that have taken place once for all, and the worshiper becomes part of a new reality, a new age, by faith in the proclaimed message. During the fourth and fifth centuries, mysteriological notions of worship and sacraments came increasingly to dominate Christian consciousness and experience.[28]

It is apparent that the church had only a slight grasp of the biblical theology of infant baptism. Infants were baptized, but the fact seemed something of an embarrassment. While paedobaptist theology stresses the continuities between birth and the rebirth of baptism, Justin Mar-

27. Jeremias, *Infant Baptism in the First Four Centuries,* 87–94, 99.

28. Alexander Schmemann, *Introduction to Liturgical Theology* (Crestwood, N.Y.: St. Vladimir's Seminary Press, 1966), 103–10.

tyr emphasized their differences: the baptized person is not a "child of necessity and of ignorance, but of choice and of knowledge, who attains the forgiveness of sins formerly committed, after he has decided to be born again and has repented of his sins."[29] This statement is embedded in a characteristically Stoic contrast of nature and freedom, and indicates that Justin failed to see baptism genuinely as a birth because of the alien philosophical categories he brought to the question. Even the extrabiblical term *sacramentum,* introduced into Latin Christianity by Tertullian, created pressure toward confessional, rather than covenantal, baptism. In Latin, a *sacramentum* was an oath of loyalty, taken, for example, by a soldier entering the Roman army, and as such was a consciously chosen act. Tertullian explicitly drew analogies with the Christian *sacramenta,* so it is hardly surprising that he had trouble grasping the point of infant baptism.[30]

The remarkable fact about baptism in the early church is that infant baptism emerged from under these pressures as the dominant practice of the church. The church was rescued from Baptist theology and practice by Augustine of Hippo. His theology of infant baptism developed in the midst of polemics against Pelagius and his followers, and accordingly emphasized that infant baptism was a deliverance from original sin and damnation. Infant sin fascinated and appalled Augustine:

> I have personally watched and studied a jealous baby. He could not yet speak and, pale with jealousy and bitterness, glared at his brother sharing his mother's milk. Who is unaware of this fact of experience? Mothers and nurses claim to charm it away by their own private remedies. But it can hardly be innocence, when the source of milk is flowing richly and abundantly, not to endure a share going to one's blood brother, who is in profound need, dependent for life exclusively on that one food.[31]

29. Justin Martyr, *Apology,* 1.61.

30. See Searle, "Infant Baptism Reconsidered," 21.

31. Augustine, *Confessions,* 1.7.11. This is the translation of Henry Chadwick (Oxford: Oxford University Press, 1991), 9.

Given this deep sense of infant sin, Augustine naturally emphasized that infants needed to be saved:

> Whether it be a newborn infant or a decrepit old man—since no one should be barred from baptism—just so, there is no one who does not die to sin in baptism. Infants die to original sin only; adults, to all those sins which they have added, through their evil living, to the burden they brought with them at birth.[32]

At the very least, he treats infant and adult baptism as closely parallel in meaning and effect. Because both infant and adult are sinners, both need the cleansing bath.

The other leg of Augustine's theology of infant baptism comes from his conviction that sinners can be delivered only by union with the death and resurrection of Christ, which is communicated in baptism. Echoing Jesus' words to Nicodemus, he wrote that "whoever is born according to the flesh must be re-born in the spirit, so that he may (thus) not only attain the kingdom of God but also be freed from sin's damnation." Since "one does not come to Christ in any other way" than through baptism, "the little ones should not be kept away from the grace of the forgiveness of sins." So central is union with Christ in baptism that Augustine thinks it appropriate to use *baptism* and *salvation* interchangeably:

> Punic Christians speak of baptism simply with the very felicitous name, salvation, and call the sacrament of Christ's body life. Whence comes that if not, as indeed I believe, from the ancient apostolic tradition, to which Christians hold fast, that apart from baptism and participation in the Lord's table no one can come either to the kingdom of God, or to salvation and eternal life.[33]

32. Augustine, *Enchiridion,* 8.43, in Finn, *Early Christian Baptism and the Catechumenate,* 152.

33. All quotations in this paragraph are from Augustine's anti-Pelagian treatise *Concerning the Merit and Remission of Sins and Concerning Baptism of Infants,* quoted in Neunheuser, *Baptism and Confirmation,* 125–26.

The fact that Augustine developed his theology of infant baptism in the middle of a debate about sin and grace is an historical accident, but for the most part a happy one. Prior to Augustine, no one had grasped the radical character of sin; as Peter Cramer says, neither Tertullian, Cyprian, nor Ambrose "could bring himself to believe that the guilt was wholly beyond the reach of human will and effort."[34] None, in short, recognized the radical helplessness of man or the radical necessity of being born again into Christ. In this sense, then, the triumph of Augustine's theology of infant baptism was simply a triumph of the gospel of grace. And, in this respect, Warfield was wrong when he claimed that there was tension between Augustine's ecclesiology and his soteriology.

By the latter part of the first millennium, baptismal practice had developed in accordance with (semi-)Augustinian theology. Instead of sheepishly applying an elaborate ritual designed for adults to infants, the church applied the simple water of apostolic baptism to infants for their salvation. Early medieval writers recommended early and radically simplified baptism, not delaying it to the "baptismal seasons" of Easter and Pentecost, as had been done in some places during the patristic period. Aelfric of Winchester's Pastoral Letter, dated in the late tenth century, suggests that "if an unbaptized child is brought suddenly to the mass-priest, . . . he must baptize it immediately in haste, so that it does not die heathen." In another letter, he recommended a simple rite that included only a blessing on the water and the pronouncement "I baptize you." Then "if the child comes up out of the water alive, he is saved."[35]

At the moment of paedobaptist triumph, however, alien influences were at work. These quotations support Mark Searle's claim that the history of infant baptism is closely tied to the question of emergency baptism. Searle explains:

34. Cramer, *Baptism and Change in the Early Middle Ages,* 118.

35. Quoted in Cramer, *Baptism and Change in the Early Middle Ages,* 136–39. Cramer, by the way, does not consider this a positive development.

> Although the eighth-century supplement to the Hadrianum contained a form of catechumenate and initiation liturgy suitably abbreviated for infants, it is significant that this did not apparently catch on. Instead, infant baptism was increasingly celebrated using the much older Gelasian Order for the Making of a Catechumen or for Baptizing. But this rite was nothing other than a rite for baptizing the dying! So common did its use become in the Middle Ages that it eventually came to serve as the basis for the rite of infant baptism in the Roman Ritual of 1614.[36]

The demand that baptism be performed as soon as possible (*quamprimum* baptism) was supported at the Council of Florence in 1442, precisely because of the danger of infant mortality: "Concerning children: because of the danger of death, which occurs frequently enough . . . the Council admonishes that holy baptism is not to be delayed for 40 or 80 days or for some other period of time, as some are wont to do, but they should be baptized as soon as conveniently possible."[37] Although the practice being enjoined is Cyprianic and Augustinian, the theology is attenuated. Apart from emergencies, baptisms were ornate, complicated, and adult. Tensions between advocacy of infant baptism and a standard liturgy that assumed adult baptism remained throughout the Middle Ages and into the modern period.

At the same time, pressures in the early medieval church led to a serious diminution of the import of infant baptism. In most cases, in the patristic period, baptism was part of a larger set of rituals that made up Christian initiation. Water baptism was often followed by anointing (or many anointings), and then immediately by first communion. This patristic practice declared without question that the person being baptized was being admitted to the fellowship of the church, and to the fellowship of the Lord's Table in particular. The story of the breakdown of this rite is obscure, but it seems that the main cause was the determination that only a bishop could administer the oil of confirmation. Since bishops were not always easy to come by, many

36. Searle, "Infant Baptism Reconsidered," 18–19.

37. Quoted in Searle, "Infant Baptism Reconsidered," 19.

would be baptized without receiving the full initiation rite. Initiation would be completed when the bishop made his next visit to the local area. Eventually, confirmation developed into an entirely distinct sacrament.[38] Inevitably, this robbed infant baptism of much of its significance. Beasley-Murray complains that current paedobaptist practice, particularly in churches with a strong view of confirmation, "leaves the unconfirmed baptized in an ambiguous position with regard to the church" and "reduces the significance of baptism in a manner unknown to Apostolic theology."[39] Paedobaptists can only concede the point.

Having conceded the point, however, the answer is not to abandon paedobaptism, but to establish a more fully paedobaptist theology and practice. The most serious threat to paedobaptism is posed, not by Baptists, but by compromised paedobaptists, who shrink from the full implications of their position and who fail to embody their theology in practice. Were the church to become predominantly Baptist, the story would indeed be a tragedy, but the centuries-long farce of schizophrenic paedobaptism is hardly preferable.

We have not yet reached the comic finale in the story of baptism, and our confidence that the story is a tragicomedy must be part of a larger confidence that history is a tragicomedy. That is an act of faith.

38. The full story is told in J. D. C. Fisher, *Christian Initiation: Baptism in the Medieval West: A Study in the Disintegration of the Primitive Rite of Initiation* (London: SPCK, 1965).

39. Beasley-Murray, *Baptism in the New Testament,* 370.

13

The Polemics of Anabaptism from the Reformation Onward

GREGG STRAWBRIDGE

As I sit at my desk in Lancaster County, Pennsylvania, composing and editing this essay, I hear horse-drawn buggies passing by, carrying descendants of the early protesters of infant baptism. Today we live at peace with one another, but it was not always so.

Baptismal Waters Divided: The Early History

Reformation sacramentology is a sad study, filled with accounts of bitter polemics, schism, unrest, and even execution. One may catch a glimpse of the pain, seeing Zwingli at Marburg, or a drowning protester in Zurich, or a banished "sacramentarian" in the Palatinate. The same holy waters of baptism, intended to bring union to God and his people, continue to be a cause of ecclesiastical divisions.

The question of who should be baptized seems to be perennially discussed in Reformed dogmatics. It is often relegated to nonessential status today, but early in the Protestant movement the question became a matter of supreme importance—most notably when some followers of Ulrich Zwingli forged a "radical reformation." Many paid for their theological convictions with their lives.[1]

Zwingli may have been somewhat ambivalent on infant baptism in his earlier years, but when the question came to a head in 1524, he opposed the Anabaptists.[2] Although Zwingli had been somewhat successful in many of his efforts at reformation, the group that became known as the Anabaptists proposed deeper changes, even cutting the umbilical cord to civil society. "They discarded infant baptism, rejected all state ordinances affecting the Church, opposed the collection of tithes, and denied that the Church was properly composed of all members of the community."[3] Zwingli sought to persuade representatives of the Anabaptist movement in meetings held on January 10 and 17, 1525. Even so, Hubmaier, Grebel, and Manz, who represented the Anabaptists at those conferences, did not abandon their position. Civil action to suppress all Anabaptist teaching followed. But in defiance of this suppression, the decisive action took place at Zollikon on February 7, 1525: Grebel rebaptized Blaurock, and later Blaurock rebaptized others. George H. Williams refers to this as "the final act, rebaptism and rupture with magisterial Protestantism."[4] Their act was political, as much as religious. After further conferences and more magisterial attempts to persuade them, including imprisonment, in November of the same year, the extreme sanction was finally imposed: death by drowning.[5] Ironically, however, martyrdom is an almost infallible means of dissemination and conversion.[6]

1. George H. Williams, *The Radical Reformation* (Philadelphia: Westminster, 1962).

2. G. W. Bromiley, introduction to Zwingli's "Of Baptism," in *Zwingli and Bullinger,* ed. G. W. Bromiley (Philadelphia: Westminster, 1953), 119.

3. John T. McNeill, *The History and Character of Calvinism* (New York: Oxford University Press, 1967), 41.

4. George Huntston Williams, introduction to "Letters to Thomas Müntzer by Conrad Grebel and Friends," in *Spiritual and Anabaptist Writers,* ed. George Huntston Williams and Angel M. Mergal (Philadelphia: Westminster, 1957), 72.

5. Bromiley, introduction to Zwingli's "Of Baptism," 120.

6. George Huntston Williams, in the introduction to "Trial and Martyrdom of Michael Sattler," in *Spiritual and Anabaptist Writers,* ed. Williams and Mergal, writes that the document

To what extent the well-known Swiss Anabaptists, Hubmaier, Blaurock, Grebel, and Manz, were revolutionary in their approach is debatable.[7] McNeill notes, "There was a strong fanatical strain in the movement, though this was not prominent in Zurich."[8] However, Grebel had been influenced by the violent leader of the peasants' revolt, Thomas Müntzer (1490–1525). Grebel wrote to Müntzer on September 5, 1524, "On the matter of baptism thy book pleases us well, and we desire to be further instructed by thee."[9] The letter goes on to speak of infant baptism as "a senseless, blasphemous abomination, contrary to all Scripture."[10]

F. Nigel Lee presents a well-supported argument that Anabaptists emerged from medieval Romanist influences, especial the Petrobusians, and were mostly communistic and revolutionary.[11] His work is framed as a response to Leonard Verduin.[12] Lee cites evidence that the revolutionary Thomas Müntzer preached the abandonment of infant baptism after being in the circle of Zwickau prophets (Nicholas Storch, Thomas Drechsel, and Marcus Stuebner) in 1521, and that the Swiss Anabaptists were of the same mind as Müntzer.[13] It may be that the Anabaptist rejection of infant baptism was being spread as early as 1522—certainly the documentary evidence points to a time prior to 1524.[14] As cited in the letter to Müntzer, he was connected to the Swiss Anabaptists, like Grebel, Castelberg, Mantz,

is "illustrative of the martyr theology which *sustained the whole Anabaptist movement*" (p. 137, emphasis added).

7. It should be noted that the term *Anabaptist* covers a great deal of theological and historical territory. Williams divides Anabaptists into three main groups: evangelical, revolutionary, and contemplative ("Introduction," in *Spiritual and Anabaptist Writers,* ed. Williams and Mergal, 28–29).

8. McNeill, *History and Character of Calvinism,* 41.

9. "Letters to Thomas Müntzer," in *Spiritual and Anabaptist Writers,* ed. Williams and Mergal, 80.

10. Ibid., 81.

11. F. Nigel Lee, *Anabaptists and Their Stepchildren* (Dallas: Commonwealth Publications, 1992).

12. Leonard Verduin, *The Reformers and Their Stepchildren* (Grand Rapids: Eerdmans, 1961).

13. Williams calls this "the Old Protestant thesis" ("Introduction," in *Spiritual and Anabaptist Writers,* ed. Williams and Mergal, 27).

14. Cf. Grebel's letter to Müntzer, September 5, 1524 ("Letters to Thomas Müntzer," in *Spiritual and Anabaptist Writers,* ed. Williams and Mergal, 73–83).

Ockenfuss, Pur, Aberli, and "other brethren of thine in Christ."[15] In a second letter, or "Postscript," Grebel added the names of Pannicellus, Hujuff, "thy countryman of Halle, thy brethren, and seven new young *Müntzers* against Luther" (emphasis added).[16] Perhaps Lee is substantially correct in characterizing the early Anabaptists as revolutionary and proto-communistic. Far from being pacifistic New-Testament-only biblicists, they referred to themselves as "Müntzers against Luther."[17]

Despite revolutionary tendencies within the overall Anabaptist movement, the distinctive convictions of the more pacifist contingent were articulated in the seven articles of the Schleitheim Confession. This confession, also known as the Brüderliche Vereinigung or the Schleitheim Brotherly Union Confession, was written under the leadership of Michael Sattler of Stauffen, Germany. The articles were ratified on February 24, 1527, during an assembly of Anabaptists in the northern Swiss village of Schleitheim. This Confession is an important primary source for early Anabaptism. In literature that is sympathetic to the movement, the qualification is often made that this Confession was not a complete confession of faith, expressing the full doctrinal system of its adherents. Rather, it focused on the distinctives of the movement. From the beginning, these articles were used in polemics. Zwingli translated them into Latin in order to refute them, and Calvin used a French translation of the Seven Articles in his refutation of Anabaptism published in 1544.[18]

There is great vehemence against infant baptism, labeling it (in the very first article) "the highest and chief abomination of the pope."[19] The proof offered in this article is "the foundation and testimony of the Apostles," citing six passages which illustrate or command bap-

15. These men all signed Grebel's letter to Müntzer (ibid., 82–83).

16. Ibid., 85.

17. Ibid.

18. See Mark Noll, ed., *Confessions and Catechisms of the Reformation* (Grand Rapids: Baker, 1991), for an informative introduction and discussion.

19. We are following the text given by John Howard Yoder, *The Legacy of Michael Sattler* (Scottdale, Pa.: Herald Press, 1973).

tism. Here we see the germ of the antipaedobaptist polemic, which is threefold: (1) infant baptism is not explicitly warranted by the New Testament; (2) believer's baptism is apostolic; (3) infant baptism is an abomination of the papacy.

Baptismal Waters and Membership Charters

In addition to rejecting infant baptism, the Anabaptists had other concerns. They fundamentally worked to reconstitute the membership of the church. This is evident in the Schleitheim Confession. Verduin even points to evidence that

> in some instances at least, the Anabaptism of the sixteenth century did not in its earliest manifestations assail infant baptism as such but rather the "christening" of the fallen Church. We read that in the earliest days of Anabaptism in the Wassenberg area, infant baptism was not as such repudiated; what was repudiated was the "christening" ritual. . . . We see then that rebaptism did not necessarily go hand in hand with a rejection of pedobaptism. It is said that Michael Sattler, one of the first to lose his life for the cause of Restitutionism, was at the first rather kindly disposed toward infant baptism.[20]

Verduin argues persuasively that the more important issue in Anabaptist development was the rejection of a "Constantinian" approach to church membership, favoring instead voluntarism and the separatism of the church from the state. That is, they looked upon the church not as a political institution, but as a voluntary association. According to the Anabaptists, when one pulls out the thread of infant baptism, the seam of church–state Christianity is unraveled.

It may be observed here that this part of the Anabaptist vision has been largely realized. Their vision of the separation and even isolation

20. Verduin, *The Reformers and Their Stepchildren,* 196–97. Apparently Sattler's views changed by 1527, since his Confession states that infant baptism is the highest and chief abomination of the pope.

of church and state and voluntary church membership is unhesitatingly accepted by the evangelical world, especially in the United States.[21] This may even be so in many ostensibly Reformed paedobaptist churches. On the other hand, the full flowering of Reformation Calvinism urged a "godly commonwealth" consisting of a "free church" and a "free state," but both under God and his law. Calvinism separated the power of the sword from the keys of the kingdom. This is all easier said than done, as subsequent history shows.[22] Unrealized as it may be today, Calvinism's conception of church-state relations is an alternative to Anabaptist isolation, and it is distinct from the Romanist concept of church domination of the state or the Erastian concept of state domination of the church.[23]

Through the influence of the Anabaptists and later the English and American Baptists, the Protestant world has been persistently divided by Anabaptist polemics. Williams's comments are interesting here. He distinguishes between the English (Calvinistic) Baptists and the previous Anabaptists, noting that the Baptists never abandoned an interest in the state and were "thus able to participate directly in the formation of our modern open, responsible democracy in a way which was never vouchsafed to the still more heroic and ethically resolute Anabaptists of sixteenth-century Germany."[24]

THE WATERS DEFINED

Let us define the issue sharply. The question of this debate, historically and theologically, is whether it is proper to baptize confessing

21. This excludes, of course, those revolutionary Anabaptists, especially the Münsterites, who were seeking to create a polygamous theocracy (see Williams, "Introduction," in *Spiritual and Anabaptist Writers,* ed. Williams and Mergal, 23).

22. See W. Stanford Reid, ed., *John Calvin: His Influence in the Western World* (Grand Rapids: Zondervan, 1982), esp. Richard C. Gamble, "Switzerland: Triumph and Decline," 66; J. D. Douglas, "Calvin's Contribution to Scotland," 217–37; George M. Marsden, "America's 'Christian' Origins: Puritan New England as a Case Study," 241–60.

23. In our day, it has been the Reconstructionists, such as Rousas J. Rushdoony, who have been the chief spokesmen for the Calvinist view. Seen in the best light, they have been urging renewed Calvinism. However, they are popularly misconstrued as proponents of theocracy.

24. Williams, "Introduction," in *Spiritual and Anabaptist Writers,* ed. Williams and Mergal, 25.

Christians' infants or their young children, who are incapable of professing the faith. Of course, all parties agree that adult converts must profess the faith before being baptized. The Westminster Larger Catechism, question 166, for example, in answer to the question, "Unto whom is baptism to be administered?" answers:

> Baptism is not to be administered to any that are out of the visible church, and so strangers from the covenant of promise, till they profess their faith in Christ, and obedience to him, but infants descended from parents, either both, or but one of them, professing faith in Christ, and obedience to him, are in that respect within the covenant, and to be baptized.

So at issue is what is to be done with the children of Christians, not with adult converts. Or, to put it another way, the Anabaptists hold to antipaedobaptism or *exclusive* believer's baptism.

To make way in this dispute, one must open the book of hermeneutics. It is generally recognized that one's view of the proper recipients of baptism is inextricably linked to the interpretive procedures and assumptions that one brings to the text. One's interpretive assumptions wield the most influence in matters that are not explicitly addressed by the Bible. Of course, there is no explicit statement in Scripture about the "infant baptism" of a Christian's child. Let me hasten to add, however, that neither is there an explicit case of a Christian's child who grows up and is baptized as a professing believer. Both sides of the argument lack an explicit textual basis for what to do with the children of Christians. A failure to recognize this as the *status questionis* will result in many explosive clashes between the battleships, but all to no avail.

Early in the debate, the lack of an explicit scriptural basis for infant baptism was acknowledged. As Zwingli retorted to the Anabaptists, "Your argument runs as follows: We do not find that the apostles baptized infants: therefore we ought not to baptize them."[25] This argu-

25. Zwingli, "Of Baptism," in *Zwingli and Bullinger*, ed. Bromiley, 147.

ment may be labeled "the explicit warrant objection." Essentially, it states that without explicit biblical warrant, infant baptism is illegitimate. The standard reply of Zwingli and many who followed him in the magisterial Protestant tradition was to present a rather cogent *reductio ad absurdum*. That is, they showed the incoherence of rejecting a belief or practice merely from its lack of explicit mention in the Bible. Originally, Zwingli pointed out the incoherence of the argument that Acts 19 contains a rebaptism by Paul of those followers of John the Baptist who had been initially baptized by Apollos. Zwingli does the *reductio* by arguing that Scripture does not tell us explicitly that Apollos baptized them, and so, following the explicit warrant principle, Apollos didn't baptize them. Thus, Zwingli demonstrated the incoherence of the explicit warrant objection. Calvin, Ursinus, and Witsius followed with other examples, such as the lack of an explicit warrant for women to receive communion.

SEPARATING THE WATERS: TYPES OF ANTIPAEDOBAPTISTS

Beginning with the historic Anabaptists of the sixteenth century, many other varieties of antipaedobaptists have emerged. Mike Renihan, in his Oxford dissertation on John Tombes, has provided helpful categories for the various types of antipaedobaptists:

a. Anabaptists—The primal sixteenth century continental movement, considered above.
b. Baptists—Those flowing from the English puritan context, of two distinct types: General (Arminian) Baptists and Particular (Calvinistic) Baptists.[26]

26. Renihan cites Barry White to explain the differences between the General and the Particular Baptists: "Both groups shared a very similar position on many aspects of the doctrine of the church. For example, they both believed that the visible church of Christians was composed of gathered congregations of believing men and women and they both believed in and practised (at least from 1642) believer's baptism by immersion. Nevertheless, they consistently organise

c. Abaptists—Quakers and others sects who denied the necessity of any baptism.
d. Anglican Antipaedobaptists—John Tombes (1603–1676) represents this small contingent of those who argued against the validity of infant baptism, while remaining in the established church (until the Great Ejection of puritan ministers in 1662).[27]

While the designation "antipaedobaptist" may at first glance seem offensive, it is the best overarching term for all those who deny the validity of infant baptism. Following Renihan, I will use it, precisely because there is no dispute about the validity of "believer's baptism" as such. All of Christendom agrees (except for the fringe Abaptists) that it is proper to baptize new converts after they make a confession of faith. There is unity on believer's baptism after all! There is no dispute as to the propriety of the post-confession baptisms of the men of Israel (Acts 2), the eunuch (Acts 8), the adult men and women and Simon the heretic in Samaria (Acts 8), Saul (Acts 9), Cornelius (Acts 10), Lydia and the Philippian jailer (Acts 16), Crispus (Acts 18; 1 Cor. 1:14), the twelve disciples in Ephesus (Acts 19), Gaius (1 Cor. 1:14), and Stephanas (1 Cor. 1:16). But what is to be done with the children in households of such followers of our covenant Lord?

It may be helpful to organize the waves of antipaedobaptist polemics into three distinct tides: (1) Anabaptist polemics proper, (2) Puritan Baptist polemics developed, and (3) New Covenant Baptist polemics triumphant. Basically, (1) Anabaptist polemics proper presented two basic arguments, the explicit warrant objection and the papal argument (that infant baptism is an abomination of the pope). (2) The Puritan Baptist polemical development was especially inspired by the Puritan separatists, empowered by a more radical conception of the

---

separately, differed in their view of inter-congregational relationships and the ministry and, on the whole flourished in different parts of the country" (Mike Renihan, *Antipaedobaptism in the Thought of John Tombes: An Untold Story from Puritan England* [Auburn, Mass.: B & R Press, 2001], 22).

27. Ibid., 21.

constituents of the church, and armed with selected New Testament concepts, such as that baptism is immersion into the death, burial, and resurrection of Christ (Rom. 6:3–4, as read by Baptists). This position was stated in the Baptist Confession of 1644 and then the Confession of 1689.[28] They understood baptism to entail immersion, in contrast to the Anabaptists proper, who did not immerse, but administered the water by pouring. (3) New Covenant Baptist polemics triumphant has come of age in this century. Calvinistic theology has crossed denomination lines, especially into Baptist circles. Their theological framework builds upon the standard covenant theology developed by Zwingli, Bullinger, Calvin, Witsius, Owen, and the Westminster Confession. Their position is that only regenerate individuals are members of the new covenant, and hence that only these are to receive the ordinance that signifies membership in the covenant. Their arguments include mature conceptions of the explicit warrant objection, balanced historical treatments of the development of antipaedobaptism, and a view of covenant theology that links regeneration, membership in the new covenant, and baptism.

Where Do the Covenant Waters Lead?

By applying the distinctive hermeneutic of Reformed, redemptive-historical, covenant theology, perhaps more can be accomplished than by merely stating the explicit warrant objection. At first glance, one might think that this too is a hopeless path to follow, since those within the redemptive-historical, covenant theology family are preeminently paedobaptist in the first place. While that may be true historically or even quantitatively, the substantive advances of antipaedobaptist polemics are now made by Baptists who appeal to Reformed principles of hermeneutics and theological method to support their case. There has arisen a vital movement of Calvinistic Baptists who disdain a New Testament–only, dispensational approach and explicitly appeal

28. The 1689 Baptist Confession (London Confession) is merely a revision of the Westminster Confession.

to covenant theology. They advocate a "Baptist covenant theology." Reformed Baptists recognize that New Testament–only appeals lack substance.

For example, David Kingdon defends the Baptist position as a Calvinistic, covenantal theologian:

> A great deal of Baptist apologetic, so it seems to me, has failed to come to terms with the indubitable fact that the covenant of grace, although it exhibits diversity of administration in the time of promise and in the time of fulfilment, is none-the-less one covenant. . . . Baptists will never seriously disturb Reformed Paedobaptists until they see this. The divisive, atomistic approach of so much of the contemporary Baptist apologetic is about as effective at this point as a shotgun against a Sherman tank.[29]

And Southern Baptist Founder's Conference pioneer Fred Malone writes, "Stated briefly, as a covenant theologian I have come to believe that according to the Bible, the only proper subjects for Christian baptism are disciples of Christ."[30] In another widely distributed booklet, the Reformed Baptist Richard C. Barcellos writes:

> Historically, Covenant Theology has been the parent of infant baptism. This essay assumes that a proper understanding of the progressive nature of the biblical covenants, and the replacement of the Old Covenant by the New Covenant, seriously challenges historic Covenant Theology, and yet does not demand Dispensationalism or Antinomianism. . . . It will be argued that a consistent adherence to Covenant Theology refutes infant baptism and upholds, even demands believers' baptism within the covenantal structure of the Bible.[31]

29. David Kingdon, *Children of Abraham* (Worthing, England: Henry E. Walter, 1973), 20–21.

30. Fred Malone, *A String of Pearls Unstrung: A Theological Journey into Believers' Baptism* (Cape Coral, Fla.: Founders Press, 1998), 1.

31. Richard C. Barcellos, *Paedoism or Credoism? A Reformed Baptist Argument for Believers' Baptism Based on Covenant Theology* (Fullerton, Calif.: Reformed Baptist Publications, 1997), 1.

In a widely cited text, the late professor Paul King Jewett writes:

> The theological conception sometimes called covenant theology which undergirds the Paedobaptist argument at this point, is too grand, too challenging, too persistent to be ignored with impunity. The dogmatician who slights it despises his own reputation. That is perhaps to concede that the Baptists as a whole have not been outstanding theologians; the stream of their rebuttal has run so thin at this juncture that only the hollow eyes of predisposition could fail to see its inadequacy and judge the counter arguments superior.[32]

Within this movement, all appeals lead to Jewett, who is certainly a most eloquent spokesman for their position. As the Reformed Baptist Greg Welty says, "In my readings on the subject of baptism, Paul K. Jewett's, *Infant Baptism and the Covenant of Grace* was a revolutionary treatment of the subject."[33] His defense of the Baptist position is certainly one of the most highly rated of this century. A succinct version of his arguments may be found in *The Zondervan Pictorial Encyclopedia of the Bible,* alongside John Murray's defense of infant baptism.[34] He argues as follows:

> With the advent of Messiah—the promised seed *par excellence*—and the Pentecostal effusion of the Spirit, the salvation contained in the promise to Israel was brought nigh. No longer was it a hope on the distant horizon but rather an accomplished fact in history. Then—and for our discussion, this THEN is of capital significance—the temporal, earthly, typical elements of the old dispensation were dropped from the great house of salvation as scaffolding from the finished edifice. It is our contention that the Paedobaptists, in framing their argument from cir-

32. Paul K. Jewett, *Infant Baptism and the Covenant of Grace* (Grand Rapids: Eerdmans, 1978), 20.

33. Greg Welty, *A Critical Evaluation of Paedobaptism* (Fullerton, Calif.: Reformed Baptist Publications, 1996), 1.

34. P. Jewett, "Baptism (Baptist View)," in *The Zondervan Pictorial Encyclopedia of the Bible,* ed. Merrill C. Tenney (Grand Rapids: Zondervan, 1975), 1:466-68.

> cumcision, have failed to keep this significant historical development in clear focus. Proceeding from the basically correct postulate that baptism stands in the place of circumcision, they have urged this analogy to a distortion. They have so far pressed the *unity* of the covenant as to suppress the *diversity* of its administration. They have, to be specific, Christianized the Old Testament and Judaized the New.[35]

In unfolding his position, Jewett charges the Reformed paedobaptist "with an error in biblical theology." The standard paedobaptist argument that infant baptism is justified on the same grounds as infant circumcision "involves the fundamental error of failing to recognize the historical character of revelation."[36] As Welty says,

> His [Jewett's] basic identification of the problem as one of biblical theology was quite insightful. Avoiding a blatantly dispensational approach, he applies the Reformed emphasis on unity and progress in redemptive history to the sacraments themselves, thus beating the paedobaptists at their own game of continuity and discontinuity.[37]

When one remembers that covenant theology was formally christened by Zwingli in response to the Anabaptists, it is an interesting thesis that if Zwingli, Bullinger, and Calvin had been more consistent in their covenant theology, they would have become Anabaptists. What they considered to be the most biblically robust reply to Anabaptism, had the scales of Constantinian prejudice been removed, would actually have put them on the Damascus road to antipaedobaptism! This claim is also interesting because the standard Protestant arguments for infant baptism appeal to the very same theological and hermeneutical foundation: covenant theology. Remove covenant theology, and infant baptism in the Reformation tradition is left in the air with no foundation.

So, this thesis deserves some attention. There has been much discussion of the exegetical, theological, and historical issues since Jew-

35. Jewett, *Infant Baptism and the Covenant of Grace*, 91.

36. Ibid., 8.

37. Welty, *A Critical Evaluation of Paedobaptism*, 2.

ett advanced his thesis. The proponents on both sides have sharpened their polemical tools. Let us briefly consider how Jewett has articulated the best contemporary case for the antipaedobaptist cause.

Jewett argues that the paedobaptist interprets Old Testament circumcision in purely spiritual terms, following the New Testament descriptions of baptism and heart circumcision, and fails to see any of the temporal aspects of it. On the other hand, the paedobaptist sees New Testament baptism as almost purely objective and external (like the external administration of circumcision). Jewett charges the paedobaptist position with a significant hermeneutical error, flowing from an error in biblical theology. The paedobaptist emphasizes "the inward and spiritual blessings sealed by baptism as the key to the interpretation of the Old Testament rite of circumcision" and interprets "circumcision exclusively in terms of baptism."[38] Jewett wants to maintain a biblical theology of circumcision that takes the Old Testament as formative and only then permits the New Testament material to speak. So, while recognizing an essential unity between circumcision and baptism, he avoids the full import of the paedobaptist interpretation of circumcision by recognizing the earthly, physical aspects of the covenant with Abraham, along with the spiritual aspects that are typological of the New Testament era (children of Abraham by faith). "To put it in still a third way, paedobaptists rightly stress the unity of redemptive history, while wrongly ignoring the *movement* of that redemptive history. Thus their error is fundamentally one of *biblical theology,* of understanding the *progressive unfolding* of God's redemptive purposes *in history.*"[39]

Jewett defends his contention with a high degree of scholarship and considerable rhetorical power and polemical prowess. He demonstrates a meticulous knowledge of the Reformation debate and the diverse sacramental views of the entire church. The teeth of his argument against the paedobaptist view is that circumcision was different from baptism precisely in its lack of any spiritual criterion for recep-

38. Jewett, *Infant Baptism and the Covenant of Grace,* 97.

39. Welty, *A Critical Evaluation of Paedobaptism,* 2.

tion. A physical and/or household connection was all that was needed in order to grant the propriety of receiving circumcision, and no spiritual qualification was necessary to receive it, even for adult proselytes.[40] Jewett argues that this is not true for baptism, and that the singular criterion for receiving it is spiritual.

Jewett's argument raises a significant issue for the student of Reformed dogmatics: Does a fully developed biblical theology utilizing a covenantal hermeneutic yield a baptistic sacramentology and thus preclude infant baptism?

THE SPIRITUALITY OF CIRCUMCISION IN THE OLD TESTAMENT

Let us begin our examination of covenant theology by considering the criterion for receiving circumcision. According to Jewett, a physical and/or household connection was all that was needed in order to receive this sign. No spiritual qualification was necessary in order to receive circumcision, even for adult proselytes. For Jewett, the convincing proof of this is the circumcision of Abraham's adult household members, as well as Ishmael (Gen. 17) and the sons of Keturah (Gen. 25). These adults were not required to make any kind of spiritual confession, and the "children of Abraham" did not receive "the covenant," nor were they spiritually qualified.

Do the admittedly exceptional cases of Ishmael and the sons of Keturah disprove the thesis that circumcision is the sacramental equivalent of baptism? Do they prove that this sign of the covenant is illegitimately placed on covenant members' children? Well, on the one hand, it could be argued that these individuals lacked the criterion of Israelite covenant membership, and hence that circumcision differs from baptism (being, as Jewett argues, part of the scaffolding). On the other hand, it could be argued that such candidates possessed the true *spiritual criterion* of membership in the covenant of grace as it extended beyond ethnic Israel. Could these not be foundational planks in the

40. Jewett, *Infant Baptism and the Covenant of Grace*, 98.

great house, unseen yet supportive? After all, our Lord teaches that many will come from east and west to sit at the table with Abraham, Isaac, and Jacob (Matt. 8:11).

Arguing from Jewett's premises, if circumcision had a twofold meaning, signifying both "the temporal, earthly, typical elements of the old dispensation"[41] (physical descent from Abraham) and also "renewal and cleansing of heart"[42] (spiritual descent from Abraham), why must we presume that Ishmael and the sons of Keturah participated in the former, but not the latter? Perhaps the circumcision of Abraham's physical, but non-Israelite offspring, Ishmael and the sons of Keturah, signified the *spiritual, not the physical, covenant realities.* I believe a good case can be made for this.

First, it might be observed that those who glibly speak of circumcision being a "national sign" are mistaken, since Ishmael received the sign, yet was not in the nation of Israel (Gen. 17:20–25). Second, in the biblical theology of Genesis, circumcision has spiritual significance, since in the "covenant of circumcision" (Acts 7:8) the Lord is "to be God to you and to your descendants after you" (Gen. 17:7). This is manifestly spiritual in nature. Third, circumcision was given as "the sign of the covenant between Me and you" (Gen. 17:11). This is likewise manifestly spiritual, not temporal or earthly. If anyone doubts this, we have the later apostolic teaching that Abraham "received the sign of circumcision, a seal of the righteousness of the faith which he had while uncircumcised" (Rom. 4:11). Fourth, Ishmael was circumcised on the same day as Abraham (Gen. 17:26). It would be strikingly inconsistent if the same ritual act, administered on the same day, was "a seal of the righteousness of the faith" for Abraham, but only a sign of physical descent for teenage Ishmael (age 13), signifying only the allegedly earthly aspects of the covenant (which was through Isaac!). Nothing in Genesis 17 explicitly denies that when Ishmael received circumcision, he did so as one expressing trust in the God of Abraham. But even if it turns out that he did not have the reality signified (as many "believers" baptized today do not), this does not change the ex-

41. Ibid., 91.
42. Ibid., 86.

press declaration that circumcision was the Abrahamic seal of the righteousness of faith. Of course, Ishmael was not the miracle seed of promise, but this is not to say that he did not have a right to the Abrahamic sign.[43] The lesson for Abraham, in making Isaac the child of promise, was to have faith in a God who is able to give life to the dead (womb) (Heb. 11:12) and even raise a dead heir (Heb. 11:19).

Fifth, we are not expressly told that the sons of Keturah were circumcised (Gen. 25:4), but it may be inferred from Genesis 17. Since Abraham obeyed God (Gen. 18:19), and since they were born into his household, they were presumably circumcised. We are not told of the spiritual state of any of Keturah's children.[44] However, we are told what Abraham was commanded to do: "For I have chosen him [Abraham], so that he may command his children and his household after him to keep the way of the Lord by doing righteousness and justice, so that the Lord may bring upon Abraham what He has spoken about him" (Gen. 18:19). And since the Lord brought about what he promised to Abraham, we can be sure that he did indeed "command his children [including the sons of Keturah] and his household [including the adults in it] . . . to keep the way of the Lord by doing righteousness and justice." If "doing righteousness and justice" is dependent on one's "circumcised heart" or "the righteousness of faith" or "justification by faith," then Abraham, being the father of the faithful, surely taught these truths to all who were under his headship.

Sixth and finally, since circumcision was a sign and seal of the righteousness of faith to Abraham, and he himself administered this seal of the righteousness of faith to many of his own children, it is all the more certain that these circumcisions represented to Abraham

43. There is no explicit reference to Ishmael in the New Testament to indicate his eternal destiny. In Galatians 4 Paul tells us, "This is *allegorically speaking* [*allēgoreō*], for these women are two covenants: one proceeding from Mount Sinai bearing children who are to be slaves; she is Hagar" (v. 24). The typology is that Hagar and Ishmael picture the Jews awaiting the fullness of the promise. But as those rejecting Christ, they are in bondage rather than true Israelites. There is a pattern from Ishmael to Israel in history. See James B. Jordan's article, "Call Me Ishmael" (www.biblicalhorizons/bh/bh117.htm).

44. The Midianites (descendants of Midian, a son of Keturah) played an interesting role in the history of the Jews, with both Joseph and Jethro, "the priest of Midian" (Moses' father-in-law).

what was spiritually significant and covenantally promised. Calvin was right in arguing against the Anabaptists: "For what will they bring forward to impugn infant baptism that may not be turned back against circumcision?"[45]

CARNALITY IN THE RECIPIENTS OF THE NEW COVENANT SIGNS

The sharp sword of the covenantal Baptist polemic cuts two ways: it lops off the spirituality of the previous covenant administration and the covenantal faithfulness of those who received the signs of the old covenant, while with the back swing it filets any carnality from those who receive the signs of the new covenant. If it can be demonstrated that the new covenant signs were intentionally given by Jesus and the apostles to some who were carnal, unregenerate, or reprobate, then it appears that a self-consistent biblical theology does not comport with the view of Jewett.

According to Jewett, only regenerate people are "in the new covenant" and thus are properly to receive the signs of the covenant.[46] Since the children of believers are not regenerate, he argues that it is improper to give the sign of the covenant to them until they give evidence of faith, namely, by demonstrating their regeneration publicly. However, if it can be proved that there are people under new covenant obligations (i.e., "in the covenant") who become apostates, then the claim that only regenerate people are in the new covenant will be shown to be false. And if this is false, then so is the view of baptism that is based upon it.

Several passages teach that there are people *set apart* in the new covenant (without the full blessings of salvation) who indeed fall away.

45. John Calvin, *Institutes of the Christian Religion,* ed. John T. McNeill, trans. Ford Lewis Battles (Philadelphia: Westminster, 1960), 4.16.9.

46. The phrase "in the covenant" or "in the new covenant" is not, strictly speaking, found in the Bible. But it is all right to use it, so long as it is defined. Here it essentially means "included in the contract" or "covenanted with, or under the stipulations of, the covenant."

Thus, there are unregenerate members of the new covenant. For example, Hebrews 10:29–31:

> How much severer punishment do you think he will deserve who has trampled under foot the Son of God, and has regarded as unclean the blood of the covenant by which he was sanctified, and has insulted the Spirit of grace? For we know Him who said, "Vengeance is Mine, I will repay." And again, "The Lord will judge His people." It is a terrifying thing to fall into the hands of the living God.

Would we not find the richest biblical-theological soil in the fertile mind of the writer to the Hebrews? Yes, since he was thinking and arguing about the relationship between the old covenant administrations and the new covenant administration. For example, only ten verses before the above passage, the writer cites the preeminent new covenant passage (Jer. 31:33–34). The writer argues that some individuals who have been "sanctified" (*hagiazō*, "set apart" or "consecrated") in "His people" (the visible people of God) may commit apostasy.[47] Of course, these individuals were never regenerate. In the Greek translation of the Old Testament, the term *hagiazō* often refers to the consecration of the visible people of God (Ex. 19:10, 14 LXX; cf. Heb. 9:13–20). The imagery of Hebrews 10:29 is drawn directly from this ceremonial typology. Those who have been consecrated by the blood of the covenant in the visible church (Heb. 9:19–20) may "have once been enlightened and have tasted of the heavenly gift and have been made partakers of the Holy Spirit, and have tasted the good word of God and the powers of the age to come, and then have fallen away" (Heb. 6:4–6). They did not lose their salvation, but they did become covenant *breakers*. To do this, they must have been recognized covenant

47. A minority of interpreters take the implied "he" in "the blood of the covenant by which *he was sanctified* (*hēgiasthē* [third person singular])" as referring to Christ. However, the grammar certainly does not necessitate that interpretation. Such a view seems to be an *ad hoc* response to the theological difficulties of a baptistic Calvinism, which are alleviated in the general Reformed view of the covenant with its internal and legal dimensions. Nevertheless, the point above still stands, apart from this question, since this apostate is still part of "His people" (v. 30).

members. Hebrews frequently speaks of those who "shrink back to destruction" (10:39), who "[come] short of the grace of God" (12:15), who are "like Esau" (12:16–17), who "neglect so great a salvation" (2:3), who "have tasted of the heavenly gift . . . and then have fallen away" (6:4–6), who "harden [their] hearts" and "fall, through following the same example of disobedience" (4:7, 11), and who "throw away [their] confidence" (10:35)—those who are, in terms of covenant theology, *new covenant breakers.*

Jesus expresses the same idea with the vine/branch covenant metaphor: "Every branch *in Me* that does not bear fruit, He takes away. . . . If anyone does not abide *in Me,* he is thrown away as a branch and dries up; and they gather them, and cast them into the fire and they are burned" (John 15:2, 6). Those in view here are unregenerate covenant members, who turn out to be covenant breakers.

Paul teaches that in God's covenantal dealings "some of the branches were broken off, and you [Gentiles], being a wild olive, were grafted in among them and became partakers with them of the rich root of the olive tree. . . . Do not be conceited, but fear; for if God did not spare the natural branches, *He will not spare you, either*" (Rom. 11:13–21). This passage expressly teaches that those in covenant with God can be "broken off." Surely regenerate people cannot be broken off. Therefore, not all who are members of the new covenant are regenerate. Similarly, Peter says, "For it is time for judgment to begin with the household of God; and if it begins with us first, what will be the outcome for those who do not obey the gospel of God?" (1 Peter 4:17). These statements are quite meaningless if no one in the covenant can be broken off or judged.

The assertion that only regenerate people are in the new covenant really amounts to saying that the older covenant administrations were with the *visible people of God,* but that the new covenant is only with the *invisible people of God.* It is true that the fulfillment of the new covenant is seen only in regenerate people who walk by faith (something also true in the previous covenant administrations, by the way).[48]

48. Many texts support this assertion, but it will suffice to point out the entire chapter of Hebrews 11.

However, it does not follow that the new covenant administration deals only with the invisible people of God (i.e., the regenerate).

Those who validly partake of the signs of the new covenant must be members of that covenant. But we find people in the New Testament who do so, yet were not regenerate. We find that baptism was given to Simon the sorcerer (Acts 8:13), who turned out to be a great heretic. And when Jesus inaugurated the covenant with these words, "Drink from it, all of you; for this is My blood of the covenant, which is poured out for many for forgiveness of sins," Judas, called a *disciple,* drank of that cup and then became the *arch covenant breaker* (Matt. 26:27–28). As these examples show, not only the regenerate have been members of the new covenant. It is simply not possible to entirely exclude the unregenerate from participation in the covenant community.

Many passages teach that the new covenant has stipulations for judgment (Matt. 16:19; 1 Cor. 11:29–30, 34; Heb. 10:30–31; 1 Peter 4:17), so membership in it cannot be exclusively for the elect.[49] Many other passages teach that the kingdom (in its new covenant manifestation) includes both regenerate and unregenerate people (Matt. 8:12; 13:24–31, 41, 47–50; 21:43; 25:1–13; Luke 13:28; Rev. 11:15). And virtually every prophecy and exposition of the new covenant expressly includes the children of believers in it (Deut. 30:6; Jer. 30:9, 18–22; 31:1, 17, 33–37; 32:15–18, 37–40; 33:22–26; Zech. 10:6–9; Joel 2:1–29; Isa. 44:3; 59:20–21; Mal. 4:5–6; Luke 1:17; 2:49–50; Acts 2:39; 3:25; 13:32–33; Rom. 4:13–17). Many Baptists discuss the *locus classicus* of the new covenant, Jeremiah 31:31–34. However, none that I know of include or even make reference to verses 35–37! These emphatically include the offspring of Israel within the scope of the new covenant:

> Thus says the LORD, who gives the sun for light by day and the fixed order of the moon and the stars for light by night, who stirs up the sea so that its waves roar; the LORD of hosts is His name: "If this fixed order

49. For more, see my appendix, "The New Covenant," in "Infant Baptism: Does the Bible Teach It?" (2000), online at http://www.WordMp3.com.

> departs from before Me," declares the LORD, "then the offspring of Israel also will cease from being a nation before Me forever." Thus says the LORD, "If the heavens above can be measured, and the foundations of the earth searched out below, then I will also cast off all the offspring of Israel for all that they have done," declares the LORD.

We have God's promise to include "the offspring of Israel" in the covenant. This prophetic word as to their inclusion in the covenant is at least as good as a minor child's "profession" of faith. And visible signs are to be given to visible members of the covenant community, as had ever been done until our Anabaptist friends arose. Children are fit for the sacrament of baptism by their explicit inclusion in the new covenant, by their explicit inclusion in the kingdom (Matt. 18), by their explicit inclusion in the church (Eph. 6; Col. 3), by the pattern of household baptisms (of the nine named individuals who are baptized in the New Testament, five have their households baptized, two do not have households, and Simon and Gaius are the others), and by the fact that the covenant promises extend to a thousand generations—which is inclusive of the years before and after 1525.

CLOSING POLEMIC

As shown above, the polemics of Anabaptism fail to demonstrate that paedobaptism is an error in biblical theology when specifically tested by the spirituality question. A strong case can be made for paedobaptism on the basis of covenant theology in the precise terms of a developmental biblical theology. Abraham is the father of many nations, and the covenant promises extended to him and his seed are to be received by all the families of the earth. Children are to receive the visible covenant signs by right of covenant membership, as first granted to Abraham; their membership has not been revoked.

Although the place of the children of Christians in baptism is not settled by explicit scriptural testimony, the paedobaptist's case appears compelling from the explicit inclusion of Christian children in the new covenant promises (Deut. 30:6; Jer. 31:36–37), from their explicit inclusion in the church (Eph. 6:1–4; 1 Cor. 7:14), and from their explicit inclusion in the kingdom (Matt. 19:14; Mark 10:14; Luke 18:16). We can close the argument from truly necessary inferences by drawing upon the continuity of the covenant people, the continuity of covenant purposes, and even the practice of household baptism.

As Warfield said, "The question of the Subjects of Baptism is one of that class of problems the solution of which hangs upon a previous question. According as is our doctrine of the Church, so will be our doctrine of the Subjects of Baptism."[50]

50. Benjamin B. Warfield, "The Polemics of Infant Baptism," in *The Works of Benjamin B. Warfield,* vol. 9, *Studies in Theology* (1932; reprint, Grand Rapids: Baker, 1981), 389.

14

Baptism and Children: Their Place in the Old and New Testaments

DOUGLAS WILSON

The prospect of writing a short essay on the subject of infant baptism is daunting, in part because of how clearly I remember those years when the kind of argumentation that I am about to present seemed entirely nonsensical to me. I have no desire to exasperate my baptistic brethren, yet at the same time it is my prayer and hope that multiple passages of Scripture will speak clearly to this vexing subject from an unexpected quarter.

During my years as a convinced Baptist, my approach was the same as what I have heard numerous times from others. If you want to understand Christian baptism, the thinking goes, then simply get a concordance and look up every passage that contains such words as *baptism, baptize,* and *baptist.* Countless Christians have done this and come away with the conviction that a person first believes in the Lord Jesus Christ and then is baptized. And further, we don't find any examples of an infant being baptized. So why make this complicated?

The procedure of turning to the Scriptures is of course not wrong. I hope that my argument below suggests the opposite. But there is a problem, and it is that of limiting the range of words to be looked up in the concordance. We must also consider what the Bible teaches about children, generations, promises, covenants, olive trees, olive shoots, descendants, and more.

The debate about infant baptism is fundamentally a debate about *children*, and not really a debate about baptism at all. A proponent of believer's baptism could consistently offer baptism to the infant John the Baptist, after being assured by the scriptural narrative that John was regenerate from the womb. The problem arises with those children about whom we have no specific revelation. What does the Bible teach about the children of believers *as a class?* If we have determined that the children of believers are promised to us by God and received by God himself, and that we are commanded to receive them, then we may safely argue from that status to their baptism. To illustrate this method, we know, for example, that believing women are in Christ (Gal. 3:28) and are faithful recipients of baptism (Acts 8:12), and so we can easily infer that they should partake of the Lord's Supper, even though the Bible does not record one instance of women partaking of that sacrament—and nowhere specifically commands that they should. We reason from their position in Christ to the sacrament. We must not begin with the scriptural silence on their partaking of the sacrament (along with hermeneutical assumptions about the need for "express warrant") and raise doubts about their position in Christ.

This is why a robust theology of children is a precondition for fruitful debate on the subject of infant baptism. When we banish thoughts of water from our minds, and consider the children of believers simply as children, we find an abundance of scriptural teaching. And in this regard, perhaps I may share an autobiographical detail. I learned the Scripture's teaching about children from my father, who remains to this day a settled Baptist. He is the one who taught me to take the many texts about children at face value—and I did so, long before I came to paedobaptist convictions. The reason for my doctrinal shift came only when I read an essay that linked what I had long believed about children with the waters of baptism.[1] In my mind, there was no reason to move from the New Testament texts on baptism up the steep hill to the baptism of infants. But when the motion went the other way, starting from what Scripture says about children, all the disturbed pebbles soon became an avalanche, and the whole thing was impossible for me to stop—despite how much I wanted it to stop.

A Review of Texts

The Bible is not silent on the subject of our children. Both the Old and the New Testament unite in teaching that children are a blessing, that they are to be brought up within the covenant of God, and that God promises his kindness to them and to *their* children in turn. We need to study these passages carefully, without being scared that the subject of baptism may eventually arise and unsettle everything. It is our duty to learn from all of God's Word.

Many key texts address this matter of generational faithfulness. Before considering them, it must be noted that the great force of these passages is cumulative. Paul Jewett once commented that when baptism is considered as an isolated subject, the paedobaptist case is weak, in his view. But when the discussion moves to the topic of the covenant, the paedobaptist case becomes a juggernaut. It is a similar situation here. I would urge the Baptist reader to avoid interacting with these verses individually as he works through them, and instead to consider them first all together. Then, having looked at them assembled together, the treatment of individual passages will be oriented to the flow of the argument.

Marriage is a creation ordinance, and the purposes behind marriage will remain the same as long as marriage endures. Because the

1. The essay was Robert S. Rayburn's article, "The Presbyterian Doctrines of Covenant Children, Covenant Nurture and Covenant Succession," in *Presbyterion* 22 (1996): 76–109, also available online at http://www.faithtacoma.org.

new covenant has not overthrown the institution of marriage, it also has not overthrown the *reason* for marriage:

> And did not he make one? Yet had he the residue of the spirit. And wherefore one? That he might seek a godly seed. Therefore take heed to your spirit, and let none deal treacherously against the wife of his youth. (Mal. 2:15)

Why does God make a man and a woman one spirit and one flesh? The reason is that he is seeking godly seed, godly offspring. An ethical exhortation follows immediately: The men in this passage have to take heed to their spirit and not betray the wife of their youth, their wife by covenant. It follows that such unfaithfulness to one's wife by covenant interferes with God's purpose and intent for believing marriage, which is believing children. If this is God's purpose, it should of course be our purpose. If parents have the same intention for their offspring that God does, then that intention is for godly seed. This refers to purpose and intention, not to wishful thinking. Of course, many believing parents think it would be wonderful to have believing children, but they do not think of it as the reason for having children. But just as a man plows a field with the intention of a harvest, or opens a business with the assumption that it will prosper, so Christian parents are to bring children into the world with the intention that they will walk with God.

As we consider God's covenant promises, we have to recognize that they are unchangeable precisely because *he* is unchangeable:

> Of old hast thou laid the foundation of the earth: and the heavens are the work of thy hands. They shall perish, but thou shalt endure: yea, all of them shall wax old like a garment; as a vesture shalt thou change them, and they shall be changed: But thou art the same, and thy years shall have no end. (Ps. 102:25–27)

Of course, every Christian knows that God does not change. This is why we are not consumed. But what does this unchanging nature of God have to do with our children? Everything—the promises of God do not shrink between the old and new covenants, and this is because God does not change. This is made explicit in the next verse: "The children of thy servants shall continue, and their seed shall be established before thee" (v. 28). Creation changes, and heaven and earth wear thin like an old pair of jeans. But God does not change, and this is why the children of his servants will continue, and *their seed will be established* in the presence of God.

In the Ten Commandments, God told the people that covenant blessings and curses were connected to whether or not they bowed down to idols. If idolatry was committed, then God would visit iniquity to the third and fourth generations. But for those who were obedient in love, he would show mercy to thousands:

> Thou shalt not bow down thyself unto them, nor serve them: for I the LORD thy God am a jealous God, visiting the iniquity of the fathers upon the children unto the third and fourth generation of them that hate me, and shewing mercy unto thousands of them that love me and keep my commandments. (Deut. 5:9–10)

Thousands of what? The implication is that his mercy extends to thousands of generations. But we do not have to guess, because the point is made explicit two chapters later: "Know therefore that the LORD thy God, he is God, the faithful God, which keepeth covenant and mercy with them that love him and keep his commandments to *a thousand generations*" (Deut. 7:9). It is important to note here that this generational blessing is one of mercy. God is not blessing all the descendants of pharisaical boasters. Generational faithfulness is not on the basis of works. These parents trust God for their own salvation and for the salvation of their children, because they are sinners relying on nothing other than God's gracious promise to show mercy.

God famously established his covenant with Abraham, and this covenant was not limited to Abraham as a believing individual. It included his seed after him:

> And I will establish my covenant between me and thee and thy seed after thee in their generations for *an everlasting covenant,* to be a God unto thee, *and to thy seed after thee.* And I will give unto thee, *and to thy seed after thee,* the land wherein thou art a stranger, all the land of Canaan, for an everlasting possession, and I will be their God. And God said unto Abraham, Thou shalt keep my covenant therefore, thou, *and thy seed after thee* in their generations. (Gen. 17:7–9)

God was promising the world to Abraham, and not just the land of Canaan. Abraham knew this, and rejoiced to see the day of Christ. "For the promise, that he should be the heir of the world, was not to Abraham, *or to his seed,* through the law, but through the righteousness of faith" (Rom. 4:13). God promised that the meek would inherit the earth. This promise was given to Abraham and to his seed on the basis of faith. This is important to note, because no one is claiming that children of believers are automatically sent off to heaven (*ex opere operato*). These promises are extended by God, and only faith can apprehend them. The promise does not come automatically to the children according to the flesh. No covenant child is automatically saved. But whenever a child is born into a believing home, the parents are invited to do what Abraham was invited to do—and that is to believe a promise. Faith is central.

Together with all the prophets, Ezekiel looked forward to the time of the new covenant, the time when the new David would rule over his people. His vision of this time is glorious:

> And David my servant shall be king over them; and they all shall have one shepherd: they shall also walk in my judgments, and observe my statutes, and do them. And they shall dwell in the land that I have given unto Jacob my servant, wherein your fathers have dwelt; and they shall

> dwell therein, *even they, and their children, and their children's children for ever:* and my servant David shall be their prince for ever. Moreover I will make a covenant of peace with them; it shall be *an everlasting covenant with them:* and I will place them, and multiply them, and will set my sanctuary in the midst of them for evermore. My tabernacle also shall be with them: yea, I will be their God, and they shall be my people. (Ezek. 37:24–27)

The promise is that God will be our God, and we will be his people. It is not that he will be our God, and we will be his individuals. In the time of the new covenant, God establishes a people, and promises that they will be faithful, along with their children and grandchildren. To seven generations? No, more than that—mercy is shown to seventy times seven. Isaiah longs for this great day as well:

> As for me, this is my covenant with them, saith the LORD; My spirit that is upon thee, and my words which I have put in thy mouth, shall not depart out of thy mouth, nor out of the mouth of thy seed, nor out of the mouth of thy seed's seed, saith the LORD, from henceforth and for ever. (Isa. 59:21)

This is the covenant, and every sinful parent should tremble with joy when he reads these words—provided he reads them in faith. God's Spirit is upon us as our portion in the covenant. His words will be in our mouths, and will not depart from us. More than this, his words will not depart from the mouths of our children or grandchildren.

As the gospel progresses gloriously in the world, the impact on descendants is equally glorious:

> They shall not build, and another inhabit; they shall not plant, and another eat: for as the days of a tree are the days of my people, and mine elect shall long enjoy the work of their hands. They shall not labour in vain, nor bring forth for trouble; for they are the seed of the blessed of the LORD, *and their offspring with them.* (Isa. 65:22–23)

Are we the seed of the blessed of the Lord? If we are, then what of our children? They come with us. They are blessed along with us.

God is truly kind to those who fear him. His mercy extends to them. Again, it is his mercy and kindness that extend to the generations of his saints:

> But the mercy of the Lord is from everlasting to everlasting upon them that fear him, and *his righteousness unto children's children;* to such as keep his covenant, and to those that remember his commandments to do them. (Ps. 103:17–18)

These promises are made to those who keep covenant (which can only be done through faith), and whose obedience to his commandments proceeds from that faith. When this happens, God forgives their sins and remembers their lawless deeds no more. He bestows his mercy from everlasting to everlasting. He pours out his righteousness upon grandchildren. In the kindness of God, at the time of writing this, I have four grandchildren, and so the promise is not a hypothetical one for me. I have four grandchildren to whom God will show mercy and righteousness. And in his kindness, he has even offered promises concerning *their* children.

Some might complain that I am applying promises of historical and temporal blessing from the Old Testament to the spiritual world of new covenant blessings, and that this can only result in confusion.

The problem with this response is the treatment given to such passages within the New Testament. For example, we find that our Lord's mother quoted the passage from Psalm 103 just quoted above. She understood the promise as coming to fruition in the child within her. She did not think that her Son was the one who would abrogate all these promises. He was the one in whom they were all yea and amen. She put it this way, when she quoted Psalm 103 in her gratitude:

> For he hath regarded the low estate of his handmaiden: for, behold, from henceforth all generations shall call me blessed. For he that is

> mighty hath done to me great things; and holy is his name. And *his mercy is on them that fear him from generation to generation.* (Luke 1:48–50)

Too many Christians think that God made many temporal and historical promises concerning generations and descendants in the Old Testament, but that they did not come to fulfillment because of unbelief. Then, in the new covenant, this kind of promise is abrogated or spiritualized. But Mary understood the promises differently. She saw that God's covenant kindness, promised to generation after generation, was to be fulfilled through her Son. This fulfillment was to be true fulfillment. Because the Messiah came, God's mercy could be extended to generation after generation.

The promises of God in the Old Testament do not hit a brick wall when they reach New Testament times. Rather, they come to fruition. Consider how the apostle Paul treats a promise to the Israelite families gathered around the foot of Mt. Sinai:

> Children, obey your parents in the Lord: for this is right. Honour thy father and mother; (which is the first commandment *with promise;*) that it may be well with thee, and thou mayest live long *on the earth.* And, ye fathers, provoke not your children to wrath: but bring them up in the nurture and admonition of the Lord. (Eph. 6:1–4)

This was the first commandment with a promise. But a promise to whom? The promise was for Israelites under the old covenant, and it had to do with long life in the land of Canaan after the Israelites displaced the pagan nations there. But notice how Paul treats it. He picks it up and applies the commandment, along with the promise annexed to it, to Gentile families in the city of Ephesus in the Roman province of Asia under the new covenant. The land of Canaan is expanded to include the whole earth. What is the basis for this glorious expansion?

> Wherefore remember, that ye being in time past Gentiles in the flesh, who are called Uncircumcision by that which is called the Circumci-

> sion in the flesh made by hands; that at that time ye were without Christ, *being aliens from the commonwealth of Israel, and strangers from the covenants of promise,* having no hope, and without God in the world: But now in Christ Jesus ye who sometimes were far off are made nigh by the blood of Christ. (Eph. 2:11–13)

In days past, Gentiles were outside the commonwealth of Israel. But now they have been brought near. Before the coming of Christ, they were strangers to the covenants of promise. But now, through the blood of Christ, they have been brought near to the covenants of promise. This is why a command given to Israelite children as part of the Sinaitic covenant is passed on to Gentile children in Ephesus, along with the promise. And note that we have not passed from flesh-and-blood children in the Old Testament to "spiritual" children in the New. We have flesh-and-blood Jewish children in Deuteronomy and flesh-and-blood Gentile children in Ephesus. And the promise covers both groups *in this life.*

These Gentile children are to be brought up in the "*paideia* of the Lord." They are to receive a Christian education from the ground up. They are received as covenantally clean from the beginning. The children of at least one Christian parent were to be considered *hagia,* that is, "holy ones." The word we normally use to translate this is *saints.* "For the unbelieving husband is sanctified by the wife, and the unbelieving wife is sanctified by the husband: else were your children unclean; but now are they holy" (1 Cor. 7:14). The children of saints are saints.

This is stated on the basis of God's promise to his people in the Old Testament. Those who were tempted to despair because of Israel's dismal history were encouraged to look forward. Let God be true and every man a liar. God promises our children to us. Because of unbelief, the promises slip through our fingers. But God in His kindness promised us a day when even this problem would be solved by his grace:

> Now when they heard this, they were pricked in their heart, and said unto Peter and to the rest of the apostles, Men and brethren, what shall

> we do? Then Peter said unto them, Repent, and be baptized every one of you in the name of Jesus Christ for the remission of sins, and ye shall receive the gift of the Holy Ghost. For the promise is unto you, and to your children, and to all that are afar off, even as many as the Lord our God shall call. (Acts 2:37–39)

Peter refers to a promise that extends to his listeners *and to their children.* This promise is that of the coming effusion of the Holy Spirit, and throughout the Old Testament children are routinely included as recipients of this blessing. And because the Scriptures speak this way, Peter does not hesitate to speak this way. The promise is for us, and for our children, and for those who are far off, and why stop there? It is for their children too. When the Spirit is poured out from heaven in this glorious baptism, the water gets everyone wet.

In the chapter after his famous prophecy of the new covenant, Jeremiah continues his discussion of it:

> And they shall be my people, and I will be their God: And I will give them one heart, and one way, that they may fear me for ever, for the good of them, *and of their children after them:* And I will make an everlasting covenant with them, that I will not turn away from them, to do them good; but I will put my fear in their hearts, that they shall not depart from me. (Jer. 32:38–40)

In the new covenant, they will all know the Lord, from the least of them to the greatest. As Jeremiah makes clear here, the children do too. The children are included.

As the stage is set for the arrival of Christ, the last prophet in the Old Testament shows us how God will prepare the way for the Messiah. The way is not prepared by annihilating the parent-child relationship, but rather by restoring it. An angel said to Zacharias, "And he shall go before him in the spirit and power of Elias, to turn the hearts of the fathers to the children, and the disobedient to the wisdom of the just; to make ready a people prepared for the Lord" (Luke

1:17). The angel knew that the Old Testament promised that families would be put right in the coming of the Messiah. And yet, in our day, we have people saying that the advent of the Messiah is not related to the turning of fathers' hearts to the spiritual condition of their children. But the Scriptures require it. The new covenant has better promises (Heb. 8:6), not worse ones!

Jesus did not arrive in a vacuum. He did not teach new doctrines *ex nihilo.* He was steeped in the Scriptures, and consequently taught that children belong in our midst. We are disciples, following the Lord, and as adults can fall into the trap of thinking that our understanding and maturity is worthy of the Lord, while that of little children is not worthy of Him. "But Jesus said, Suffer little children, and forbid them not, to come unto me: for of such is the kingdom of heaven. And he laid his hands on them, and departed thence" (Matt. 19:14–15; cf. Mark 10:14). We say that to be converted, children need to become more like adults. But Jesus said that to be converted, adults need to become more like children. And these children include infants, as Luke expressly mentions:

> And they brought unto him also infants, that he would touch them: but when his disciples saw it, they rebuked them. But Jesus called them unto him, and said, Suffer little children to come unto me, and forbid them not: for of such is the kingdom of God. (Luke 18:15–16)

The kingdom of God is a come one, come all, kind of thing. Everyone is invited, from the least to the greatest. The Spirit is poured out on old men and young maidens. This is not the time when access to God begins to narrow; rather, it grows and widens to encompass the whole world. So may we then come into the Christian faith as a household? Of course! (Acts 3:25; 1 Cor. 1:16):

> And a certain woman named Lydia, a seller of purple, of the city of Thyatira, which worshipped God, heard us: whose heart the Lord opened, that she attended unto the things which were spoken of Paul.

> And when *she was baptized, and her household,* she besought us, saying, If ye have judged me to be faithful to the Lord, come into my house, and abide there. And she constrained us. (Acts 16:14–15)

This is exactly what God promised to Abraham—that he would be a blessing to all the families and households of earth (Acts 3:25). But our argument, that "household" includes infants, does not depend, as many assume, upon the assumption that Lydia's household contained infants, or that the Philippian jailer's did. Rather, it depends upon the assumption that her household was *a household.* Over the centuries, the faith has grown by individuals, families, tribes, and sometimes even nations, and it did this rather consistently until the early part of the nineteenth century, when individualists made it necessary to come into the covenant one at a time. We did this because we believed that a certain level of maturity and wisdom was necessary before we could praise God rightly. But God has different ideas about what constitutes praise that is worthy of him: "Out of the mouth of babes and sucklings hast thou ordained strength because of thine enemies, that thou mightest still the enemy and the avenger" (Ps. 8:2). When the evangelical invitation is issued to a household, no assumption is made about the ages of those in it. But if it does contain babes and sucklings, they will not be excluded from adding their voices to ours in the praise of God.

A Theology of Children

We are faced with an inescapable reality. God has placed our children in our presence, and we are in covenant with the God who has done so. We will either treat our children as though they are in this covenant together with us, and teach them the terms of it, or we will treat them as strangers to that covenant, as outsiders. If we treat them as strangers to the covenant, if we say it is not possible for us to disciple our children in evangelical faith, bringing them up in it, then we will have to live with the unhappy consequences of covenant members training up covenant strangers. This would be hard enough, but if we are training them up as covenant strangers when the promises of God have brought them near, then we are not just laboring against Adamic sin in our children (as many parents assume), but are also swimming against the tide of God's promises. Too often we assume that things are going badly because our child's sin is interfering with our parental wisdom. Perhaps we should consider whether our theology is interfering with God's parental grace. We discipline our children in unbelief—not believing God's promises and hence not believing indications of his word in our children—and over time, our children finally give up and learn the lessons of our unbelief, which are more conducive to the flesh anyway.

Many say that the nature of faith is that it cannot be "taught" to our children. That may be, but we can certainly teach them to doubt. And with regard to the first point, faith cannot be taught without warrant from God, but what I have sought to show is that we do have warrant from God. Are our children included in the Great Commission? Disciple the nations, we are told. How? By baptizing them and teaching them obedience (Matt. 28:19–20). So, on the authority of God's promises and commands, we should disciple our children by baptizing them and teaching them to obey in true faith.

The only alternative is to refuse them baptism and to refuse to teach them obedience, because we are busy instilling doubts and scruples. Instead of equipping our children with the shield of faith that extinguishes flaming darts, we too often throw the darts ourselves. But how do we do this? A small girl comes up to her father and says that she believes in Jesus. She is four years old. Now, what is the father to do? He must either believe her or disbelieve her. If he disbelieves her, he is teaching her to doubt her profession, just as he doubts it. She thinks she loves Jesus, but her father, an older and wiser Christian, declines to have her baptized or to ask the elders to bring her to the table. She knows that in a certain fundamental sense, she is still considered "out." She must be outside for a reason. Her belief that she loves Jesus must therefore be erroneous, and she must learn to doubt other similar affections as they arise. "True" faith is always just around the corner, and is something that apparently happens (miraculously) to other people. For many children taught this way, this is the way it remains. They leave the faith, breaking the hearts of those parents who (unwittingly) taught them to do so.

This is nothing other than teaching our little ones to doubt the promises of God. We may say that we are doing it for the sake of maintaining true evangelical zeal, not letting anyone in until they display it, but we are actually killing the heart of true covenant faithfulness over generations. We have made dramatic conversions out of paganism the norm, and then, having placed this expectation on our covenant children, we have slowly driven them into nominalism through the false but very common standard of the "flashy testimony." But God told Christian parents to bring up their children in such a way that they have a really boring testimony. This is what it means to bring children up in the nurture and admonition of the Lord (Eph. 6:4). Children are to grow up in an environment dominated by the Word of God, and *they are to be a natural and organic part of that environment.* We are not to think of the dinner table as surrounded mostly with Israelites, but with the newly arrived Amalekite sitting sullenly off to the side in his high chair. Our homes are to be considered as part of the covenantal olive tree, and this certainly includes the olive shoots around the table (Ps. 128).

When we look for dramatic "Damascus road conversion experiences" in our children, we are setting up a false standard. We may be doing this in the name of a high view of conversion, but we are actually setting the stage for compromises that have been seen before in the history of the church. And this refusal to think of our children covenantally is at the heart of the church's current disarray. This began, for us, in the infamous halfway covenant of New England. That covenant came about, not because standards of coming to the Table were lowered, but rather because those standards were unbiblically and artificially high. In order to come to the Table, baptized children growing up in the church had to demonstrate that they had had a *real* conversion experience. In other words, the burden of proof was on the children to show that they should be allowed "in." This made the unmistakable point that they were still "out."

Baptists create this alien mentality in children by refusing to baptize them. Presbyterians do it by banning children from the Table. But virtually all American Christians do it, and they do it because they do not have a biblical theology of generations. And, having taught our children to doubt the promises and leave the covenant, we take the fact that they do leave as incontrovertible evidence that we were right in excluding them in the first place. We require children to grow big and strong so that we might give them some food after they have done so. Then, when they starve to death, we take it as proving that we were right in not feeding them. Wisdom is vindicated by her children, but in our case, they don't stick around.

I know that these words may seem harsh, and it is not my intent to give offense. But I have to say that our Lord issued some of his sternest warnings to those who caused the little ones to stumble. And I also have to say that it is my conviction that we have adopted a theology in the American church which leads to the stumbling of little ones. In my view, the only way out of such a horrible situation is some plain speaking, followed by repentance. Rather that than a millstone around the neck.

Conclusion

Paradigms are hard to shake. I know that some will think I have just quoted a bunch of verses, but have not "made the case." And in no way can any of our contributions be thought to have answered all questions or settled all problems. But I believe that we can consider the root of the matter addressed. On the Last Day, my deepest desire is to imitate the Lord's joy in us, and stand before God, able to say, "Here am I, and the children you have given me."

For those who love to be convinced—"How wonderful would this be if it *were* true!"—perhaps one last comment may help. Returning to our earlier example of women and the Lord's Supper, let us conclude with a thought experiment. Suppose for a moment that we had no reference to women receiving baptism in the New Testament. Suppose further that the subject had become controversial in the church, and that we were now debating it. And now let us take the additional step of assuming that all the passages we have cited above were to be found in the Scriptures, but that they were worded a little differently. They all referred to women, and not to children or children's children.

In other words, we knew from Scripture that God had made a covenant with believers and their wives. God had promised to pour out his Spirit on women, and that his Word would not depart from the mouths of these women forever. The seed of the Lord, and their wives with them, would be greatly blessed by God. God would dwell with them, and with their wives, and would make an everlasting covenant with them. And so forth. Would anyone have a problem baptizing women on such a basis? Would the evidence be considered slender?

15

In Jesus' Name, Amen

R. C. SPROUL JR.

I don't remember the man's name or the exact time of the event. It was sometime during the heyday of the Moral Majority, and the man in question had some loose connection with the Rev. Jerry Falwell. Mr. Falwell no doubt wanted to sever that connection when the man in question hit the news. Mr. Falwell usually picked his words with care, but not this associate. What he said that made its way into the national news was something like this: "God doesn't hear the prayers of Muslims and Buddhists." This was said, of course, well before the violent attack on the United States by militant Muslims led us to sink even more deeply into feel-good ecumenism. Nevertheless, there was a great stir that someone—a man of the cloth, no less—could make such a bigoted, narrow-minded comment.

I had my concerns as well. I had no trouble with anyone saying that God is at war with all those who will not profess Christ. I had no trouble with anyone saying that God's wrath burns hot against such people. I just wanted to be sure that no one was denying God's omniscience. Of course God hears the prayers of Muslims and Buddhists, in the sense that he knows what they are saying. God not only is immediately aware of the prayers of Muslims and Buddhists, but also was aware of them before they were even uttered. He did, after all, ordain them.

But of course God doesn't hear their prayers, in the sense of listening as a father would listen to his son. He doesn't even entertain their requests. God does not take in all the supplications made across the globe, prioritize them on the basis of how sanctified the supplicant is, and then answer them in that order, sometimes getting to the requests of the heathen (on days when Christians aren't making so many requests), and sometimes pushing the delete button when his e-mail in-box is particularly crowded.

The distinction between one kind of hearing and the other kind of hearing is based upon the person bringing the request. Whether you are a Buddhist or a Christian makes all the difference in the world. You may stand outside a local courtroom, screaming your lungs out to a local judge. If it's a hot day and the windows are open, you may be heard. But it takes an invitation to receive a hearing from the judge.

God is the judge of all the earth. He is also the only judge who always judges rightly. But there is only one attorney, only one advocate, who actually has what it takes to be granted a hearing. That advocate is of course his only begotten Son. The truly supreme court is strictly a family affair. The one true judge is rather particular. Anyone seeking to avoid a contempt of court citation cannot come into the courtroom wearing just anything. He doesn't take it well when someone wearing flip-flops and sweatpants tries to enter his most august chambers. And you cannot find a place at the bar, either, if you are dressed in the finest Saville Row suit. To enter these chambers, you must be spotless, inside and out. This is why Christ alone appears before the judge.

What has any of this to do with baptism and family worship? Everything. For when we worship, we enter into the courts of God. When we worship, we come before the presence of this great and terrible judge. And when he charges you with contempt of court, you stay in prison forever.

The church that I serve has what some would call a rather liturgical service. We read prayers together. We sing service music together. Liturgies are tools of remembrance. They are not unlike the stones that God ordered to be placed in the center of the Jordan River to commemorate the time when the children of Israel walked across the river on dry ground to enter the Promised Land. Every service of worship is liturgical, for every service is designed to help us remember. Those who look down their noses at our liturgy fear that our worship habits will become just that, habits—that we will remember to use the tools of remembrance, without remembering what they were designed to help us remember. They fear that without knowledge, these things will become rote. It's a legitimate concern, but one that applies to everyone's liturgies. When we return thanks before we eat God's provision at a meal, we are using a tool to help us remember that God gives us our daily bread. Despite this reminder, however, we all too often mumble our way through the prayer, hoping our food won't grow cold.

But it is not just prayers that can become rote, but also the parts of our prayers. Many of us, if we are careful, close our prayers in a rather liturgical way. Having brought forth our adoration, confession, thanksgiving, and supplications, we close with the words "In Jesus' name, amen." I wouldn't be surprised if half the people who close their prayers in this way have no idea what they are saying. What they are saying has to do with how we can even appear before the just judge.

What we are doing is reminding God, who needs no reminding, and reminding ourselves, who do need reminding, how it is that we are able to appear before him. We are acknowledging to God that in ourselves we cannot come into his courtroom. We are still sinners. God not only cannot "hear" sinners, but cannot even "look" upon them. "In Jesus' name" is a concise way of saying, "Oh great and holy God, we can only come before you with these prayers because we are clothed in the righteousness of Christ. It is because his blood covers our sins, and his righteousness has become our own, that we bring these things before you." It affirms that if we were to try to stand before God without the work of Christ on our behalf, we would be instantly destroyed.

Of course, it is not only in our prayers that we enter into God's presence. If we would sing his praises, we must do so in his presence. We know that while we are all always *coram Deo,* before God's face, believers and unbelievers alike, when we come to him with our songs of praise we are inviting him to pay attention (keeping in mind, of course, that God is always immediately aware of all things). And if we do so, we had better be covered in the blood and righteousness of his Son.

Like any father, I love my children. They are a delight to me, truly a great reward and blessing from my own heavenly Father. Because I love them, I am not too permissive. My love for them does not lead me to allow them to do whatever they please. When I say "No!" to my daughter Erin Claire as she reaches out to touch the hot stove, I do so not as a cruel tyrant, but as a loving father who does not want to see her get hurt. There is, however, a far greater danger to my children than a hot stove. The greatest danger is a hot eternity, to fall into the hands of the living God.

My love for my children, I pray, does not lead me to forget what the Bible teaches about my children. They are indeed a blessing, a source of joy, but they are also, in themselves, under the wrath of God. They were, like David, conceived in sin. They justly deserve God's displeasure. They, like their father, are not in a position, in themselves, to come before the living God. They too, like their father, must be covered by Christ.

That little liturgical element at the end of our prayers, "in Jesus' name," is not a magical incantation. Those words are not the equivalent of "open sesame," the magic words that open the door to God's courtroom. When we say those words, we do not bring Christ's covering over us, but affirm that Christ's covering has already been placed over us. If Christ hasn't truly covered us, we only add to the wrath of God, as sinners trying to barge into his courtroom.

This brings us back to baptism and family worship. There are a host of different ways in which people understand baptism. There are those, both some who affirm paedobaptism and some who affirm adult baptism, who believe that the water works the magic. These are sacerdotalists, who believe that the working of the work covers those baptized with the work of Christ. Those who hold to this position, of course, deny the doctrine of justification by faith alone, and so are not baptizing anyone into the Christ of the Bible.

Then there are those who believe that the water is water, and that, when we baptize an infant, we are dedicating our child to God, saying in essence, "Lord, here is your child. We hope you'll save him one day." Then there are those who fall somewhere in between these two views. They deny that baptism is merely a wet dedication, and deny that baptism ushers anyone into the kingdom. Instead, baptism increases the odds that God will one day redeem the children. It invites the children to partake of the means of grace (at least some of them), to come under the discipline of the church and the preaching of the Word. Finally, there are the believer's baptists, who affirm that we ought not to baptize anyone unless and until he makes a credible profession of faith in Christ.

All of these views, excluding those that are sacerdotal, assert that we have no reason to believe that the baptized are in fact covered by the blood of Christ and credited with the righteousness of Christ, until we hear from them a credible profession of faith. So how and why do we lead little ones into the presence of God?

There seems to be some kind of schizophrenia when our understandings of baptism and family worship come together. With respect to baptism, we think that our little ones, who have not yet been "confirmed," are inside the church, but not inside the faith. But when we have family worship, we see them as inside the faith. We lead these little ones into the throne room of the Most High, all the while believing that they can't truly pray "in Jesus' name." I'm sure there are parents who are more consistent in this, who maintain the same understanding of baptism, but who are more cautious about how they treat the prayers and praise of their children. I'm sure also that there aren't too many who are this consistent.

There is, however, another option, one that does not require us to adopt an *ex opere operato* understanding of baptism, but does allow us to bring our children before God in worship. Baptism is the sign of faith. We can deny sacerdotalism, and yet affirm that we ought to treat our covenant children as believers. We need not create two different covenants, as some tend to do. Instead, we can affirm that, as far as we know, our covenant children are in fact in the covenant, in the church, in the kingdom, in the faith, and so we may, believing them to be covered by Christ, bring them before God in worship. Their baptism neither causes this to happen nor is an ironclad guarantee. Instead, it is the sign of faith. The baptized child may yet be unregenerate. The child may in fact be a reprobate. But our assumption, based on the covenant promises of God, is that the child is in, all the way in, until he or she gives contrary evidence and is eventually excommunicated.

This view is consistent with how God worked in the old covenant. A son was born and was given the mark of the covenant. Jewish parents did not wait in fear and trepidation, hoping and praying that one day this covenant child would embrace the faith and be brought into the kingdom. God required no rite of "confirmation" when the child reached a certain age. No Hebrew ever walked down an aisle or made a decision. Instead, he was raised within the covenant community.

Some may object that the old covenant was an earthly covenant. God had promised Abraham that he would give him a land that he would show him. He promised also that he would give him a son, and through him a mighty nation. He promised Abraham also that he would be a blessing to all the nations. But all of these promises, though they are astounding in their grace, cannot be compared with the greatest promise, that the Lord would be God to Abraham and to his seed.

How does one have God as his God? There is only one way, through the mediatorial work of the Son. All those, under the old covenant or the new, who are not in union with Christ are at war with the Father. Abraham had peace with God, and the sign of that peace was circumcision. The promises, then, were not merely earthly, but heavenly. The sign symbolized God's covenant blessing.

Others may object that not all Israel was Israel. Paul himself said so. How can circumcision be a sign of belief when some had the sign and did not believe? Wouldn't it make more sense to give the sign of belief only to those who actually believe? Of course some were given the sign who did not believe. The sign is a sign, not a guarantee, a peek into the Lamb's book of life. The same is true of covenant baptism. Because we are not sacerdotalists, we affirm that indeed some are given the sign of faith who do not have faith. Not all who are of the new covenant community are of the new covenant community. The trouble with this objection is that it objects to too much. Those who baptize covenant children are not alone in this dilemma. Even in baptistic churches there are those who are given the sign of faith who are in fact not in the faith. That someone lacks the thing signified does not mean that they should not have been given the sign. The trouble is that we just don't know who are the elect of God and who are not. Neither circumcision, paedobaptism, nor believer's baptism can get past that fact.

Others still might object that little children do not have the capacity for faith. If such is the case, we must infer two things. First, all those who die in infancy spend eternity facing the wrath of God. The Scripture affirms both that we are sinners from the beginning, and that there is only one way to escape the wrath of God, by believing on the Lord Jesus Christ. Those who cannot believe cannot escape. Second, we must not take those who cannot have faith into the heavenly temple. If they have no faith, they are not covered by Christ. If they are not covered by Christ, then God's courtroom is not a safe place for them to appear.

There is every reason to believe that little children do not have the capacity to believe the gospel. They lack that which is necessary. The good news, however, is that no person has the capacity to believe the gospel. Not one of us can believe on our own, not because we aren't smart enough, but because we are not good enough. What stops the little children from believing is not an underdeveloped brain, but a wicked heart. But God is stronger than both underdeveloped brains and wicked hearts. And if God can work the miracle of regeneration in a sinner like me, he can certainly do it in a little baby. He can even do it in the womb. When Elizabeth came to visit Mary, the Scripture tells us, John the Baptist leapt in his mother's womb. The unregenerate do not leap in the presence of Christ; they cower. John, even in the womb, had been given new life.

The question comes down to this: how do we see our covenant children? How are we to look at them, when we cannot see into their hearts and cannot see into the Lamb's book of life? If we look at them as potential converts, hot prospects, then we will treat family worship one way. We will perhaps instruct them, witness to them, evangelize them. We will warn them of the wrath to come, and remind them of the very point I am trying to make, that until you come repenting, claiming the blood of Christ, by no means seek to enter into the presence of God.

If, on the other hand, we look at them as young servants of the king, as recipients of the grace of God, then our family worship will look different. It will be most different in that it will be *family worship.* We will come as a family into the presence of God and will ascribe to him the glory that is due his name. We will receive instruction from the captain of the Lord's hosts, knowing that we are among those hosts—that we, and our children, are soldiers in the army of God. We will rejoice in the redemption wrought for us in Christ. We will bring before God our prayers and petitions, as children before a loving father.

Our earthly goal (remembering that we do family worship ultimately for the glory of God and not for the benefits that we might receive) will not be conversion, but sanctification. We, in practicing family worship, will be acting in obedience to God's command that we raise our children in the nurture and admonition of the Lord. Of course we will still preach the gospel to our children, just as the gospel continues to be preached in faithful pulpits all across the world. We do not forget the gospel once we have been saved, but continue to grow into it. And we want the same for our covenant children.

If we learn to see our children as being in the one true covenant, then, and only then, can we not only pray for them, but pray with them. Only then can we bring them to the great and terrible judge of all the world, because we believe that the one who is our advocate, who stands and speaks for us, has already been lifted up to receive what is our due. Only then can we be confident that he truly hears the prayers of our children. Only then can they rightly pray, "In Jesus' name, amen."

About the Contributors

Joel R. Beeke (Ph.D., Westminster Theological Seminary) is president and professor of systematic theology and homiletics at Puritan Reformed Theological Seminary, pastor of the Heritage Netherlands Reformed Congregation in Grand Rapids, Michigan, and editor of *Banner of Sovereign Grace Truth.* He has written numerous books, most recently *Truth That Frees: A Workbook on Reformed Doctrine for Young Adults, A Reader's Guide to Reformed Literature, Puritan Evangelism,* and *The Quest for Full Assurance: The Legacy of Calvin and His Successors.*

Lyle D. Bierma (Ph.D., Duke University) is professor of systematic theology at Calvin Theological Seminary in Grand Rapids, Michigan. He also serves as editor of the *Calvin Theological Journal.* His most recent publications are *German Calvinism in the Confessional Age: The Covenant Theology of Caspar Olevianus* and *The Doctrine of the Sacraments in the Heidelberg Catechism.* He is an ordained minister in the Christian Reformed Church in North America.

Randy Booth is pastor of Grace Covenant Presbyterian Church in Nacogdoches, Texas, and serves on the faculty of the Dabney Theological Study Center in Monroe, Louisiana. He is the director of Covenant Media Foundation, cofounder of Veritas Classical Christian School in Texarkana, Arkansas, and the founding board chairman of Regents Academy in Nacogdoches, Texas. He is the author of several published articles and the book *Children of the Promise: The Biblical Case for Infant Baptism.*

Bryan Chapell (Ph.D., Southern Illinois University) is president and professor of practical theology at Covenant Theological Seminary. He began teaching at Covenant Seminary in 1984, after ten years in pastoral ministry. He is the author of *Christ-Centered Preaching, Standing Your Ground, In the Grip of Grace, Using Illustrations to Preach with Power, Each for the Other, The Wonder of It All,* and many articles.

Daniel M. Doriani (Ph.D., Westminster Theological Seminary) is senior pastor of Central Presbyterian Church in St. Louis and adjunct professor of New Testament at Covenant Theological Seminary. His publications include *Putting the Truth to Work: The Theory and Practice of Biblical Application, Life of a God-Made Man, Getting the Message: A Plan for Interpreting and Applying the Bible, David the Anointed,* and a number of articles.

Ray B. Lanning (M.Div., Westminster Theological Seminary) is pastor of the Associate Reformed Presbyterian Church of Grand Rapids. He has done graduate work at Calvin Theological Seminary. He has written a variety of articles for various periodicals, and coauthored chapters in various books with Joel R. Beeke. Ordained to the ministry in 1977, he has served Presbyterian and Reformed churches in various parts of North America.

Peter J. Leithart (Ph.D., University of Cambridge) is an ordained minister in the Presbyterian Church in America, and teaches theology and literature at New St. Andrews College in Moscow, Idaho. He writes a regular column on worship for *Credenda/Agenda,* has published several books on theology and literature, and his doctoral dissertation, "The Priesthood of the Plebs: The Baptismal Transformation of Antique Order," is forthcoming from Wipf & Stock Publishers.

Jeffrey D. Niell (M.A., Fuller Theological Seminary) is the pastor of Emmanuel Covenant Church (CRE) in Phoenix, Arizona. He has coauthored *The Same Sex Controversy.*

Joseph A. Pipa Jr. (Ph.D., Westminster Theological Seminary) is president and professor of historical and systematic theology at

Greenville Presbyterian Theological Seminary. He is the author of many articles and the books *Root and Branch, William Perkins and the Development of Puritan Preaching,* and *The Lord's Day,* and contributed to *Whatever Happened to the Reformation? Onward Christian Soldiers, Did God Create in Six Days? Written for Our Instruction: The Sufficiency of Scripture for All of Life,* and *Sanctification: Growing in Grace.*

Richard L. Pratt Jr. (Th.D., Harvard University) chairs the Old Testament department at Reformed Theological Seminary in Orlando, Florida. He is the author of several books, including *Pray with Your Eyes Open, Designed for Dignity, He Gave Us Stories,* and *1 and 2 Chronicles.* He is also a contributor to *The Literary Guide to the Bible* and the author of numerous journal articles.

Mark Ross (Ph.D., University of Liverpool) is the associate pastor of First Presbyterian Church (ARP) in Columbia, South Carolina. He serves as an adjunct professor at Columbia Biblical Seminary.

R. C. Sproul Jr. (D.Min., Whitefield Theological Seminary) is associate pastor of teaching at Saint Peter Presbyterian Church in Bristol, Tennessee (Reformed Presbyterian Church, General Assembly), the director of the Highlands Study Center in Meadowview, Virginia, and the editor of *Tabletalk* magazine. He is the author of several books, including *Almighty over All, Tearing Down Strongholds,* and *Eternity in Our Hearts.*

Gregg Strawbridge (Ph.D., University of Southern Mississippi) is the pastor of All Saints' Presbyterian Church (CRE) in Lancaster, Pennsylvania. He is the director of WordMp3.com, an online audio library, and has held adjunct professor appointments at Columbia International University, William Carey College, and the University of Southern Mississippi. He is the author of several booklets, articles, and reviews, including *Classical and Christian Education* and *Infant Baptism: Does the Bible Teach It?*

Cornelis P. Venema (Ph.D., Princeton Theological Seminary) is president and professor of doctrinal studies at Mid-America Reformed Seminary in Dyer, Indiana. He serves as a coeditor of the *Mid-America Journal of Theology* and as associate pastor of the First Christian Reformed Church of South Holland, Illinois. He is the author of *But for the Grace of God: An Exposition of the Canons of Dort, What We Believe: An Exposition of the Apostle's Creed, The Promise of the Future,* and a study of Heinrich Bullinger's doctrine of predestination (forthcoming).

Jonathan M. Watt (Ph.D., University of Pittsburgh) served for eighteen years as pastor of Reformed Presbyterian Church of North America congregations, in New Kensington, Pennsylvania; Cambridge, Massachusetts; and Beaver Falls, Pennsylvania. He is currently assistant professor of biblical studies at Geneva College in Beaver Falls, Pennsylvania, and adjunct professor of biblical and historical studies at the Reformed Presbyterian Theological Seminary in Pittsburgh, Pennsylvania. He is the author of one book and various papers and articles in the area of biblical sociolinguistics.

Douglas Wilson (M.A., University of Idaho) is the pastor of Christ Church in Moscow, Idaho (CRE), the editor of *Credenda/Agenda,* and a teacher at New St. Andrews College in Moscow, Idaho. He is the author of numerous books and publications, including *Recovering the Lost Tools of Learning, Persuasions, Reforming Marriage, To a Thousand Generations,* and *Future Men.*

Index of Scripture

Index of Subjects and Names